SAGE was founded in 1965 by Sara Miller McCune to support the dissemination of usable knowledge by publishing innovative and high-quality research and teaching content. Today, we publish over 900 journals, including those of more than 100 learned societies, more than 800 new books per year, and a growing range of library products including archives, data, case studies, reports, and video. SAGE remains majority owned by our founder, and after Sara's lifetime will become owned by a charitable trust that secures our continued independence.

Los Angeles | London | New Delhi | Singapore | Washington DC | Melbourne

Advance Praise

The book *Financing International Trade: Banking Theories and Applications* by Dr Gargi Sanati is a comprehensive practical guide for the practitioners engaged in Trade Finance and Foreign Exchange Markets. The topics covered are otherwise not available in academic textbooks. This book is an outcome of her experience in training bankers engaged in the professions. Dr Sanati has added a great value by blending theories with applications in a separately covered area of knowledge in trade finance.

—Dr Achintan Bhattacharya
Former Director, NIBM
Ex Joint Secretary of Department of Financial Service, Ministry of Finance, Government of India

This book by Dr Gargi Sanati fills the long existing gap felt by both bankers and postgraduate students for an authentic read in the area of International Trade Finance. The simple and smooth flowing approach of the author makes it easy for the reader to understand the intricacies of the documentation involved in International Trade. The illuminating caselets add value to the in-depth understanding of the subject matter.

—Shri V. Rajagopal
Visiting Faculty Forex and Technical Analysis and Head Trainer of Forex Bourse Game Conducted by
NIBM, BOI, IIBF and IIIMs
Former Chief Dealer, Kotak Mahindra Bank and ICICI Bank

With pleasure I read the new book on trade finance products scripted by Dr Gargi Sanati and observed that the contents of the book are quite comprehensive and narrating all trade finance products with processes and procedures, rules and regulations, and risks and mitigates. I also found that the book is written in a simple lucid style. The book will serve as a reference guide to all the MBA and postgraduate students, and it would contribute to the guidance of trade bankers who have recently been posted to the international business departments.

—Shri Jayant Keskar
Former DGM, International Banking and Operation, IDBI Bank

Dr Gargi Sanati, a Research Scholar in Advanced Econometrics, inadvertently found herself in the realm of Foreign Exchange and Trade Finance at NIBM Pune.

It is her sheer passion toward academic research that she immersed herself into the domain of Trade Finance. She interacted with practitioners, experts, and relentlessly forayed into the universe. During my many visits to NIBM, I recollect watching Gargi pick our brains to gain a deep understanding about the subject matter through our knowledge and experience.

She has put together a comprehensive volume consisting of practical examples and regulatory information on the topics of International Finance, FX Banking and Cross-Border Trade. I highly recommend this book to students bankers/corporates and wish her great success!

—Shri Harit Dhruv
Currently working as a Consultant in Bassein Bank
Former Forex Dealer, Oriental Bank of Commerce

Bankers, corporates, and students of International Trade would find reference to this book invaluable in terms of its contents and scope, painstakingly compiled for a comprehensive coverage on all areas including exchange rates.

—Shri M. V. Subramaniam
Senior Dealer in Forex Treasury, Oriental Bank of Commerce
Joint General Manager, Essar Group Treasury
Corporate Trainer and Consultant, Forex and Risk Management

The book is a worthy compendium on International Trade Finance from a practitioner's perspective. The text is well organized, written in a simple and lucid manner, and covers the entire gamut of procedures that goes behind financing foreign trade. Besides serving as a handbook for trade professionals, it can eminently be used as a text to teach trade finance to student in international management. The perspective it brings on the trade credit is the capstone of the book.

—Dr Mridul Saggar
Adviser and Head of International Department, Reserve Bank of India

This is a pioneering textbook on Financing International Trade in India, rigorous and meticulous in style. This book is equally relevant for the scholars and public policymakers in International Finance and Trade.

—Dr Lekha S. Chakraborty
NIPFP, New Delhi

We hardly find any textbook having coverage on the payment methods and banking products to facilitate export and import business. This book bridges this long pending gap and offers a perfect blend of theory and practices and would help MBA students of finance, bankers, and policymakers.

—Dr Pinaki Chakraborty
National institute of Public Finance and Policy, New Delhi

Financing International Trade

Financing International Trade

Banking Theories and Applications

Gargi Sanati

Assistant Professor

Department of Money International Banking & Finance

National Institute of Bank Management (NIBM), Pune

Los Angeles | London | New Delhi
Singapore | Washington DC | Melbourne

First published in 2017 by

SAGE Publications India Pvt Ltd
B1/I-1 Mohan Cooperative Industrial Area
Mathura Road, New Delhi 110 044, India
www.sagepub.in

SAGE Publications Inc
2455 Teller Road
Thousand Oaks, California 91320, USA

SAGE Publications Ltd
1 Oliver's Yard, 55 City Road
London EC1Y 1SP, United Kingdom

SAGE Publications Asia-Pacific Pte Ltd
3 Church Street
#10-04 Samsung Hub
Singapore 049483

Published by Vivek Mehra for SAGE Publications India Pvt Ltd, typeset in 10/13 pt Minion by Zaza Eunice, Hosur, Tamil Nadu, India and printed at Saurabh Printers Pvt Ltd, Greater Noida.

Library of Congress Cataloging-in-Publication Data Available

ISBN: 978-93-864-4617-6 (PB)

SAGE Team: Amit Kumar, Indrani Dutta, Sunil Koli, Shobhna Paul and Ritu Chopra

To
My Father and Mother

Thank you for choosing a SAGE product!
If you have any comment, observation or feedback,
I would like to personally hear from you.
Please write to me at **contactceo@sagepub.in**

Vivek Mehra, Managing Director and CEO, SAGE India.

Bulk Sales

SAGE India offers special discounts
for bulk institutional purchases.
*For queries/orders/inspection copy requests
write to* **textbooksales@sagepub.in**

Publishing

Would you like to publish a textbook with SAGE?
Please send your proposal to **publishtextbook@sagepub.in**

Get to know more about SAGE

Be invited to SAGE events, get on our mailing list.
Write today to **marketing@sagepub.in**

Brief Contents

Brief Contents

Detailed Contents

List of Abbreviations

ACU	:	Asian Clearing Union
AD	:	Authorized dealers
ADB	:	Asian Development Bank
BG	:	Bank guarantee
BIPC	:	Bank branchwise individual packing credit
BL	:	Bill of lading
BOLT	:	Built own lease transfer
BOOT	:	Build own operate transfer
BOT	:	Build operate transfer
CBDT	:	Central Board of Direct Tax
CECA	:	Comprehensive economic cooperation agreements
CENVAT	:	Central Value Added Tax
CEPA	:	Comprehensive economic partnerships agreements
CFR	:	Cost and freight
CIF	:	Cost, insurance and freight
CIN	:	Corporate Identity Number
CISG	:	Contract of international sales of goods
CMR	:	Contract of the international carriage of goods by road
COTIF	:	Convention concerning international carriage by rail
CPT	:	Carriage paid to
CQCTD	:	Committee on Quality Complaints and Trade Disputes
DA	:	Documents against acceptance
DAF	:	Delivered at frontier
DAP	:	Delivered at place
DAT	:	Delivered at terminal
DC	:	Development commissioner
DDP	:	Delivered duty paid
DDU	:	Delivered duty unpaid
DEQ	:	Delivered ex quay
DES	:	Delivered ex ship
DFTP	:	Duty free tariff preference
DGFT	:	Directorate General of Foreign Trade

DIN	:	Director identification number
DOR	:	Department of Revenue
DP	:	Documents against payment
DTA	:	Domestic tariff area
EC&GC	:	Export Credit & Guarantee Corporation Ltd
ECB	:	External commercial borrowings
ECGC	:	Export Credit Guarantee Corporation of India
EDI	:	Economic development initiatives
EDPMS	:	Export data processing and monitoring system
EEFC	:	Exchange earners' foreign currency
EO	:	Export obligation
EODG	:	Export obligation discharge certificate
EOU	:	Export Oriented Units
EPCG	:	Export promotion of capital goods
ERIC	:	Export Risk Insurance Corporation
EUC	:	End user certificate
EXIM Bank	:	Export-Import Bank of India
FAS	:	Free alongside ship
FBL	:	FIATA bill of lading
FBL	:	FIATA waybill
FCA	:	Free carrier
FEDAI	:	Foreign Exchange Dealers Association of India
FEMA	:	Foreign Exchange Management Act
FERA	:	Foreign Exchange Regulation Act
FIATA	:	International Federation of Freight Forwarders Associations
FOB	:	Free onboard
FTP	:	Foreign Trade Policy
GSP	:	Generalized system of preferences
ICC	:	International Chamber of Commerce
ICRA Ltd	:	Investment Information and Credit Rating Agency Ltd
IEC	:	Import export code
IEM	:	Industrial entrepreneur memorandum
IFA	:	International Forfaiting Association
IL	:	Industrial license
INCOTERMS	:	International commercial terms
INPC	:	Individual packing credit
IPR	:	Intellectual property rights
IRDA	:	Insurance Regulatory and Development Authority
ISBP	:	International standard banking practice
ISP	:	International standby practices
LC	:	Letter of credit
LDC	:	Least developed countries
LI	:	Letter of intent
LIBOR	:	London inter-bank offered rate

LoA	:	Letter of approval
LoC	:	Letter of comfort
LOP	:	Letter of permission
LoU	:	Letter of undertaking
MCA	:	Ministry of Corporate Affairs
MEIS	:	Merchandise export from India scheme
MRI	:	Magnetic resonance imagining
NAFTA	:	North American Free Trade Agreement
NEE	:	Net foreign exchange earning
NTP	:	Normal transit period
PNB	:	Punjab National Bank
PTA	:	Preferential trading agreement
RAPC	:	Running account packing credit facility
RCMC	:	Registration Cum Membership Certificate
SAL	:	Specific approval list
SBLC	:	Standby letter of credit
SC	:	Surety cover
SCOMET	:	Special chemicals, organisms, materials, equipment and technologies
SEIS	:	Service exports from India scheme
SEZ	:	Special Economic Zone
SWIFT	:	Society for worldwide interbank financial telecommunication
TC	:	Trade credits
UCP	:	Uniform rules for documentary credit
URC	:	Uniform rules for collections
URDG	:	Uniform rules for demand guarantee
VKGUY	:	Vishesh Krishi and Gram Udyog Yojana
WR	:	Whole turnover
WTPC	:	Whole turnover packing credit
WTPS	:	Whole turnover post-shipment credit

LoA	:	Letter of approval
LoC	:	Letter of comfort
LOP	:	Letter of permission
LoU	:	Letter of undertaking
MCA	:	Ministry of Corporate Affairs
MEIS	:	Merchandise export from India scheme
MRI	:	Magnetic resonance imagining
NAFTA	:	North American Free Trade Agreement
NFE	:	Net foreign exchange earning
NTP	:	Normal transit period
PNB	:	Punjab National Bank
PTA	:	Preferential trading agreement
RAPC	:	Running account packing credit facility
RCMC	:	Registration Cum Membership Certificate
SAL	:	Specific approval list
SBLC	:	Standby letter of credit
SC	:	Surety cover
SCOMET	:	Special chemicals, organisms, materials, equipment and technologies
SEIS	:	Service exports from India scheme
SEZ	:	Special Economic Zone
SWIFT	:	Society for worldwide interbank financial telecommunication
TC	:	Trade credits
UCP	:	Uniform rules for documentary credit
URC	:	Uniform rules for collections
URDG	:	Uniform rules for demand guarantee
VKGUY	:	Vishesh Krishi and Gram Udyog Yojana
WT	:	Whole turnover
WTPC	:	Whole turnover packing credit
WTPS	:	Whole turnover post-shipment credit

Foreword

The book on international trade finance by Dr Gargi Sanati is an excellent attempt to cover a vast ground in a complex subject in which there are not many authentic books.

Today, international trade plays a key role in global economic development. Hence, it is an important business activity center for all the multinational banks operating in various geographies. Without clear knowledge of the rules, regulations, and practices governing international trade and finance, it will be impossible for any bank to develop this key business area as a profit center. This book will certainly be a great aid to practitioners working in an international trade finance environment to establish and sustain their footprints.

The chapter on Forex markets provides the much needed insights into the arithmetic part too, which many books do not dare to enter into. I am sure that even the Forex dealers will stand immensely benefited in honing up their expertise.

Researchers will find this a great compendium of information which will be an invaluable input for their research.

All in all, an excellent book to fill a vacuum.

Shri G. Mahalingam
Whole Time Member, SEBI and Former Executive Director, Reserve Bank of India

Preface

This book is intended to cover all the aspects of the implementation of international trade through the banking channel. There are many books on international trade and finance that mostly cover the economic and business theory and hardly deal with anything related to the practical aspects of financing international trade. For a student of economics, finance or business management, it is very important to understand the practicality of the execution of trade with other countries. This book is intended to introduce students to the new domain of payment methods and different products under letter of credit (LC), for example, back-to-back LC, transferable LC, standby LC (SBLC), red clause and green clause LC and their usage for exporters and importers. It provides a complete coverage on the dynamics of the LC mechanism through different caselets related to Uniform Rules for Customs and Practices or UCP 600 and International Standard Banking Practices or ISBP 745, which are required to be understood by exporters, importers and bankers.

The main objective of this book is to bridge the existing gap between the theory and practices related to international finance. In this book, we discuss FEMA guidelines, banking theories related to International Chamber of Commerce (ICC) rules and the role of banks as an issuing bank, an advising bank, a nominated bank, a negotiating bank and a confirming bank. Given the increasing demand and the development in the area, this book explores the role and responsibility of a practitioner banker, which remained as a very gray area in the mainstream literature of finance and economics and was hardly discussed in the area of international finance. This book is an attempt to reach MBA students and practitioners in the banking domain, given the growing proportion of commerce happening across borders. The functionality of SBLC or bank guarantees is also a very gray area in the mainstream academic arena. This book is designed to address the utilization of these products in international trade with the applications related to ISP 98 and URDG 758.

This book discusses in detail all the steps of executing an export or import deal, right from signing a contract, managing pre-shipment credit and booking a forward contract to hedge the exchange rate risk till the closing of the deal. It discusses the application of ICC rules through caselets, which helps an Indian exporter to take necessary actions when the payment is denied by a party overseas, or how an Indian importer can simply deny the payment if there is documentary noncompliance. Also, this book explains the role of a guarantee cover in international trade and its application. Moreover, the book is designed to facilitate exporters and the importers in using INCOTERMS (international commercial terms) that define the division of risk and cost between the buyer and the seller. Use of a bill of lading as a transport document is another area that was largely ignored and is covered in this book. In addition to export finance or pre- and post-shipment finance, this book provides a detailed coverage on import finance or buyer's credit and suppliers' credit.

We also intend to bridge the knowledge gap in terms of hedging the foreign exchange risk in international trade. Existing international finance textbooks are reluctant to employ the practical way of covering exchange rate risk through examples interbank deals. Right from bid and offer rate, this book also covers the importance of understanding value dates and their implementation in converting INR into foreign currency and vice versa at different settlement dates. Also, it explains the booking of merchant deals and how these deals create positions in the banking book under exchange position and fund position, and how do the interbank dealers covers the nostro position.

This book has evolved over a number of years of my teaching international banking and trade finance. As a student of economics and having specialization in financial economics, I had never received any opportunity to learn this subject before I joined the National Institute of Bank Management (NIBM), Pune. I was assigned to develop a course in trade finance, which was not taught exclusively before in NIBM. After developing the subject, I conceived the idea of writing a book in this area with the expectation that students now would have a handy reference to depend on. I am immensely thankful to NIBM, especially to Dr Asish Saha, the then director, for giving me an opportunity to contribute to an area of practical banking that is closely related to international trade. I am deeply indebted to all the bankers whom I met and whose sessions I attended right from the beginning and learnt the subject.

I am sure that this book will contribute to the existing knowledge of international finance and will definitely be a good read for all management students and bankers who are working in Forex, and also for the academicians who are interested in doing research in the related areas.

Acknowledgments

First, I would like to acknowledge the encouragement of Ms Indrayani Deekshit, ex-Banker, Bank of Maharashtra; Management and Forex Consultant, with whom the book was initially proposed to be written. She contributed the content of merchanting trade, presented in Chapter 9. The untimely demise of Ms Deekshit had left the task much more difficult; however, I have received constant support and guidance from Shri Jayant Keskar, ex-Banker, IDBI Bank. I sincerely acknowledge the invaluable help of Shri Appaji Apte, ex-Banker, Bank of Maharashtra, for sharing his experience, which helped in developing the caselets related to ICC guidelines. My heartfelt gratitude to Shri Arvind Salvi, ex-Banker, RBI, for his exquisite contribution in writing the relevant content on FEMA.

Also, I am deeply indebted to Shri V. Rajagopal, Shri Harit Dhruv and Shri M. V. Subramaniam for their constant support and help in building my base in terms of Forex dealing and interbank transactions. The entire operational gamut of managing foreign exchange risk was learnt from these three eminent foreign exchange dealers. Being a student of economics, I must acknowledge that there is a huge gap between the theoretical and practical applications of hedging foreign exchange.

I have learned a lot from my students and the participants of the executive program held at NIBM for middle- and senior-level bankers. The titles of the programs are as follows: (a) Financing International Trade, (b) Foreign Exchange Business and Trade Finance, (c) Forex Dealing with Bourse Game, and (d) Integrated Treasury Management with Bourse Game. Most of the case studies and contents of this book were taught to them and well discussed in the classroom.

My deepest obligations to Dr Asish Saha, former Director of NIBM, who encouraged me to develop the subject. He was the first person to let me know of the gap in the existing academic knowledge that requires bridging. I am extremely obliged to Dr Achintan Bhattacharya, Director, NIBM, for his inspiration and support, especially at the time when I lost some chapters due to the crashing of my laptop's hard disc. Without his support, it would not have been possible to submit the manuscript on time. I am also thankful to Dr Lekha Chakraborty, Professor at NIPFP; Dr Pinaki Chakraborty, Professor at NIPFP; for their support and encouragement. My heartfelt thanks to Dr Arindam Bandyopadhyay and Prof Sanjay Basu for their constant encouragement to do research. My sincere gratitude to all the professionals and teachers from whose lectures I developed the subject. Also, I deeply acknowledge the guidance and support of the editors of SAGE. A special thanks to Ms Indrani Dutta, Senior Development Editor, SAGE.

In the end, I want to express my profound thanks to my father who stood by me through all my troubles to share my feelings and helped me to overcome the difficulties of my life. I am also thankful to my husband Anirban; my mother, my parents-in-law, my little sister, Ivy and my *didi* for being there for me with all their love and affection.

About the Author

Gargi Sanati, PhD, is currently Assistant Professor at NIBM, Pune. Specializing in trade finance and Forex dealings, Dr Sanati's key area of teaching and research is interbank cover operations through Forex swap. Other areas of her research interest include financial integration at the domestic and international fronts, examination of India as a bank-or market-based economy, impact of universal banking and stochastic and technical analysis for forecasting. She plays a lead role in coordinating and teaching a number of executive programs in the area of financing international trade, Forex dealing and bourse game.

Dr Sanati has published a number of research papers related to packing credit or pre-shipment credit. She played a key role in a consultancy project "Impact Assessment Study of Interest Subvention Scheme" undertaken by the Directorate General of Foreign Trade, Ministry of Commerce, Government of India. She has also closely worked on the preparation of the treasury manual of a bank (the name of which cannot be disclosed).

Dr Sanati completed her masters and MPhil in economics from the University of Kalyani and received her PhD degree from the Centre of Development Studies, Jawaharlal Nehru University (JNU), in the year 2013.

International Trade Finance and Payment Methods

1.1 Trade Finance in Today's Context

Trade finance is in general related to the methods of payment, products, and procedures of financing the production cycle in an exporting sector. It is specifically linked to underlying international trade transactions where exporters are assured of payment and importers are assured of good-quality products. Commercial banks play a significant role in turning export opportunities into actual sales; moreover, a product such as a letter of credit (LC) ensures payments for such sales by effectively managing the risks associated with international business. Trade finance is of vital importance to the global economy, with the World Trade Organization estimating that 80%–90% of global trade is reliant on this method of financing. Figure 1.1 represents the significant distributions of the products and payment methods of all the countries together for export and import accounts.

Figure 1.1   Products in Export–Import Business

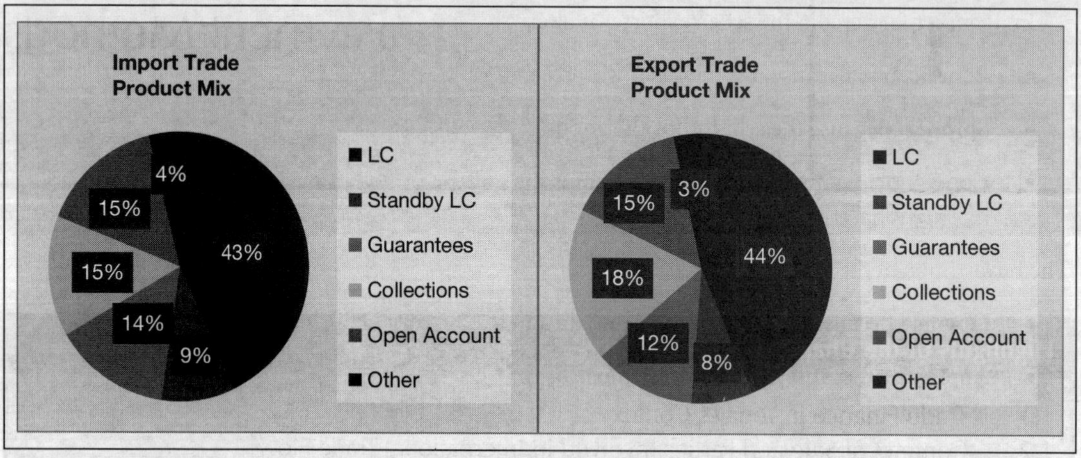

Import Trade Product Mix

- LC
- Standby LC
- Guarantees
- Collections
- Open Account
- Other

4%, 15%, 43%, 15%, 14%, 9%

Export Trade Product Mix

- LC
- Standby LC
- Guarantees
- Collections
- Open Account
- Other

3%, 15%, 44%, 18%, 12%, 8%

SOURCE: Adapted from ICC Report "Rethinking Trade and Finance," 2015.

The global trade finance market, although vibrant and liquid, it hardly kept any systematically maintained databases before 2009. The International Chamber of Commerce (ICC) has started developing a detailed worldwide database on payment methods and related trade transactions only since 2009. More specifically, this initiative is a consequence of stress situations experienced by most of the countries immediately after the Lehman bankruptcy. Lack of trust and funding strains at European banks had raised concerns about possible disruptions in payment chains across countries. On the other hand, the development of new structured products led to an incipient structural change.

Global and domestic banks have played an active role in developing a wide range of products to help their customers manage international payment obligations. Also, these banks are predominantly the source of the required working capital in the form of either pre-shipment finance or post-shipment finance and that too at the lowest possible interest cost.

1.2 Contract of Sale and Parties Involved in International Trade Flow

This section describes the contract of sale and different parties involved in international trade finance in connection to the payment methods they use. The main parties of trade financing are (a) exporter, (b) importer, and (c) banks. A contract of sale is established between the exporter and importer with the specification of price, quantity, products, delivery, and payment terms. The contract of sale is the principal contract, which is followed by other contractual agreements such as payment methods and the terms of payment, bill of lading (BL), international commercial terms (INCOTERMS), insurance document, and so on.

There is one standard format of the contract of sale, popularly known as the Contract of International Sales of Goods (CISG). It is established as per the convention of the United Nations, and as of May 2016, it has been ratified by 85 states that account for a significant proportion of world trade, making it one of the most successful international uniform laws. However, Hong Kong, India, South Africa, Taiwan, and the United Kingdom are the only major trading countries that have not yet ratified the CISG.

In documentary credit, the seller/exporter is alternatively referred to as:

- **Beneficiary:** Because it is the seller who receives payment from the LC.

- **Shipper:** Because the seller ships the goods.

- **Consignor:** Again, because the seller ships the goods; sometimes referred to as "consignment" in international transport.

The buyer/importer is alternatively referred to as:

- **Opener:** Because the importer "opens" the credit to begin the process.

- **Applicant:** Because the importer must begin the process by submitting a "credit application" to a bank.

- **Account party:** Because the importer's application to open credit creates an "account" relationship with the issuing bank and it is supervised by an account officer.

For establishing any international trade transaction, the importer or exporter requires an import–export code (IEC). It is issued by the Directorate General of Foreign Trade (DGFT), Ministry of Commerce, India.

Banks: Mostly, the commercial banks authorized to deal in foreign exchange help in the trade finance process. However, depending on the payment methods involved, the risk and responsibility vary across the banks. Especially, a bank when involved in a LC transaction undertakes more responsibility than it does for the other payment methods. We discuss the role of these banks together with the payment methods.

1.3 Payment Methods: Associated Risk and Parties Involved

International trade finance involves four different payment methods: (a) advance payment, (b) open account, (c) documentary collection, and (d) documentary credit or LC transaction.

We now describe the details of the payment methods in international trade finance and the risks associated with each of the payment methods (see Figure 1.2).

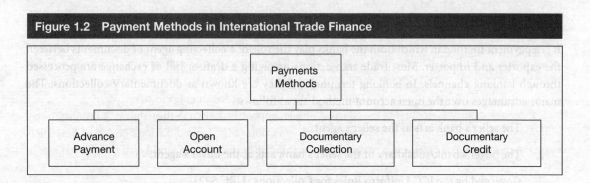

Figure 1.2   Payment Methods in International Trade Finance

1.3.1 Advance Payment

Under this, the exporter will not ship the goods until the buyer remits the payment to the exporter. The important characteristics of advance payment are:

1. Riskiest proposal for the importer as the importer pays early.

2. The exporter is doubtful about the importer who is the "first-time" buyer and/or whose credit-worthiness is unknown to the exporter.

3. The exporter is selling to a country that is in financial difficulty and under country risk. Country risk is a little different from sovereign risk. Country risk comprises financial, economic, and political risk.

This method provides the supplier the greatest degree of protection. Most buyers, however, are not willing to bear all the risk by prepaying an order. Many a times the advance is paid in part.

1.3.2 Open Account

Under this payment system, the exporter dispatches the goods directly to the importer on an agreement of payment at a later date. Sometimes payment is made after the goods are sold by the buyer. The major characteristics of this payment method are:

1. Risk of nonpayment fully lies with exporter.

2. Legal remedies to enforce payment are very difficult.

3. No bank finance is involved.

4. Cheapest method of receiving payment.

5. Takes place usually among subsidiary–parent companies, creditworthy buyers or buyers with a long-standing trade relationship.

Despite the risks involved, open account transactions are widely utilized, particularly among the industrialized countries. This is considered to be the most preferred payment method as it involves lesser cost than other bank intermediary transactions. Many times open account transaction is used in international market through the service of factoring and forfaiting. Sometimes, open account transaction is used with the support of SBLC.

1.3.3 Documentary Collection

It is a payment method in which both the banks play the role of a collecting agent of documents between the exporter and importer. Most trade transactions involving a draft or bill of exchange are processed through banking channels. In banking terminology, they are known as documentary collections. The major advantages over the open account method are as follows:

1. The seller's bank acts as the seller's agent.

2. The buyer's bank/subsidiary of the seller's bank acts as the buyer's agent.

3. Governed by the ICC Uniform Rules for Collections (URC 522).

4. From the seller's point of view, if the seller needs to take action against nonpayment, he or she can take legal action.

5. From the buyer's point of view, payment is made only after the goods are received.

As per the definition of documentary collection in ICC guideline URC 522, documentary collection involves the following parties:

1. **The principal (the drawer):** The exporter who arranges the collection of documents and delivers them to his or her bank with collection instructions.

2. **The remitting bank:** The exporter's bank that forwards the documents together with the exporter's instructions to the collection bank.

3. **The collecting bank:** Any bank (other than the remitting bank) involved in the processing of the collection and that would normally be the remitting bank's correspondent in the importer's country.

4. **The presenting bank:** The importer's bank that presents the collection documents to the drawee (importer) and collects the payment or obtains the acceptance from the drawee. The collecting and presenting bank are often the same.

5. **The drawee:** The importer to whom the documents are presented for payment or acceptance.

Now, we would discuss a case to understand the flow chart of the documents and payment involving the aforementioned parties.

Case Study

Say, ABC Malaysia, a retail trader, has signed a purchase agreement on November 1 with a cloth company in Bangladesh. The order value of the garments is USD 1 million. Shipment is to be made on November 25. As per the agreement, the Bangladesh company has to deliver 10,000 shirts to ABC Malaysia. The cloth company ships the goods and submits the documents to its bank, say East Bank (See Figure 1.3).

There are two types of collections, depending on the bill of exchange involved. A bill of exchange or draft is a promise drawn by the exporter, instructing the buyer to pay the face amount of the draft upon presentation. The draft represents the exporter's formal demand on payment from the buyer. There are two types of drafts:

a. Sight draft, which is involved with collection under documents against payment (DP), and

b. Usance draft, which is involved with collection under documents against acceptance (DA).

1. Collection under Documents against Payment or DP: If shipment is made under a sight draft, the collecting bank is instructed to deliver documents only against payment. It is a practice that provides the exporter with some protection, since the banks will release the shipping documents only according to the exporter's instructions. Let's say the previously mentioned transaction involves DP, and it is under sight draft. The important characteristics of the documents and payment are as described here:

a. The buyer needs the shipping documents to pick up the merchandise. Sometimes goods reach the dock much earlier than documents reach the bank.

b. If the goods are not as per the ordered quality, the importer would lose as payment is already made.

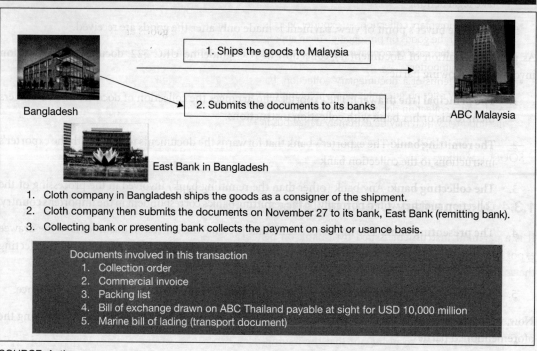

Figure 1.3   Transaction Flow under Documentary Collection

1. Ships the goods to Malaysia

Bangladesh

2. Submits the documents to its banks

ABC Malaysia

East Bank in Bangladesh

1. Cloth company in Bangladesh ships the goods as a consigner of the shipment.
2. Cloth company then submits the documents on November 27 to its bank, East Bank (remitting bank).
3. Collecting bank or presenting bank collects the payment on sight or usance basis.

Documents involved in this transaction
1. Collection order
2. Commercial invoice
3. Packing list
4. Bill of exchange drawn on ABC Thailand payable at sight for USD 10,000 million
5. Marine bill of lading (transport document)

SOURCE: Author.

  c. If for any reason, the collecting bank overlooks the instructions on sight payment and delivers documents before getting paid, it faces the risk of having to recompense the seller for the loss.

Now, if the transaction is under DA and it involves a usance draft, the flow of the documents and payments is as discussed further.

2. Collection under Documents against Acceptance or DA: If a shipment is made under a time draft or a usance draft, the exporter provides instructions to the buyer's bank to release shipping DA. This method of payment is referred to as DA:

  a. By accepting the draft, the buyer promises to pay the exporter at the specified future date. Consequently, the buyer is able to obtain the merchandise and check the quality of the goods prior to payment. It might create the risk of nonpayment to the exporter.

  b. It is the buyer's responsibility to honor the draft at maturity. In this case, the exporter provides the financing in terms of time and is dependent upon the buyer's financial integrity to pay the draft at maturity.

  c. The added risk is that if the buyer fails to pay the draft at maturity, the bank is not obligated to honor payment. The exporter assumes all the risk and must analyze the buyer accordingly.

  d. Sometimes after checking goods, the importer refuses to pay; so the seller may have to arrange some other customer in the same country or in a different country.

Box 1.1   Risk in Documentary Collections

- Under documentary collection, an exporter bears less risk compared to an importer. The importer can take control over the goods on presentation of an appropriate document of title together with a bill of exchange or draft. In the case of nonpayment, the draft provides the legal support to the exporter for protesting against the importer.
- Under the terms of a documentary collection, banks are only concerned with the exchange of documents. They offer no guarantee of payment, **unless the buyer's bank avals an accepted bill of exchange**. Avalizing a collection document means bank undertakes unconditional payment obligation on behalf of the importer, which may be extremely dangerous from a bank's point of view.

SOURCE: Author.

1.3.4 Documentary Credit or Letter of Credit

It is a payment instrument issued by a bank on behalf of the importer (buyer) promising to pay the exporter (beneficiary) upon presentation of all the documents in compliance with the terms stipulated in the credit. The main characteristics of LCs are:

- The exporter is assured of receiving payment from the issuing bank as long as he or she presents documents in accordance with the LC.

- It is important to point out that the issuing bank is obligated to honor drawings under the LC regardless of the buyer's ability or willingness to pay.

- On the other hand, the importer does not have to pay for the goods until shipment is made and documents are presented in good order. However, the importer must still rely upon the exporter to ship the goods as described in the documents, since the LC does not guarantee that the goods purchased will be those invoiced and shipped.

All the LCs subject to The Uniform Customs and Practices of Documentary Credit, 2007 Revision, ICC Publication No. 600 (UCP), are considered to be irrevocable LCs. Under UCP 600, all LCs are treated as irrevocable, even if there is no indication to that effect. An irrevocable LC cannot be amended or cancelled without the consent of the issuing bank, the confirming bank (if any) and the exporter. This allows the exporter to procure the goods or prepare them for shipment with the assurance that payment will be received if the stipulated documents are presented and the terms and condition of the credit are complied with. At present, there is no existence of a revocable LC that allows the importer to amend or even cancel the LC; as it provides no security to the exporter.

The LC mechanism and the flow of documents and payments in Figure 1.4 are represented as follows:

1. ABC Exporter, USA, and Renuka Importer, India, establish a sales contract between them. In this, the exporter insists on payment by LC, mainly to avoid credit risk in the transaction. It is more often practiced if the buyer is not known much to the exporter and if there is any information on weak creditworthiness. If there is any country risk, then the exporter gets protection under confirmed LC.

2. The importer then initiates the LC mechanism by giving an application to its bank, Bank of Baroda, India (known as issuing bank), for issuing an LC.

Figure 1.4   The Flow of Documents and Payments under Letter of Credit Transaction

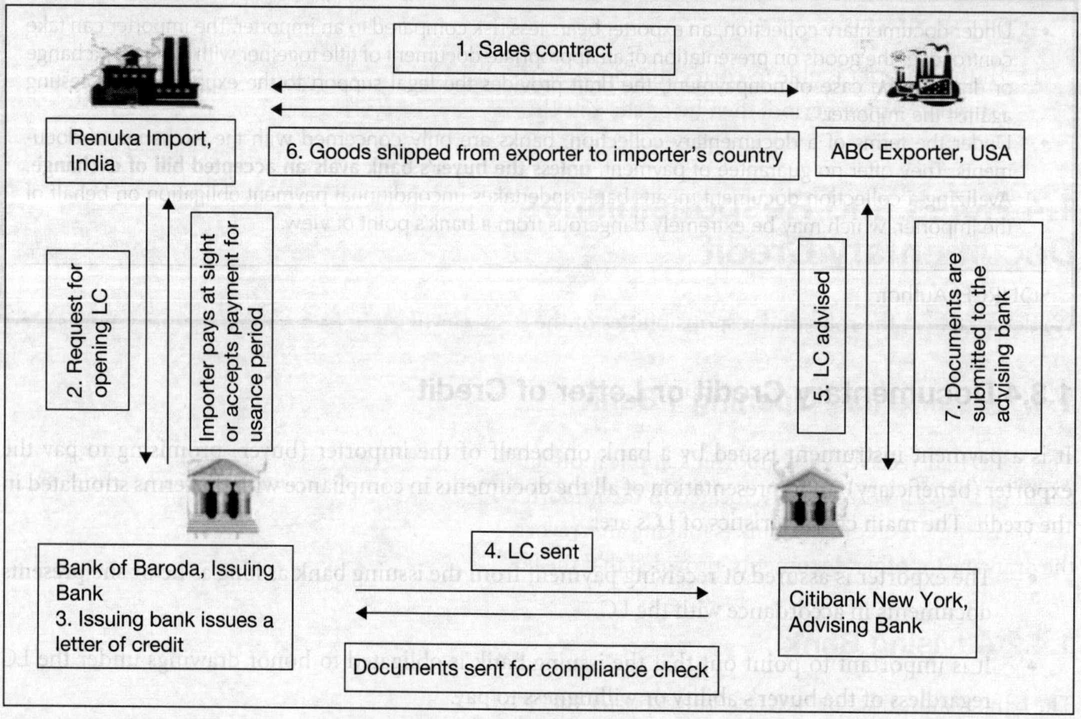

SOURCE: Author. The idea is conceived from the guidelines of FEDAI Publication 2015, titled Documentary Credits and Standby Credits.

3. Given that the internal credit department approves the credit facility, an issuing bank issues LC through the Society for Worldwide Interbank Financial Telecommunication (SWIFT) in favor of the beneficiary or exporter. By opening an LC, Bank of Baroda undertakes the payment obligation irrespective of the ability of the importer to pay.

4. Then the issuing bank sends the LC to the advising bank or the exporter bank, Citibank New York, USA.

5. Citibank advises or notifies ABC Exporter about the LC without undertaking the payment obligation unless and until it plays the role of a confirming bank.

6. The exporter ships the goods as per the terms and conditions of the credit.

7. The exporter submits all the documents asked by the credit along with a BL—a shipping document and a bill of exchange or draft representing the issuing bank's payment obligation to the exporter's bank within 21 days from the date of shipment and within the validity of the credit.

8. All the documents are sent to the issuing bank.

9. The issuing bank checks the documents. If the documents comply with the payment terms, then the importer either initiates the payment under a sight draft or accepts the future payment obligation under a usance draft.

10. If the documents do not comply, then Bank of Baroda cites a documentary discrepancy and notifies ABC Exporter through the advising bank within five banking days from the date of sighting the documents.

11. If the exporter is able to correct the documents as per the LC terms and resubmits them within a stipulated time period, then he or she gets the payment or else the payment gets rejected.

1.4 Roles and Responsibilities of Banks under Documentary Credit

We describe here the roles and responsibilities of the banks involved in international trade finance.

1.4.1 Issuing (or "Opening") Bank

The bank that receives the importer's application and agrees to "issue" the credit. The issuing bank is commonly, but not necessarily, located in the importer's country.

By issuing the credit, the bank is making an irrevocable undertaking to pay the beneficiary the value of the draft and/or other documents, provided that the terms and conditions of the credit are complied with.

1.4.2 Advising Bank

The bank that notifies or "advises" the exporter that a credit has been opened in the exporter's favor.

By advising a credit, the bank is only acting as an outlet for the issuing bank; the advising bank does not take any further risk. The advising bank only has the responsibility of satisfying itself as to the apparent authenticity of the credit and ensuring that the advice of the credit (to the beneficiary) accurately reflects the terms and conditions of the credit received.

The advising bank is commonly, but not necessarily, located in the exporter's country.

The advising bank may be named differently depending on its role in a transaction:

1. Nominated Bank

2. Negotiating Bank

3. Confirming Bank

4. Paying Bank

1.4.2.1 Nominated Bank

The bank that is stipulated in a credit as authorized to honor (pay, issue a deferred payment undertaking or accept drafts) or negotiate.

Unless a credit expressly states that it is available only with the issuing bank, it should nominate some other bank.

If the credit is of the "freely available" variety, any bank qualifies as a nominated bank. A nominated bank is not normally bound to pay under the credit, unless it has added its confirmation to the credit and has become a confirming bank.

1.4.2.2 Negotiating Bank

The bank that examines the documents presented by the exporter, then negotiates the credit (i.e., in the case of a usance draft, the bank either advances or agrees to advance funds to the beneficiary on or before the maturity date of the draft). This negotiation is usually done "with recourse," which means that if the issuing bank fails to reimburse the negotiating bank, the negotiating bank will recover the funds advanced to the exporter.

1.4.2.3 Confirming Bank

The bank (normally also the advising bank) that adds its own irrevocable undertaking (known as confirmation) in addition to that given by the issuing bank.

Confirmation allows the exporter to be paid by a bank in the exporter's own country, or by a bank that the exporter otherwise trusts.

The confirming bank irrevocably commits itself to pay the exporter upon presentation of conforming documents.

1.4.2.4 Paying (or "Paying Agent") Bank

The bank that reviews the documents presented by the exporter and, if they comply with the terms and conditions of the credit, arranges payment to the exporter. A paying bank's main risk is paying against documents that turn out to contain discrepancies, in which case it may not be able to recover the funds from the issuing bank.

However, a bank acting as paying agent may refuse to pay the exporter if the issuing bank's account is not sufficient to cover the draft (this applies where the bank has not added its confirmation to the LC).

1.4.3 A Sample Letter of Credit

```
Sender: Bank of Baroda, Kolkata, India
Receiver: Citibank, Texas, USA

40A: Form of Documentary Credit:
     Irrevocable
20:  Documentary Credit No:
     LC25198042
31C: Date of Issue:
     110608
31D: Date and Place of Expiry:
     110724 Texas
51A: Applicant Bank:
     BARBINBBIBB
     Bank of Baroda, Kolkata, India
50:  Applicant:
     Renuka Imports,
     Mumbai, India
59:  Beneficiary:
     ABC Exporter
     19 Main Road, New York, USA
```

32B: Currency Code Amount:
   Currency: US$ (USD)
   Amount: 10,000
41D: Available with/by Name:
   Any Bank
   By Negotiation
42C: Drafts at:
   Sight for 100 PCT of invoice value
42A: Drawee:
   BOB,
   Bank of Baroda,
   Kolkata, India
43P: Partial Shipments:
   Allowed
43T: Transshipment:
   Not Allowed
44A: On Board:
   Port of Houston, Texas, USA
44B: For Transportation to:
   Howrah, India
44C: Latest Date of Shipment:
   110714
45A: Descriptions of Goods and/or Services
   Contract No: HLSZ048-GY-01
   Commodity:
   1.   T-shirts
        Quantity: 1000
        Unit price: USD 10
        Documents required:
        • Signed commercial invoice in five copies indicating LC number and contract number HLSZ48-GY-01.
        • A copy of rail waybills consigned to the applicant name and address with the stamp of shipping.
        • Certificate of quantity in three copies.
        • Certificate of quality in three copies issued by the beneficiary.
        • Beneficiary's certified copy of cable/telex dispatched to accounts within 72 hours after last shipment, advising shipping number and date, contract number, LC number, commodity, quantity, weight, and value of shipment.
47A. Additional Conditions:
   One extra nonnegotiable copy of the previously mentioned documents should also be sent to the issuing bank for its file.
71B: Charges:
   All banking charges and interest outside India are for the beneficiary's account.
48:   Period for Presentation
   Documents to be presented within 21 days after the issuance of the transport document but within the validity of the credit.
49:   Confirmation Instructions:
   Without
78:   Instructions to Pay/Acc/Neg Bank
        A discrepant document fee of USD 60 plus telex/SWIFT charges for each set of documents contained within a presentation will be deducted from proceeds if the documents contain discrepancies.
Unless otherwise stated, this credit is subject to UCP 600 by ICC.

(Continued)

(Continued)

All documents should be sent in two covers to the following address:

Bank of Baroda, Kolkata, India, 700141

This LC is opened through SWIFT by the message type 700. Although most of the fields of the LC are self-explanatory, we would specifically describe field numbers 41D, 42C, 43P, 43T, 48 and 49.

   41D: It describes whether the LC is a restricted or freely available type. As in this LC, we see that it is available by any bank; therefore, we can say that the exporter can go for negotiating his or her documents to any bank. This kind of credit is known as *freely available credit*. If a name of the particular bank, say, Citibank Texas, is written in this field, then the exporter is free to negotiate his or her documents only with Citibank Texas. This second kind of credit is known as *restricted credit*.

   42C: It describes that the credit involves a sight draft. It necessarily means that the importer has to pay as and when documents are sighted by him or her.

   43P: It refers to the condition whether the LC allows any partial shipment to happen or not. If this field is left blank, it means the LC is silent about it. Then, partial shipment is allowed. Otherwise, the LC has to prohibit partial shipment with a mention of it.

   By definition of UCP 600, the time limit for a bank to determine a complying presentation is five banking days. A presentation consisting of more than one set of transport documents evidencing shipment commencing by the same means of conveyance and for the same journey, provided the documents indicate the same destination, will not be regarded as covering a partial shipment, even if they indicate different dates of shipment or different ports of loading, places of taking in charge or dispatch.

   For example, we do not consider it partial shipment if ship A goes from Nhava Sheva Port, Mumbai, to Sri Lanka on August 16 by waterway and then the same ship gets another loading from Kochi, Kerala, on August 18 for the same destination, having two BLs or transport documents involved. This is because in the above case we have the same means of conveyance, that is, ship A going to the same destination having more than one BL. However, two ships A and B going to the same destinations by the same mode of transport (waterway) would be considered as partial shipment even if the ships start on the same day.

   43T: It refers to transshipment, and it means unloading from one vessel and reloading to another vessel during carriage from the port of loading to the port of discharge stated in the credit.

   48: It states that the documents are to be presented within 21 days after the issuance of the transport document but within the validity of the credit. If they are not presented accordingly, the documents are considered to be stale documents. In this case, the documents may be rejected for payment unless the LC explicitly mentions that stale documents are allowed.

   49: The advising bank or some other bank in the exporter's country may be requested to add confirmation under this field. We have already discussed that it is to avoid the problem of payment due to country risk. However, it may be noted that whether the bank would add or not add the confirmation is up to the bank.

1.5 Export Bill Negotiation/Purchase and Discount

Having understood the LC mechanism and payment flow, we will now discuss in detail the concepts of negotiation, purchase and discount. In the banking parlance, purchase or discount is used when the transactions are not under LC. If documentary collection involves a sight draft, then the process of presentation of documents and related advance made by the bank, if any, is known as the purchase of bill. If under documentary collection the Usance draft is used, then the aforementioned activity is termed as discounting the bill. However, the term negotiation is used when a transaction is under documentary credit.

   Negotiation takes the form of an advance while the funds or documents are in the banking system, and is normally "with recourse" in the event (that) the issuer fails to reimburse the nominated bank. "With recourse" means that the bank that is negotiating with the exporter can call back the money if the importer is not paying.

If an exporter negotiates the documents with the advising bank, which is nominated for negotiation, then the advising bank is called the negotiating bank. After the shipment of the goods, the exporter prepares necessary documents, such as commercial invoice, packing list, certificate of origin, BL or airway bill, bill of exchange, quality certificate and other documents specifically mentioned in the LC, and submits them to the negotiating bank. As the trade transaction is under LC, the bank verifies whether the documents are complying with the terms and conditions of the credit and then negotiates the export bills. Under negotiation, the invoice amount is credited to the exporter's account after deducting the necessary bank charges. After the realization of credit amount from the overseas buyer, the exporter pays back the bank with the interest rate.

1.6 Normal Transit Period

This is the period taken for realization of export proceeds. The normal transit period (NTP) has nothing to do with the goods in transit. Instead, it refers to the period after which documents are received by the issuing bank and the export payment is made to the nostro account of the exporter's bank. For example, if there is sight draft, then as per the recommendation of the Foreign Exchange Dealers Association of India (FEDAI), 25 days NTP is allowed to the exporter, from the date of shipment. As this trade transaction is under sight draft, it is not possible to know the exact date or day of sight to the importer or receiving the payment. Thus, the calculation of maturity is a major problem. So the exporter is allowed to negotiate his or her documents for 25 days. Now if the payment is received, say, on the 10th day, then the bank adjusts the interest rate that is charged to the exporter.

This NTP is also allowed for the usance draft if the draft is drawn with the condition, say, 90 days after sight. For example,

SPACE BELOW FOR ACCEPTANCE STAMP FORM : 3221		DRAWER'S OR FORWARDING BANK'S NUMBER
Drawn Under Bank of Thailand 21.01.2016 **L/C 324 / 1437** **Royal Bank of Scotland International** **Trade Centre L/C 68924**	Due	**324 / 1437**
AT 90 DAYS SIGHT FOR VALUE RECEIVED PAY TO THE ORDER OF THE **ROYAL BANK OF SCOTLAND** THE SUM OF		RECEIVING BANK'S NUMBER 68924
Fifty Five Thousand **US dollars $ 55,000.00 US** To, *Royal Bank of Scotland* *International Trade Centre* *Any City, Any Province*	**ABC Silk Trading Inc.** **Saritha S., Director**	

If an exporter wants to negotiate on this bill of exchange, then 25 days NTP would be added to 90 days.

1.7 Checklist for Documentary Credit

For the exporter:

As payment under documentary credit methods is subject to documentary compliance, an exporter has to be extra careful in documentary management (Jimenez, 2012). The following steps are must:

1. The exporter must check the terms and conditions of the credit once advised and request for amendment if any of the terms and conditions are difficult to comply with.

2. Prepare the exact documents called for in the credit.

3. Verify the type of the documentary credit:

   a. Insurance certificate, or

   b. Insurance policy.

4. Prepare the documents as required by the credit.

5. Avoid presentation of the documents at the last date of presentation. It is easier to present the documents at the earliest possible.

6. Any corrections in the credit should be authenticated by the issuer or by his or her agent.

For the importer:

1. Do not incorporate unnecessary clauses in the credit.

2. The terms of the credit should be same as that in the contract.

3. Do not have any conflicting documents called by the credit. For example, if the goods are shipped by a container, then it would not be wise to call for a simple BL.

4. Call for an insurance certificate, and mention who should issue the insurance certificate. This is the best safeguard measure for an importer to ensure the delivery of goods.

5. Avoid third-party documents.

6. Avoid charter party BL.

For the banks:

1. Counsel inexperienced customers on the value of an insurance certificate and the use of INCOTERMS.

2. In case an applicant wants to use INCOTERMS, say, free onboard (FOB), when goods are sent by airway, then the banker should not use such INCOTERMS. In case of wrong specification of INCOTERMS in the contract, the banker should advise changes in the contract itself to avoid conflict of data.

3. Transshipment and partial shipment is allowed in case the LC is silent about the credit.

4. Review of documents should be done within the stipulated time frame. In no condition would the maximum period of time be exceeded by the banker.

5. Banks deal in documents, not in goods.

1.8 Factoring

Factoring, since its inception in 1950 in the USA and the UK, was popularly known as "invoice financing" and was mostly practiced by small- and medium-sized enterprises. Commercial banks started taking an interest in factoring business in the 1980s; however, it was limited to domestic markets at large until the mid-1990s. Today, the factoring service includes a wide range of services, for example, credit risk assessment and protection, collection of overdue accounts, and administration of sales contracts. These services are offered by different agents or "factors" of different companies. An exporter may purchase either or all the services: finance, collection, and credit cover.

Factoring is widely used in international markets as an alternative service to bank intermediary services such as documentary collection and LC. Under open account payment methods, factoring is an important service to the exporters at a comparatively low cost. Also, the services offered by banks are often based on the a negotiable instrument, such as a bill of exchange, which does not cover a large part of the accounts receivables.

Under open account, the exporter may agree to supply to the importer with 30 or 60 days' time gap for payment and produce the invoice to a factoring organization (either a subsidiary of a bank or an independent factor). After the shipping of goods and receiving documentary evidence, the factor extends an advance to the exporter against a service charge. Generally, the advance amount is 80%–90% of the total invoice value. On the due date, the factor collects the dues from the importer. In case of an advance, the factor charges an interest over and above the service charges.

It may happen that, in addition to the export factor (the factor operating in the exporter's country), there may be an import factor in the importer's country. These factors may be subsidiaries of the same company working in two different countries. The import factor mostly takes the responsibility of checking the creditworthiness of the buyer, collects funds from the importer immediately after the receipt of goods and transfers the funds to the export factor.

1.8.1 Guidelines on Factoring (Refer RBI Master Circular on Export of Goods and Services)

1. Export factoring on nonrecourse basis

Taking into account the recommendation made by the Technical Committee on Facilities and Services to the Exporters (Chairman: Shri G. Padmanabhan), it has been decided to permit authorized dealer (AD) banks to factor the export receivables on a nonrecourse basis, so as to enable the exporters to improve their cash flow and meet their working capital requirements subject to the following conditions:

1. AD banks may take their own business decision to enter into export factoring arrangements on a nonrecourse basis. They should ensure that their client is not over-financed. Accordingly, they may determine the working capital requirement of their clients, taking into account the value of the invoices purchased for factoring. The invoices purchased should represent genuine trade invoices.

2. In case export financing has not been done by the export factor, the export factor may pass on the net value to the financing bank/institution after realizing the export proceeds.

3. The AD bank, being the export factor, should have an arrangement with the import factor for credit evaluation and collection of payment.

4. Notation should be made on the invoice that the importer has to make payment to the import factor.

5. After factoring, the export factor may close the export bills and report the same in the Export Data Processing and Monitoring System (EDPMS) of the Reserve Bank of India (RBI).

6. In case of a single factor, not involving an import factor overseas, the export factor may obtain credit evaluation details from the correspondent bank abroad.

7. Know your customer (KYC) and due diligence on the exporter shall be ensured by the export factor.

1.9 Forfaiting

The forfaiting facility is available mainly for medium-term financing, typically three to five years at a fixed or floating interest rate and popularly used for financing capital goods. According to the definition provided by International Forfaiting Association (IFA), "[f]orfaiting is a form of export finance involving the discount of trade related debt-obligations due to mature at a future date without recourse to the exporter/endorser" (Ramberg, 2008, p. 261).

Forfaiting guarantees 100% financing without recourse to the seller of the obligation. However, if the seller is an importer, the forfaiting service is provided to the importer only against an irrevocable and unconditional bank guarantee (BG) with documentary evidence of a bill of exchange, promissory notes or an LC.

For example, Renuka Import accepts a bill of exchange or a promissory note that is guaranteed by or availed by a bank in the importer's country, say, Punjab National Bank. This bill of exchange is sent to Mr John Wall in the UK for his export of cotton to Renuka Import. After receiving the draft, John endorses the draft and hands it over to his bank, Barclays, UK, and it discounts the documents without recourse. If the payment method is chosen as LC, then the issuing bank accepts the bill of exchange and the forfaiting bank negotiates the accepted draft without recourse. For this, the forfaiter needs to have some important documents, for example, (a) copy of sales contract and a bill, preferably avalized by a bank, (b) copy of invoice, (c) certificate of origin, (d) insurance certificate, and (e) copy of acceptance advice and the due date notification. As the forfaiter purchases the bill without recourse, the beneficiary has to bear the risk of nonpayment. So the forfaiter takes both political and country risk in addition to credit risk.

1.9.1 RBI Guidelines on Forfaiting (Refer Master Circular on Exports of Goods and Services)

Export-Import Bank of India (EXIM Bank) and AD Category–I banks have been permitted to undertake forfaiting, for the financing of export receivables. Remittance of commitment fee/service charges, and so on, payable by the exporter as approved by the EXIM Bank/AD Category–I banks concerned, may be done through an AD bank. Such remittances may be made in advance in one lump sum or at monthly intervals as approved by the authority concerned.

References and Resources

United Nations. (2010). *Contracts for international sales of goods.* Retrieved on October 31, 2016, from https://www.uncitral.org/pdf/english/texts/sales/cisg/V1056997-CISG-e-book.pdf

Jimenez, G. C. (2012). *ICC guide to export/import: Global standard for international trade.* ICC Publication.

Ramberg, J. (2008). *Guide to export–import basics: Vital knowledge for trading internationally.* (3rd ed., p. 261). Paris: ICC Publication.

Uniform Customs and Practices–UCP 600. *ICC guidelines to govern operation under letter of credit.* Retrieved on February 23, 2016, from www.fd.unl.pt>mhb_MA_24705

Uniform Rules for Collection–URC 522. *ICC guidelines to govern operations under collection.* Retrieved on February 23, 2016, from www.uef.fi

QUESTIONS

A. Multiple Choice Question

1. The LC issuing bank undertakes to honor its commitment if
   a. The beneficiary submits the stipulated documents according to the LC terms
   b. Packs and ships the goods according to the sales of contract
   c. LC issuing bank may refuse to honor its commitment due to the poor credit rating of the beneficiary

2. If paying bank acts as a confirming bank under LC
   a. It bears the responsibility to scrutinize the document
   b. Faces the documentary risk, wherein issuing bank may refuse to honor its commitment
   c. Paying bank can't be confirming bank
   d. a and b
   e. a and c

3. Which of the following is true with respect to a BE?
   a. This is a demand for payment issued by the exporter (drawer) to the importer (drawee) in case of documentary collection
   b. It is just a financial document
   c. It is an conditional payment obligation
   d. Both a and b
   e. All a, b, and c
   f. None of the above

4. Unrestricted LC specifically means credit is available with
   a. Advising bank

   b. Confirming bank
   c. Negotiating bank
   d. Any bank

5. After receiving the goods if importer finds the goods are not matching the quality specified in the sales contract, importer asks issuing bank to call back the payment from exporter
   a. Issuing bank can call back the payment because of the discrepancy found in the goods
   b. Issuing bank can't call back the payment as it deals only with the documents and not with the goods
   c. It depends whether the LC is with or without recourse
   d. Both a and b
   e. All a, b, and c

6. Under documentary collection
   a. Exporter is relatively safer as it involves bill of exchange, although nonpayment risk to be borne by exporter
   b. Exporter is safe only when bank adds it avalization
   c. Both a and b
   d. None of the above

7. In international trade, LCs are governed by
   a. FEMA
   b. FEDAI
   c. UCP
   d. RBI
   e. (a) and (b)
   f. (b) and (c)
   g. (a), (b) and (c)
   h. (a), (b), (c) and (d)

8. From exporter's point of view, lay out the various modes of trade transactions in ascending order of risk
   (i) Documents against payment
   (ii) Documents against agreement
   (iii) Advance payment
   (iv) Open a/c
   a. (iv), (ii), (iii). (i)
   b. (iv), (ii), (i), (iii)
   c. (iii), (ii), (i), (iv)
   d. (iii), (i), (ii), (iv)

9. Import–export code is issued by
   a. RBI
   b. DGFT
   c. FEDAI
   d. Customs department
   e. Both a and

10. As per UCP 600, time limit for a bank to determine a complying presentation is
    a. 7 banking days
    b. 5 banking days
    c. 10 banking days
    d. None of these

B. Answer the Following Questions

1. How many payment methods are involved in international trade finance?

2. What is bill of exchange? In which payment method(s) is it used?

3. What are the differences between documentary collection and documentary credit?

4. What is the role of an advising bank?

5. What is the usefulness of a confirmed letter of credit? If a bank is nominated for confirmation, is it obliged to add its confirmation? Explain.

6. What is restricted credit? What is freely available credit?

7. Does bank undertake any payment obligation under documentary collection? Is there any exception?

8. What are the differences among export bill negotiation, discount, and purchase?

9. What is negotiation with recourse?

10. What is partial shipment?

11. What is transshipment? If a letter of credit prohibits transshipment, can it happen?

12. Is it mandatory to open a letter of credit under UCP 600? Can it be opened under other UCP publications?

13. If the letter of credit is silent about partial shipment, is it allowed?

14. Explain the documentary flow of a letter of credit transaction.

15. When can an issuing bank refuse to pay? Give an example.

16. What is the difference between factoring and forfaiting?

17. Write a few important characteristics of forfaiting service.

18. For documentary collection, what all parties are involved?

19. For documentary collection, what all documents are required?

20. Suppose an exporter from India wants to export to Africa. Which payment method would the exporter opt for?

21. If an exporter from India expects country risk and the payment method is under letter of credit then what kind of special protection the exporter can look for?

22. Does the bank take any risk related to documentary collection?

23. What is avalization? Explain with an example.

24. What is the remitting bank under documentary collection?

25. What is normal transit period? Why is it applied in case of sight draft? Is it necessary to apply the NTP for the usance period?

26. A letter of credit is opened with sight draft. The below is submitted by the Indian exporter for negotiation to Indian Bank. For how many days can Indian Bank negotiate the documents?

SPACE BELOW FOR ACCEPTANCE STAMP FORM : 321 **Drawn Under Singapore Commercial Bank** **Due**…………………………. **L/C 3902 / 2389** **Royal Bank of Canada International** **January 21 19**………. **Trade Centre L/C 4567123** AT SIGHT FOR VALUE RECEIVED PAY TO THE ORDER OF THE **ROYAL BANK OF SCOTLAND** THE SUM OF *Fifty Thousand* **U.S.DOLLARS** $ 50,000.00 **U.S.** **TO**, *Royal Bank Of Scotland* *International Trade Centre* **BCD Exports LTD.** *Any City, Any Province* **Saritha S, Export Manager**	DRAWER'S OR FORWARDING BANK'S NUMBER 3902 / 2389 _____ _____ RECEIVING BANK'S NUMBER 4567123

Sample of Inland Letter of Credit

INLAND IRREVOCABLE DOCUMENTARY CREDIT	
OPENING BANK/BRANCH NAME AND ADDRESS	ILC No. Dated: Last date of Transport _____ Last date of Negotiation_____
APPLICANT NAME AND ADDRESS	**BENEFICIARY NAME AND ADDRESS**
ADVISING BANK/BRANCH NAME AND ADDRESS	Amount not exceeding ₹ _____ (In words _____)
Partial Dispatch Transshipments Allowed Allowed _____	Credit available by drafts drawn by the beneficiary on the opener and marked drawn under _____ (Bank name/branch) ILC No. _____ dated _____ for
Dispatch from _____	100% of the invoice value at 90 days usance from the date of drafts quoting this credit number.
For Transportation to _____	Our Irrevocable Credit No. Date of Dispatch : Date of Expiry : Place of Expiry :

(Continued)

(Continued)

Authorized Signatory   **Authorized Signatory**
ILC no _____
Dated _____

- **DOCUMENTS REQUIRED:** Draft for 100% of invoice value plus carrying charges, expenses and interest.
- Two copies of signed delivery orders.
- Two copies of signed commercial invoices.
- Two copies of debit notes for carrying charges, interest, and other expenses, if any, as per contract terms.
- Motor lorry receipt.
- Two copies of weight notes.

SPECIAL INSTRUCTIONS TO NEGOTIATING BANK:
- Negotiations should be marked separately on the back of the first page of this documentary credit, and this credit should accompany the draft that exhausts the credit. The negotiating bank must send the full set of documents to us in one lot by courier.
- We shall remit on due date/you claim on us provided the documents submitted are in strict conformity with LC terms.

SPECIAL INSTRUCTIONS TO ADVISING BANK:
- We request to notify the credit to the beneficiary without adding your confirmation.
- We hereby engage with drawers and/or bona fide holders that draft (s) drawn under and negotiated in conformity with terms of this credit will be duly honored on presentation and that draft(s) accepted within the terms of this credit will be duly honored at maturity except as otherwise expressly stated, this credit is subject to Uniform Customs and Practice for Documentary Credits (2007 Revision) International Chamber of Commerce, Publication no. 600.
- We hereby guarantee to protect the drawers, endorsers, and bona fide holders from any consequence that may arise in the event of nonacceptance or nonpayment of the drafts drawn in accordance with terms of this credit.

ADDITIONAL CONDITIONS:
- Tolerance in value is 5% plus/minus.
- Documents must be presented for negotiation within 30 days from the date of drafts but within the validity of credit.
- Goods should be consigned to _____ (Bank Name) _____ A/c M/s. _____ (Name of the applicant).
- Transportation prior to LC date is not acceptable.

DESCRIPTION OF GOODS:
Dispatch of _____ (nos.) of FP bales @ _____ per candy of variety _____, as per Indent no. _____ dated_____, vide Contract no. _____ dated.
This document consists of _____ signed pages.

_____   _____
Authorized Signatory   Authorized Signatory

OTHER TERMS:

1. ILC amount includes invoice value with sales tax, carrying charges, and other expenses, if any, as per the contract terms.
2. Bill of exchange.
3. Transit Insurance will be covered by the applicant.
4. Freight will be paid by the applicant.
5. All bank charges including discounting charges are on the account of opener.
6. Interest at the rate 15% per annum on the 1 above on account of the opener.
7. In case, the amount not paid on due date a penal interest @ 2% per annum will be charged over and above interest charged at clause no. 6.
8. Letter of credit is "WITHOUT RECOURSE TO DRAWERS."
9. The letter of credit is for _____ days usance from the date of bill of exchange.
10. Negotiation under this credit is allowed with _____ (CCI bank/branch name, and address).
11. The negotiating bank/branch should mark all negotiation made by it on the reverse of the original credit.
12. After negotiation the document to be presented to _____(bank name and branch) who is authorized to make payment on due date directly to negotiating bank.

Authorized Signatory   Authorized Signatory

Sample of International Letter of Credit

MDTC/f&A/TOCMPl/1/459   dated 31.01.2017

To
Dy. General Manager (MC-SH),
The State Bank of India,
24, Park Street (3rd Floor),
Kolkata-700016

Sub: Procedure and Modalities of Letter of Credit Arrangement
Ref: Your Letter No. MCSH/DGM/dated 017.12.2016.

Sir,

According to your advice and our projected scheme to allow LC facility to our customers of coal sent to us vide letter under reference. After having a rigorous appraisal of the entire modalities/procedure at our end, we have finalized the Letter of Credit Scheme and we propose for implementation of the scheme at the earliest possible. As such, a copy of the said finalized scheme along with the enclosures/annexures is attached for your perusal.

We shall allow the buyers of the coal from our very next e-auction proposed to be held on 10.02.2017 to avail such Letter of Credit facility strictly as per the aforesaid scheme.

(Continued)

(Continued)

This is for your information and necessary further action.

With regards,

Enclo: As stated.

Yours faithfully,

Signature:

_____

(Saritha S)
Managing Director

Copy to:

1) Mr Bhattacharya Damodar Coal Mining Private Limited, Kuvera Plot, Unit No. B-21, 2th Floor, 221/1B, A. J.C. Bose Road, Kolkata 700021.
2) M/s Sen and Sen Services Limited, Green City, Riverside, Sector -II, 5th Floor, Plot No. 15, Block-DP, Salt Lake City, Kolkata 700092.
3) M/s MSTC Limited, 255-B, A.J.C Bose Road, Kolkata 700030.

Managing Director

Notice for Payment through Letter of Credit

A. The successful bidder in e-auction of ABC Mineral Development and Trading Corporation Ltd (ABC MDTCL), intending to make payment of Coal Value through Letter of Credit, is informed that Letter of Credit submitted by them to ABC MDTCL will be acceptable only if
    1) A Solvency Opinion/Certificate from their banker has to be submitted by the party/ customer. Also, the party/customer must accepts the terms and conditions of e-auction and Letter of Credit in writing in his letter head under seat and signature and submits the same with the service provider.
    2) Letter of Credit should be issued by the Issuing Bank in the recommended format of ABC MDTCL.
    3) Letter of Credit is transmitted to the banker of ABC MDTCL.
    4) Letter of Credit should be a confirmed letter of credit, if issued, in physical form. Letter of Credit should have a confirmation by the Banker of ABC MDTCL.
    5) Letter of Credit is issued only by banks as per list attached in Annexure "A."
    6) Letter of Credit should be a restricted one. It is to be advised through and restricts for negotiation on State Bank of India, Alipore Branch, Alipore, Kolkata.
    7) The bidder who wins the bid has to bear all charges on Letter of Credit like Issuing Charges/Advising Charge/Confirmation Charge/ Negotiation Charge/Bill of Exchange Stamp Duty/Intent I Discount Charge for usance period etc., if availed.

B. The payment through Letter of Credit is subject to the following conditions:
    1) Letter of Credit has to be submitted on or before last date of payment intimated in the Sale Intimation Letter issued to the successful bidder.
    2) A Delivery Order has to be generated against the allocation of Letter of Credit by the successful bidder from the website of the service provider.

3) A bill of exchange to be prepared by ABC MDTCL. It must indicate the usance period same as mentioned in Letter of Credit, the amount of bill of exchange including Bank Charges/Stamp Duties/Interest Discount Charges for usance period etc.

4) After receiving all the documents, ABC MDTCL shall submit the following documents for negotiation to their bank:

   i.   Bill of Exchange, mentioning the usance period, due date, sale amount as per Proforma Invoice and bank charges including interest for usance period, drawn by ABC Mineral Development and Trading Corporation Limited.

   ii.   Proforma Invoice(s) (original+3 copies) duly signed by Authorized Signatory of ABC Mineral Development and Trading Corporation Limited.

   iii. Delivery Order (original+2 copies).

5) The original Delivery Order will be handed over to the Bidder by their bankers only on acceptance of documents. The payment would be made on maturity of bill of exchange by the Bidder's bank.

6) The Delivery Order will be made effective with the receipt of acceptance of documents by the Bidder's bank.

7) In the event of nonacceptance of documents by the Bidder's bank, the original Delivery Order issued, will be cancelled by ABC MDTCL.

C. The usance period may be decided by the bidder. However, it is subject to following:

1) Usance shall be up to a maximum 120 days.

2) Bidder has to pay all the charges, for example, stamp duty, advising bank charges, confirming bank charges, handling charges, and interest charged for the usance period by the negotiating bank. For this bank must collect an undertaking from the bidder.

Annexure "A"

List of Banks:

Nationalized Banks:

1. Allahabad Bank
2. Andhra Bank
3. Bank of Baroda
4. Bank of India
5. Bank of Maharashtra
6. Canara Bank
7. Central Bank of India
8. Corporation Bank
9. Dena bank
10. IDBI Bank
11. Indian Bank
12. Indian Overseas Bank
13. Oriental Bank of Commerce
14. Punjab & Sind Bank
15. Punjab National Bank
16. State Bank of Bikaner & Jaipur
17. State Bank of Hyderabad
18. State Bank of India
19. State Bank of Mysore
20. State Bank of Patiala
21. State Bank of Travancore
22. Syndicate Bank
23. UCO Bank
24. Union Bank of India
25. United Bank of India
26. Vijaya Bank

Private Sector Banks:

1. Axis Bank
2. Federal Bank
3. HDFC Bank
4. ICICI Bank
5. IndusInd Bank
6. Kotak Mahindra Bank
7. Yes Bank

Letter of Credit

40A	TYPE OF LC	IRREVOCABLE LETTER OF CREDIT
31D	DATE & PLACE/COUNTRY OF EXPIRY	DATE : _____ PLACE : INDIA
50	NAME & ADDRESS OF THE APPLICANT	
59	NAME & ADDRESS OF THE BENEFICIARY WITH TEL, TLX & FAX NOS.	ABC MINERAL DEVELOPMENT & TRADING CORPORATION LIMITED 13, SARAT BOSE ROAD, COMMERCIAL BUIDING, 1ND FLOOR, KOLKATA-700021 EMAIL : abcmdtcl@gmail.com TEL: 033-1234-1111, 033-1234-1112, 033-1234-1113 FAX: 033-2222-3333
	ADVISING BANK NAME, ADDRESS AND RTGS DETAIL	STATE BANK OF INDIA, ALIPORE BRANCH, ALIPORE, 25/1/1, ALIPORE ROAD, KOLKATA-700021 ACCOUNT NO: 00000011223344556 IFS CODE: SBIN0001234
	NEGOTIATING BANK	STATE BANK OF INDIA, ALIPORE BRANCH, ALIPORE, 25/1/1, ALIPORE ROAD, KOLKATA-700021 ACCOUNT NO: 00000011223344556 IFS CODE: SBIN0001234
32B	CURRENCY & AMOUNT OF CREDIT (IN FIGURES AND WORDS)	INR _____ (INR _____ CRORES ONLY)
39A	TOLERANCE LIMIT IN LC AMT	(+/-) 5%
39C	ADDITIONAL AMT PERMITTED	NIL
41A	CREDIT AVAILABLE WITH	STATE BANK OF INDIA, ALIPORE BRANCH, ALIPORE, 25/1/1, ALIPORE ROAD, KOLKATA-700021
42C	DRAFTS AT	USANCE _90_____DAYS FROM THE DATE OF DELIVERY ORDER
42A	DRAWEE	LC ISSUING BANK
42M	MIXED PAYMENT DETAILS	NOT APPLICABLE
42B	DEFERED PAYMENT DETAILS	NOT APPLICABLE
43P	PARTIAL SHIPMENTS	PERMITTED
43T	TRANSSHIPMENT	PERMITTED
44E	LOADING POINT	TRANS PADMA OPEN CAST MINES, KALYAN NAGAR, BANKURA
44F	DESTINATION	
44C	LATEST DELIVERY ORDER DATE	

45A	DESCRIPTION OF GOODS	PRODUCT-COAL SIZE - ROM / STEAM GRADE -G4 / G5 QUANTITY - (+/0)5% UNIT PRICE – INR_____ /MT FOB PACKING - BULK OTHER DETAILS-AS PER SALES INTIMATION LETTER NO - DTD - MODE OF TRANSPORT - ROAD/RAIL DESPATCH TERM- FOB
46A	DOCUMENTS REQUIRED :	
	1) BILL OF EXCHANGE MENTIONING USANCE PERIOD, DUE DATE, DELIVERY ORDER AMOUNT, AND ALSO BANK CHARGES INCLUDING INTEREST FOR USANCE PERIOD DRAWN BY ABC MINERAL DEVELOPMENT & TRADING CORPORATION LTD. 2) BENEFICIARY SIGNED PROFORMA INVOICE(S) IN ONE SET OF ORIGINAL PLUS 3 COPIES 3) ORIGIANL DELIVERY ORDER PLUS 2 COPIES OF DELIVERY ORDER	
47A	ADDITIONAL DOCUMENTS: • L/C TERMS & CONDITIONS:- 1. All DOCUMENTS SHOULD BE IN ENGLISH. DOCUMENTS PRODUCED OUT OF CARBON COPIES/COMPUTERIZED SYSTEM 15 NOT ACCEPTABLE UNLESS AUTHENTICATED OR MANUALLY SIGNED. 2. DISCREPANT DOCUMENTS SHALL NOT BE NEGOTIATED WITHOUT THE PRIOR CONSENT/ACCEPTANCE OF THE APPLICANT/ISSUING BANK. 3. All DOCUMENTS MUST BEAR THE LC NUMBER. 4. STAMP DUTY IF ANY WILL BE BORNE BY APPLICANT.	
71B	CHARGES: L/C ISSUING CHARGES/ADVISING CHARGES/CONFIRMATION CHARGES/ NEGOTIATION CHARGES/INTEREST FOR USANCE PERIOD /ANY OTHER CHARGES OF THE APPLICANT BANK ANO BENEFIIARY BANK WILL BE BORNE BY APPLICANT.	
48	PERIOD OF PRESENTATION	DOCUMENTS ARE TO BE PRESENTED WITHIN 45 DAYS FROM THE DATE OF BILL OF EXCHANGE BUT WITHIN THE VALIDITY OF THE LC
49	CONFIRMATION INSTRUCTION	WITHOUT FEE. BANKS ACCEPTABLE TO WBMOTCL AS PER LIST IN NOTICE.
50A	CREDIT TO BE ADVISED TO THE BENEFICIARY THROUGH (BANK)	STATE BANK OF INDIA, ALIPORE BRANCH, ALIPORE, 25/1/1, ALIPORE ROAD, KOLKATA-700021

REIMBURSEMENT INSTRUCTIONS:

NEGOTIATION SHOULD BE MARKED SEPARATELY ON THE BACK OF THE FIRST PAGE OF THIS DOCUMENTARY CREDIT AND THIS CREDIT SHOULD ACCOMPANY THE DRAFT THAT EXHAUSTS THE CREDIT. THE NEGOTIATIONG BANK MUST SEND THE FULL SET OF DOCUMENTS TO IS IN ONE LOT BY DTDC, IN REIMBURSEMENT, WE SHALL REMIT THE PAYMENT ON DUE DATE AS PER INSTRUCTION OF THE NEGOTIATING BANK.

(Continued)

(Continued)

> WE HEREBY ENGAGE WITH THE DRAWER AND/OR BONA-FIDE HOLDERS THAT DOCUMENTS DRAWN IN CONFORMITY WITH THE CREDIT TERMS WILL BE PAID ON PRESENTATION.
>
> UNLESS OTHERWISE EXPRSSLY STATED, THE CREDIT IS SUBJECT TO UCP (2007 REVISION) ICC PUBLICATION NO. 600.

Appendix

Documentary Credit Message Types

The following table lists all documentary credit message types defined in Category 7.

For each message type, there is a short description, an indicator whether the message type is signed (Y or N), the maximum message length for input (2,000 or 10,000 characters) and whether the use of the message requires registration with SWIFT for use in a message user group (Y or N).

MT	MT Name	Purpose	Signed (1)	Max Length	MUG
700	Issue of a Documentary Credit	Indicates the terms and conditions of a documentary credit	Y	10,000	N
701	Issue of a Documentary Credit	Continuation of MT 700	Y	10,000	N
705	Pre-Advice of a Documentary Credit	Provides brief advice of a documentary credit for which full details will follow	Y	2,000	N
707	Amendment to a Documentary Credit	Informs the receiver of amendments to the terms and conditions of a documentary credit	Y	10,000	N
708	Amendment to a Documentary Credit	Continuation of MT 707	Y	10,000	N
710	Advice of a Third Bank's Documentary Credit	Advises the receiver of the terms and conditions of a documentary credit	Y	10,000	N
711	Advice of a Third Bank's Documentary Credit	Continuation of MT 710	Y	10,000	N
720	Transfer of a Documentary Credit	Advises the transfer of a documentary credit, or part thereof, to the bank advising the second beneficiary	Y	10,000	N
721	Transfer of a Documentary Credit	Continuation of MT 720	Y	10,000	N

730	Acknowledgment	Acknowledges the receipt of a documentary credit message and may indicate that the message has been forwarded according to instructions. It may also be used to account for bank charges or to advise of acceptance or rejection of an amendment of a documentary credit	Y	2,000	N
732	Advice of Discharge	Advises that documents received with discrepancies have been taken up	Y	2,000	N
734	Advice of Refusal	Advises the refusal of documents that are not in accordance with the terms and conditions of a documentary credit	Y	10,000	N
740	Authorization to Reimburse	Requests the receiver to honor claims for reimbursement of payment(s) or negotiation(s) under a documentary credit	Y	2,000	N
742	Reimbursement Claim	Provides a reimbursement claim to the bank authorized to reimburse the sender or its branch for its payments/negotiations	Y	2,000	N
744	Notice of Non-Conforming Reimbursement Claim	Notifies the receiver that the sender considers the claim, on the face of it, as not to be in accordance with the instruction in reimbursement authorization for the reason(s) as stated in this message	Y	2,000	N
747	Amendment to an Authorization to Reimburse	Informs the reimbursing bank of amendments to the terms and conditions of a documentary credit, relative to the authorization to reimburse	Y	2,000	N
750	Advice of Discrepancy	Advises of discrepancies and requests authorization to honor documents presented that are not in accordance with the terms and conditions of the documentary credit	Y	10,000	N

(Continued)

(Continued)

752	Authorization to Pay, Accept or Negotiate	Advises a bank which has requested authorization to pay, accept, negotiate or incur a deferred payment undertaking that the presentation of the documents may be honored, notwithstanding the discrepancies, provided they are otherwise in order	Y	2,000	N
754	Advice of Payment/ Acceptance/ Negotiation	Advises that documents have been presented in accordance with the terms of a documentary credit and are being forwarded as instructed. This message type also handles the payment/negotiation	Y	2,000	N
756	Advice of Reimbursement or Payment	Advises of the reimbursement or payment for a drawing under a documentary credit in which no specific reimbursement instructions or payment provisions were given	Y	2,000	N
759	Ancillary Trade Structured Message	Requests or provides information, such as a fraud alert or a financing request, concerning an existing trade transaction such as a documentary credit, demand guarantee, standby letter of credit or an undertaking (for example, a guarantee, surety, etc.)	Y	10,000	N

SOURCE: Category 7 - Documentary Credits and Guarantees, Retrived from https://www.swift.com/node/21326 retrieved on June 29, 2017.

Format of MT 700

MT 700 Issue of a Documentary Credit

Status	Tag	Field Name	No.
M	27	Sequence of Total	1
M	40A	Form of Documentary Credit	2
M	20	Documentary Credit Number	3
O	23	Reference to Pre-Advice	4

Status	Tag	Field Name		No.
M	31C	Date of Issue		5
M	40E	Applicable Rules		6
M	31D	Date and Place of Expiry		7
O	51a	Applicant Bank		8
M	50	Applicant		9
M	59	Beneficiary		10
M	32B	Currency Code, Amount		11
O	39A	Percentage Credit Amount Tolerance		12
O	39B	Maximum Credit Amount		13
O	39C	Additional Amounts Covered		14
M	41a	Available with… By…		15
O	42C	Drafts at…		16
O	42a	Drawee		17
O	42M	Mixed Payment Details		18
O	42P	Negotiation/Deferred Payment Details		19
O	43P	Partial Shipments		20
O	43T	Transshipment		21
O	44A	Place of Taking in Charge/Dispatch from…/Place of Receipt		22

Status	Tag	Field Name	Content/Options	No.
O	44E	Port of Loading/Airport of Departure	65x	23
O	44F	Port of Discharge/Airport of Destination	65x	24
O	44B	Place of Final Destination/For Transportation to …/Place of Delivery	65x	25
O	44C	Latest Date of Shipment	6!n	26
O	44D	Shipment Period	6*65x	27
O	45A	Description of Goods and/or Services	100*65z	28
O	46A	Documents Required	100*65z	29
O	47A	Additional Conditions	100*65z	30
O	49G	Special Payment Conditions for Beneficiary	100*65z	31
O	49H	Special Payment Conditions for Receiving Bank	100*65z	32
O	71D	Charges	6*35z	33
O	48	Period for Presentation in Days	3n[/35x]	34
M	49	Confirmation Instructions	7!x	35
O	58a	Requested Confirmation Party	A or D	36

(Continued)

(Continued)

O	53a	Reimbursing Bank	A or D	37
O	78	Instructions to the Paying/Accepting/Negotiating Bank	12*65x	38
O	57a	Second Advising Bank	A, B, or D	39
O	72Z	Sender to Receiver Information	6*35z	40
M=Mandatory, O=Optional				

Regulatory and Institutional Framework

2.1 The Role of the Regulatory Bodies in Indian and in International Front

International trade and its related activities are regulated by many domestic and international regulatory bodies. The important domestic regulatory bodies primarily are the RBI, the Central Bank of India, FEDAI and the DGFT, Ministry of Commerce. The RBI plays the primary role in formulating the regulatory guidelines, whereas FEDAI helps in framing the execution process. On the other hand, DGFT provides the IEC to the exporter. There are important provisions laid down by DGFT every five years under the foreign trade policy (FTP) which give clear directions related to international trade. In this chapter, we discuss more on the Foreign Exchange Management Act (FEMA); FTP; and the role of

DGFT, EXIM Bank and the Export Credit Guarantee Corporation of India (ECGC). We discuss most of the regulatory policies of the RBI, FEDAI and ICC in different chapters with different related case studies.

2.2 Foreign Exchange Management Act, 1999, Regulatory Framework: An Overview

The Foreign Exchange Management Act, 1999 (FEMA) came into force on June 1, 2000 and replaced the Foreign Exchange Regulation Act, 1973 (FERA). The object of FERA was to conserve foreign exchange resources, whereas the object of FEMA is to facilitate external trade and payments and to promote orderly development and maintenance of the foreign exchange market in India.

2.2.1 Highlights of the FEMA

1. FEMA is more transparent in its application. It has laid down the areas where specific permission of the RBI/Government of India is required. In the rest of the cases, no such permission would be needed and a person can remit funds, acquire assets and incur liabilities in accordance with the specific provisions laid down in the Act or notifications issued by the RBI/Government of India under the Act without seeking approval of the RBI/Government of India.

2. Application of FEMA may be seen broadly from two angles, namely, capital account transactions and current account transactions. Capital account transactions relate to movement of capital, for example, transactions in property and investment, and lending and borrowing of money. Transactions that do not fall in capital account category are the current account transactions, which are permitted freely, subject to a few restrictions as given in the following paragraphs.

    a. Certain current account transactions require the RBI's permission, if they exceed a certain ceiling. Currently it is USD 250,000 per financial year.

    b. A few current account transactions need the permission of the appropriate Government of India authority, irrespective of the amount.

    c. There are eight types of current account transactions, which are totally prohibited and no transaction can, therefore, be undertaken relating to them.

[Details of (a), (b), and (c) are given in Schedules I, II, and III of the Government of India notification dated May 3, 2000, namely, Foreign Exchange Management (Current Account Transactions) Rules, 2000 as amended from time to time.]

2.2.2 Salient Features of FEMA

The salient features of FEMA are as follows:

1. The preamble of FEMA indicates its objective of "facilitating external trade" and "promoting the orderly development and maintenance of foreign exchange market in India."

2. The powers of the Government of India and the RBI have been clearly demarcated in FEMA.

3. In FEMA, the foreign exchange transactions have been clearly divided in terms of the nature of their being current account or capital account transactions.

4. In FEMA, all provisions are dependent on residential status.

5. The definition of "a person resident in India" is dependent on period of stay as well as on purpose of stay in India.

6. The powers of enforcement officials have been brought at par with income tax officials.

7. Under FEMA, arrest is possible only in cases where the offender tries to evade payment of the penalty imposed on him or her.

8. In FEMA, the prosecution will have to prove the charges against the accused.

9. In FEMA, investigation and adjudication have been segregated as is in case of other investigating authorities like income tax.

10. A concept of "compounding" has found place in FEMA. The RBI as well as Directorate of Enforcement have been empowered to compound contravention as per the authorization prescribed by the government.

11. For disposal of applications for compounding, adjudication and appeal and so on, a definite time frame has been provided in the Act itself.

12. In the repeal clause, a "sun-set" provision has been incorporated with effect that after expiry of two years from the date of commencement of FEMA, no adjudication authority will be able to take cognizance of any contravention of FERA.

2.2.3 Architect and Mechanism

FEMA 1999 has seven chapters consisting of 49 sections. Few sections are specific in nature, that is, either specifically permit or prohibit the undertaking of certain transactions. Most of the sections are required to be operationalized by notifications. These notifications need to be published in the Official Gazette of the Government of India and ratified by both the Houses of the Parliament.

The central government has been empowered to make rules, by notification, to carry out the provisions of this Act, in consultation with the RBI. These rules mainly relate to current account transactions, compounding, adjudication and so on.

The RBI has been empowered to make regulations, by notification, to carry out the provisions of this Act and the rules made thereunder, in consultation with the Government of India. These regulations mainly relate to the permissible classes of capital account transactions, the limits of admissibility of foreign exchange for such transactions and the prohibition, restriction or regulation of certain capital account transaction.

As per the Act, dealing in foreign exchange or foreign securities other than through an authorized person is prohibited. The RBI has been empowered to authorize any person to be known as an authorized person to deal in foreign exchange or in foreign securities as an AD, money changer or offshore banking unit or in any other manner as it deems fit.

The RBI has also been empowered, for the purpose of securing compliance with the provisions of this Act and of any rules, regulations, notifications or directives made thereunder, to give to authorized persons any directives in regard to making payment or doing or desisting from doing any act relating to foreign exchange or foreign security.

2.2.4 Compliance under FEMA

Regulatory framework under FEMA consists of the various provisions of the Act, notifications, rules, regulations, direction or order issued in exercise of the powers under this Act. Therefore, to comply with the regulatory framework one has to strictly follow the framework. Broadly, the following three stages are involved in compliance:

Stage 1

Before undertaking the transaction, that is, compliance with the provisions of Section 10(5) of the Act, which reads as,

> An authorised person shall, before undertaking any transaction in foreign exchange on behalf of any person, require that person to make such declaration and to give such information as will reasonably satisfy him that the transaction will not involve, and is not design for the purpose of any contravention or evasion of the provisions of this Act or of any rule, regulation, notification, direction or order made there under, and where the said person refuses to comply with any such requirement or makes only unsatisfactory compliance therewith, the authorised person shall refuse in writing to undertake the transaction and shall, if he or she has reason to believe that any such contravention or evasion as aforesaid is contemplated by the person, report the matter to the Reserve Bank.

Stage 2

While undertaking the transaction, submission of documentary evidence in support of the transaction such as purpose of the transaction, details of the beneficiary, amount, currency and so on.

Stage 3

After completion of the transaction, compliance with reporting requirements, periodical returns/statements and so on such as inflow reporting, FC-GPR, FC-TRS, ECB-2, ODI, APR and so on.

Apart from these, an authorized person is required to submit various regulatory returns specified by the RBI such as R-Return, XOS, BEF, EBW and so on.

2.2.5 Foreign Exchange Management Act, 1999 (FEMA): Penal Provisions

If any person contravenes any provisions of this Act, or contravenes any rule, regulation, notification, direction or order issued in the exercise of the powers under this Act or contravenes any condition, subject to which an authorization is issued by the RBI, they will be liable to a penalty prescribed in the Act.

The enforcement of the penal provisions operates in three ways as under:

1. Compounding: Settlement of an offence by paying monetary penalty, without litigation provided the contravener voluntary accepts the contravention committed by him or her.

2. Adjudication: Adjudicating authority levies penalty upon adjudication.

3. Sun-set clause: Treatment to cases relating to FERA period, that is, violation committed prior to FEMA regime (up to May 31, 2000).

For disposal of applications for compounding, adjudication and appeal and so on, a definite time frame has been provided in the Act, itself.

If any authorized person contravenes any direction given by the RBI under this Act or fails to file any return as directed by the RBI, the RBI may, after giving reasonable opportunity of being heard, impose on the authorized person a penalty as prescribed in the Act.

2.3 Reserve Bank of India

The RBI was established in 1935, under the Reserve Bank of India Act, 1934. The main purpose of setting up a central bank of India was, as it is stated in the Preamble of the RBI Act, "to regulate the issue of bank notes and for keeping of reserves with a view to securing monetary stability in India and generally to operate the currency and credit system of the country to its advantage."

As a central bank of the country, the RBI acts as the main autonomous regulator of the Indian banking and financial system. As an apex institution, it also monitors all the public, private and foreign commercial banks of India closely. Other than regulating Indian banks, the RBI also controls and promotes India's financial system. The RBI regulates credit, domestic and international lending, credit risk, market risk, operational risk, export and import in international markets, inward and outward remittances and so on.

The RBI is the sole authority for the issue of currency in India, other than the one rupee note/coin which is issued by the Government of India. The RBI regulates and control the supply of money in India through open market operation, repo and reverse repo transactions. The RBI operates through the following departments:

1. Consumer Education and Protection Department,

2. Corporate Strategy and Budget Department,

3. Department of Banking Regulation,

4. Department of Banking Supervision,

5. Department of Communication,

6. Department of Cooperative Bank Regulation,

7. Department of Cooperative Bank Supervision,

8. Department of Corporate Services,

9. Department of Currency Management,

10. Department of Economic and Policy Research,

11. Department of External Investments and Operations,

12. Department of Government and Bank Accounts,

13. Department of Information Technology,

14. Department of Non-Banking Regulation,

15. Department of Non-Banking Supervision,

16. Department of Payment and Settlement Systems,

17. Department of Statistics and Information Management,

18. Financial Inclusion and Development Department,

19. Financial Markets Operation Department,

20. Financial Markets Regulation Department,

21. Financial Stability Unit,

22. Foreign Exchange Department,

23. Human Resource Management Department,

24. Inspection Department,

25. Internal Debt Management Department,

26. International Department,

27. Legal Department,

28. Monetary Policy Department,

29. Premises Department,

30. Rajbhasha Department,

31. Risk Monitoring Department,

32. Secretary's Department,

33. Central Vigilance Cell.

Also, the RBI is a banker to the central government as well as to the state government. The central government is privileged to borrow any amount from the RBI, whereas state governments can borrow only up to sanctioned limits. The short-term advances to the state government are called ways and means advances.

The RBI also plays a very important role as an advisory body to the Central Government. The RBI many a time requested to render advice to the government in term of financial policies and measures concerning new loans, agricultural finance, cooperative organization, industrial finance and legislation affecting banking and credit.

As a bank for commercial banks, the RBI holds their cash reserves and lends them funds. The RBI rediscounts the bills of the commercial banks and also provides them the opportunity to maintain cash reserves and statutory liquidity reserves. The RBI is called lender of the last resort as commercial banks can approach the RBI if they are not able to meet their funds requirements from any other source.

Also, by the RBI Act of 1934 and the Banking (Companies) Regulation Act, 1949, the bank has been vested with extensive powers of supervision and control over commercial and cooperative banks.

2.4 Foreign Exchange Dealers Association of India

It is a nonprofit association of all ADs (PSU banks, foreign banks, private sector banks, cooperative banks and financial institutions) originally setup with the approval of the RBI with the objective of "furthering the interests and regulate the dealings of and between authorized dealers in Foreign Exchange both inter se, and with the public, brokers, the RBI and other bodies." It is an association of the ADs dealing in foreign exchange. In 1958, FEDAI was set up as a self-regulatory body. It is incorporated under Section 25 of The Companies Act, 1956. The primary objective of FEDAI is to frame the operational guidelines for commercial banks according to the guidelines of the RBI. This is to conduct good foreign exchange business within the bank.

On the basis of the RBI guidelines, FEDAI lays down the ground rules for the day-to-day conduct of foreign exchange activity by ADs. Though, with liberalization (and upon the recommendation of Sodhani committee), the members of FEDAI now have more freedom to determine their service charges, etc. FEDAI also acts as a facilitator between the member banks and the RBI, export organizations/chambers of commerce and other bodies, as also among the members. Besides, FEDAI governs the various forex activities including conduct of derivative business by banks.

It provides different rates such as Telegraphic Transfer (TT) buying and selling rates, and bill buying and selling rates along with the rules for export bill and import purchase or discount or negotiation. Also, it may be noted that FEDAI prescribes 25 days as the NTP for sight bill and also for usance bill for calculating maturity date under the condition say "90 days USANCE from the date of sight."

FEDAI prescribes different safeguard measures for using different LC products such as back-to-back LC, transferable LC and standby LC. It also provides guidelines for using products such as BL, packing credit, certificate of origin and so on. FEDAI describes the rate calculation for merchant deals and the application of forex derivatives or currency derivatives as a tool to hedge the open position or the foreign exchange risk.

2.5 Directorate General of Foreign Trade and Foreign Trade Policy

The export-import policy framed by the Government of India (Ministry of Commerce) is implemented by the DGFT. DGFT also looks into the proper use of the various export incentive schemes that are currently in force in our country.

We know that FTP is generally revised every five years. Given the change in the scenarios of international trade, the FTP goes through revision by the DGFT. As discussing all the policies under current FTP is beyond the spread of this chapter or the book, we discuss some of the highlights of this policy.[1]

---

[1] Available at the Government of India website on January 20, 2017. The link is dgft.gov.in/exim/2000/highlight2015.pdf. The detail FTP is available at dgft.gov.in/exim/2000/ftp2015-20E.pdf on January 30, 2017.

2.5.1 Simplification and Merger of Reward Schemes

The scheme applicable from export from India:

1. The Scheme Applicable from Export from India

Earlier there were five different schemes available for rewarding merchandise exports with different kinds of duty scrips with varying conditions (sector specific or actual user only) attached to their use. The schemes which were prevalent were (a) Focus: Product Scheme, (b) Market Linked Focus Product Scheme, (c) Focus Market Scheme, (d) Agri. Infrastructure Incentive Scrip, and (e) Vishesh Krishi and Gram Udyog Yojana (VKGUY). Now all these schemes have been merged into a single scheme, namely, Merchandise Export from India Scheme (MEIS), and there would be no conditionality attached to the scrips issued under the scheme. The description of the group of products and the country grouping under MEIS are available at Annexure-1 (see Appendix).

As per the objective of MEIS, export of notified goods to notified markets are subjective to rewards which are payable as percentage of realized free onboard (FOB) value (in free foreign exchange). The debits towards basic customs duty in the transferable reward duty credit scrips would also be allowed adjustment as duty drawback. As per the Department of Revenue (DoR) rules, currently, only the additional duty of customs/excise duty/service tax is allowed adjustment as Central Value Added Tax (CENVAT) credit or drawback.

2. Service Exports from India Scheme (SEIS)

a. Service Exports from India Scheme (SEIS) has replaced Served from India Scheme (SFIS). SEIS is more inclusive in the sense that it applies to "service providers located in India" instead of "Indian service providers" only. Thus, regardless of the constitution or profile of the service provider, SEIS provides rewards to all service providers of notified services who are providing services from India, The list of services and the rates of rewards under SEIS are in Annexure-2 (See Appendix).

b. Depending on the net foreign exchange earned, the rate of reward is decided under SEIS. There would no longer be any restriction either in terms of actual user conditions and/or in terms of the usage for specified types of goods once the reward is issued as duty credit scrip. Instead, it is freely transferable and operational for all types of goods and service tax debits on procurement of services/goods. Debits would be eligible for CENVAT credit or drawback.

3. Incentives for MEIS and SEIS

Incentives for MEIS and SEIS are available for special economic zones (SEZs) and for the units located in SEZs also.

4. Freely Transferable Duty Credit Scrips

Duty credit scrips are to be freely transferable and usable for payment of custom duty, excise duty and service tax.

a. All scrips issued under MEIS and SEIS and the goods imported against these scrips would be fully transferable.

b. The use of the scrips issued under exports from India schemes are depicted as follows: (a) Expense of customs duty for import of inputs/goods comprising capital goods, except items listed in Appendix 3A[2], (b) Payment of excise duty on domestic procurement of inputs or goods, including capital goods as per DoR notification, and (c) Payment of service tax on procurement of services as per DoR notification.

c. Under duty credit scrip, if inputs so imported are used for exports, the basic customs duty which is paid in cash or through debit can be taken back as duty drawback as per DoR Rules.

5. Status Holders

a. To provide an incentive to the business leaders who have excelled in international trade and have successfully contributed to country's foreign trade it has been proposed that these leaders be recognized as status holders. They should be given special treatment and privileges to facilitate their trade transactions in order to reduce their transaction costs and time.

b. The classification of export house, star export house, trading house, star trading house and premier trading house have been changed to one, two, three, four and five star export house respectively.

c. The new criteria for recognition of status holder has been changed from rupees to US dollar earnings according to the export performance. The status category as per the new classification is given below.

Status Category	Export Performance FOB/FOR (as converted) Value (in US$ million) during current and previous two years
One Star Export House	3
Two Star Export House	25
Three Star Export House	100
Four Star Export House	500
Five Star Export House	2,000

d. Approved Exporter Scheme—Self-certification by Status Holders

To be eligible for preferential treatment under different preferential trading agreements (PTAs), FTAs, comprehensive economic cooperation agreements (CECAs) and comprehensive economic partnerships agreements (CEPAs) which are in operation, the manufacturers who are also status holders will be permitted to self-certify their manufactured goods as originating from India. These self-certification is permitted for the goods manufactured as per their industrial entrepreneur memorandum (IEM)/industrial license (IL)/letter of intent (LOI).

---

[2] See the main Foreign Trade Policy 2015–2020, retrieved from, http://dgft.gov.in/exim/2000/ftp2015-20E.pdf retrieved on May 22, 2017.

2.5.2 Boost to "Make in India"

6. Reduced Export Obligation (EO) for domestic procurement under Export Promotion of Capital Goods (EPCG) scheme

If capital goods are procured from indigenous manufacturers, under EPCG scheme, specific EO, which is currently 90% of the normal EO (six times at the duty saved amount), has been reduced to 75%. This measure is taken to promote domestic capital goods manufacturing industry.

7. Reward for the Products with High Domestic Content

Under MEIS, higher level of rewards are available for export items with high domestic content and value addition as compared to products with high import content and less value addition.

2.5.3 Trade Facilitation and Ease of Doing Business

8. Online Filing of Documents/Applications and Paperless Trade in 24×7 Environment

a. Under FTP, the facility of online filing of various applications by the exporters/importers is already provided by DGFT. However, it excludes certain documents; certificates issued by chartered accountants/company secretary/cost accountant and so on have to be filed in physical forms. It has been decided to develop an online procedure to upload digitally signed documents by chartered accountants/company secretaries/cost accountants in order to move further towards paperless processing of reward schemes.[3]

b. To save paper, cost and time for the exporters, it has been decided that, henceforth, applications under Chapter 3 and 4 of FTP, which accounts for more than 70% of the total applications, are not required to be submitted in the hard copy format. Applications under Chapter 5 would be taken up in the next phase.

c. Exporters can upload the landing documents of export consignment as proofs for notified market digitally. This measure is taken to ease the business dealings for the exporters. The digitalization of the document can be done in the following ways:

   i. Any exporter may upload the scanned copy of the digitally signed bill of entry.

   ii. Status holders falling in the category of three star, four star or five star export house may upload scanned copies of documents.

9. Online Inter-ministerial Consultations

With the objective to reduce time for approval, it is proposed to have online inter-ministerial consultations for approval of export of special chemicals, organisms, materials, equipment and technologies (SCOMET) items, norms fixation, import authorizations and export authorization, in a phased manner. For this purpose, exporters would not be required to submit hard copies of documents.

---

[3] In the new system, it will be possible to upload online documents like the annexure attached to ANF 3B, ANF 3C and ANF 3D, which are at present signed by these signatories and submitted physically.

10. Simplification of Procedures/Processes, Digitization and E-governance

a. Procurement and submission of a certificate from an independent chartered engineer confirming the use of spares, tools, refractory and catalysts imported for final redemption of EPCG authorizations has been dispensed with under *EPCG* scheme.

b. Now the EPCG authorization holders shall be required to maintain records for a period of two years after redemption of authorizations, instead of the three years that was in operation. The government's endeavor is to gradually phase out this requirement because the relevant records, such as shipping bills and e-BRC are expected to be available in electronic mode and can be retrieved whenever required.

c. Exporter Importer Profile: Facility has been created to upload records/documents, for example IEC, manufacturing license, registration cum membership certificate (RCMC), PAN and so on in the exporter/importer profile. Once uploaded, it would not require the submission of copies of permanent records/documents repeatedly with each application.

d. Communication with Exporters/Importers: In IEC database, information such as mobile number, email address and so on has been added as compulsory fields for establishing better communication with exporters. As a part of the improved communication with the parties, SMS/email would be sent to exporters to inform them about issuance of authorizations or status of their applications.

e. Online message exchange with Central Board of Direct Tax (CBDT) and Ministry of Corporate Affairs (MCA): Online message exchange with CBDT for PAN data and with MCA for Corporate Identity Number (CIN) and Director Identification Number (DIN) data has become mandatory. This integration would obviate the need to seek information from IEC holders for subsequent amendments/update of data in IEC database.

f. Communication with Committees of DGFT: Various committees of DGFT, such as Norms Committee, Import Committee and Pre-shipment Inspection Agency, have access to the email addresses for faster communication.

11. Forthcoming E-governance Initiatives

a. DGFT is currently working on the following economic development initiatives (EDIs):

   i. The message for transmission of export reward scrips from DGFT to Customs to be passed on.

   ii. The message for transmission of bills of entry (import details) from Customs to DGFT to be passed on.

   iii. Issuance of Export Obligation Discharge Certificate (EODC) to be issued online.

   iv. Message exchange with MCA for CIN and DIN.

   v. Message exchange with CBDT for PAN.

   vi. Application fee can be paid by using debit/credit card.

   vii. Mobile applications for FTP.

12. New initiatives for EOUs, Electronic Hardware Technology Parks (EHTPs) and Software Technology Parks (STPs)

a. Export oriented units (EOUs), EHTPs and STPs can share infrastructural facilities among themselves, which will enable the units to utilize their infrastructural facilities in an optimum way. This will also help the units to avoid duplication of efforts and cost to create separate infrastructural facilities in different units.

b. Inter-unit transfer of goods and services is also possible among EOUs, EHTPs, STPs and Biotechnology parks (BTPs). This will facilitate the group of those units that source inputs centrally in order to obtain bulk discount. This will establish an effective supply chain and help in reducing the cost of transportation and other logistic costs.

c. Warehouses facility can be set up near the port of export by EOUs. This will help in reducing lead time for delivery of goods and will also address the issue of unpredictability of supply orders.

d. STP units, EHTP units and software EOUs have been allowed the facility to use all duty free equipment/goods for training purposes in order to develop the skills of their employees.

e. 100% of EOU units have been allowed facility of supply of spares/components up to 2% of the value of the manufactured articles to a buyer in domestic market for the purpose of after-sale services.

f. At present, EOU units have to achieve Positive Net Foreign Exchange Earning (NEE) cumulatively in a period of five years. A one-year extension is given in case of an adverse market condition or in case of genuine hardship.

g. For faster execution and monitoring of projects, the time period for validity of letter of permission (LOP) for EOUs/EHTP/STPI/BTP units has been revised. To enable the unit to construct the plant and install the machinery, LOP will have an initial validity of two years with one year possible extension which can be granted by the development commissioner. In case the unit has completed 2/3rd of activities, including the construction activities, extension beyond three years of the validity of LOP can be granted.

h. Currently, capital goods are allowed to be transferred from EOUs/EHTP/STPI units to other EOUs, EHTPs, STPs or SEZ units. If such transferred capital goods are rejected by the recipient, then the same can be returned to the supplying unit, without payment of duty. This facility was not there previously.

i. A simplified procedure will be provided to fast track the de-bonding/exit of STP/EHTP units. This will save time for these units and help in reduction of transaction costs.

j. EOUs having physical export turnover of ₹10 crore and above, and have been allowed the facility of fast-track clearances of import and domestic procurement. The fast-track clearances of goods is available for export production. The export production has to be pre-authenticated by procurement of a certificate which to be issued by Customs/central excise authorities. They will not have to seek procurement permission for every import consignment.

13. Facilitating and Encouraging Export of Dual Use Items (SCOMET)

a. To help the industry to plan their activity in an orderly manner and obviate the need to seek revalidation or relaxation from DGFT, validity of SCOMET export authorization has been extended from the present 12 months to 24 months.

b. Subject to certain conditions, authorization for repeat orders will be considered on automatic basis.

c. If a SCOMET item is being exported under Defense Export Offset Policy, authentication of End User Certificate (EUC) is simplified.

d. To increase responsiveness among various stakeholders, outreach programs will be conducted at different locations.

14. Facilitating and Encouraging Export of Defense Items

a. Normal EO period under advance authorization is 18 months. For export items in the group of defense, military store, aerospace and nuclear energy, EO period shall be 24 months from the date of issue of authorization or coterminus with contracted duration of the export order, whichever is later. This provision will help export of defense items and other high-technology items.

b. According to DGFT notification, a list of military stores require the NOC from the Department of Defence Production for operational purpose. A committee has been formed to create ITC (HS) codes for defense and security items for which industrial licenses are issued by DIPP.

15. e-Commerce Exports

a. Having FOB value up to ₹25,000 per consignment, goods falling in the class of handloom products, books/periodicals, leather footwear, toys and customized fashion garments shall be eligible for benefits under FTP. Such goods can be exported in manual mode through foreign post offices at New Delhi, Mumbai and Chennai.

b. Export of such goods under courier regulations shall be allowed manually on pilot basis through airports at Delhi, Mumbai and Chennai as per appropriate amendments in regulations to be made by DoR. The DoR shall fast track the implementation of EDI mode at courier terminals.

16. Duty Exemption

a. Exemption from transitional product specific safeguard duty is allowed for imports against advance authorization.

b. In order to encourage manufacturing of capital goods in India, import under EPCG authorization scheme shall not be eligible for exemption from payment of anti-dumping duty, safeguard duty and transitional product specific safeguard duty.

17. Additional Ports Allowed for Export and Import

Calicut Airport, Kerala, and Arakonam ICD, Tamil Nadu, have been notified as registered ports for import and export.

18. Duty Free Tariff Preference (DFTP) Scheme

India has already extended DTFP to 33 least developed countries (LDCs) across the globe. This is being notified under FTP.

19. Quality Complaints and Trade Disputes

a. A new chapter, namely, a chapter on quality complaints and trade disputes has been incorporated in the FTP with an endeavor to resolve quality complaints and trade disputes, between exporters and importers.

b. A committee on quality complaints and trade disputes (CQCTD) is being constituted for resolving such disputes at a faster pace in 22 offices and would have members from EPCs/FIEOs/APEDA/EICs.

20. Vishakhapatnam and Bhimavaram Added as Towns of Export Excellence

The government has already recognized 33 towns as export excellence towns. It has been decided to add Vishakhapatnam and Bhimavaram in Andhra Pradesh as towns of export excellence (Product Category– Seafood).

2.6 Export-Import Bank of India or EXIM Bank

By the "Export Import Bank of India Act" in 1981, EXIM Bank was established. The main objective of setting such an institution was threefold: First, to provide financial assistance to exporters and importers. Second, as the main coordinating financial institution to extend its support in financing export and import of goods and services which may enhance the promotion of the country's international trade. Third, the EXIM Bank plays a very important role in project export financing. Besides financing of EOUs, the EXIM Bank played its role in building associations with different other countries to boost the project export financing.

EXIM Bank largely promotes and facilitates foreign trade of India. It is the principal financial institution of the country to coordinate the working of various agencies engaged in financing exports and imports. It provides finance to:

- Commercial banks through rediscounting of short-term export bills and by way of refinance.

- Indian companies on deferred payment terms, and

- Foreign governments, financial institutions and companies.

EXIM Bank also participates in issued of guarantees such as advance payment guarantee, performance guarantees, guarantee for borrowings and so on.

ECGC–ECGC is a wholly owned company of the Government of India, which provides export credit insurance support to Indian exporters and financing banks. ECGC is the fifth largest credit insurer of the world in terms of coverage of national exports. ECGC protects exporters from the consequences of payment risk (both political and commercial risks) and thus enables them to expand their overseas business without fear of loss. It also protects the lending banker against the exporter's failure to discharge his or her liabilities, which could expose the banker to a risk of loss. In view of this, ECGC plays a very significant role in the context of export credit provided by the lending bankers.

General Insurance Corporations–They provide the transit insurance cover to exporters, commonly known as marine insurance cover.

Export Promotion Councils–These councils have been set up by the ministry of commerce (Government of India) to promote exports of different commodities. It is compulsory for every exporter to be a member of a council concerning his or her commodity of export. The councils also help their members to interact with the ministry on matters affecting the exporters. They represent the viewpoints of their members and help the government to formulate policies and the country's response at international trade forums.

As per the Memorandum of Instructions on Project Exports and Service Exports of the RBI, project exports consists the following:

1. Industrial turnkey projects
2. Civil construction contracts
3. Technical consultancy/services contracts
4. Supply of goods/equipment on deferred payment terms

We discuss these facilities as the following:

- **Industrial Turnkey Projects**: By the very nature of this project, it is complete product. It can be said that a turnkey project is supplied as a complete package in which all other related services, such as design, detailed engineering, civil construction, erection and commissioning of plants and power transmission, and distribution are supplied along with the equipment.

- **Civil Construction Projects**: This type of projects are mostly infrastructure projects related to civil works, supply of construction material and equipment.

- **Technical and Consultancy Service Contracts**: This project contract relates to skill and knowledge development through training and consultancy projects. Examples of service contracts are software exports, supervision of assembly of plants, project execution and so on.

- **Supplies Contracts**: This is related to the export of capital goods and industrial manufactures. Examples of supply contracts are supply of stainless steel slabs and ferrochrome manufacturing equipment, diesel generators, pumps and compressors.

It may be noted that if the value of the project export contracts is above USD 100 million then there is a requirement of an approval given by an inter-institutional working group involving EXIM Bank as the convener and nodal agency, the RBI—Foreign Exchange Department—and ECGC. Officials of the Ministry of Finance, Ministry of Commerce and Industry and Ministry of External Affairs, Government of India, are requested to partake in the group meetings if the project value is extremely large.

Other than project exports financing, EXIM Bank also covers fund-based and nonfund-based credit facility to deemed export contracts as defined in FTP of GOI: for example,

1. The facilities which are tenable under funding from multilateral funding agencies such as the World Bank, Asian Development Bank (ADB) and so on;

2. The facility is extended for the bid contracts secured in the international competitive bidding;

3. Foreign currency contract for which payments are expected in foreign currency.

Other than extending the export credit facility to commercial banks, EXIM Bank extends export and import credit facilities to two different entities (as per an Indian Institute of Banking and Finance (IIBF) document, see reference).

- Indian Companies

    o Post-shipment supplier's credit

    o Export project cash flow deficit financing program

o   Pre-shipment credit in rupee and foreign currency

o   Finance for export of consultancy and technology services

o   Finance for deemed export contracts

o   Capital equipment finance

o   Financing deemed export contracts secured via structures including but not restricted to build operate transfer (BOT)/build own operate transfer (BOOT)/built own lease transfer (BOLT)

o   LCs/guarantees

- For Commercial Banks in India

  o   Risk participation in funded/nonfunded facilities extended to Indian exporters

  o   Refinance of export credit

- For Overseas Entities

  o   Buyer's credit

  o   Buyer's credit under National Export Insurance Account (NEIA)

2.6.1 Export Capability Creation Loans

This loan is extended by EXIM Bank to facilitate the export promotion and increase the participation of Indian exporters in international markets. As referred in IIBF document (please see the reference) there can be three broad categories of this loan:

1.   Overseas Investment

     a.   Term Financing

     b.   Equity Investment

     c.   Working Capital Loans to JVs/WOSs

     d.   Guarantees to JVs/WOSs

2.   Export Oriented Units

     a.   Asset Creation

          i.   Equipment Finance

          ii. Project Finance

     b.   Working Capital

          i.   Medium Term

    ii.   Short-term Finance

  c.   Special Products

      i.   Export Marketing Finance

     ii.   Export Product Development Finance

    iii.   Export Vendor Development Finance

    iv.   Research & Development (R&D) Finance

     v.   Finance for Indian Educational Institutions and Setting Up Institutions Abroad

    vi.   Finance for Software Technology Parks

   vii.   Finance for Development of Minor Ports/Jetties

  viii.   Creative Industry Financing

    ix.   Project-related Nonfund-based Guarantees

     x.   Guarantees and SBLCs

    xi.   LCs

3. Financial Intermediaries

  a.   Refinance to Commercial Banks

  b.   Export Bills Rediscounting for Commercial Banks

2.6.2 Finance for MSMEs

EXIM Bank also offers support to small and medium enterprises in terms of arranging credit line from the ADB. This credit line is provided in foreign currency term loans to the micro, small and medium enterprise (MSME) borrowers in certain specific lagging states of India, namely, Assam, Madhya Pradesh, Orissa, Uttar Pradesh, Chhattisgarh, Jharkhand, Rajasthan and Uttarakhand. These foreign currency term loans can be used to get support for financing domestic capital expenditure of the borrowers in Indian Rupees, besides meeting their foreign currency capital expenditure requirements.

2.7 Export Credit Guarantee Corporation of India

The journey of ECGC started as a Private Ltd Company in 1957 as Export Risk Insurance Corporation (ERIC). The primary objective of ERIC was to provide support to exporters to mitigate their risk international trade. In 1964, the name was changed to Export Credit & Guarantee Corporation Ltd (EC&GC). In 1983 the name was changed to **Export Guarantee Corporation of India Ltd (ECGC) and changed to the present ECGC Ltd** w.e.f. 8.8.2014. It is a Government of India Enterprise functioning under the administrative control of the Ministry of Commerce & Industry.

There are many types of insurance covers under export credit insurance:

- **Credit Insurance Cover to Exporters**: In international trade the exporter is subject to credit risk losses in export of goods and services. Credit insurance provides cover to exporters against such credit risk losses which may be short, medium and long term in nature.

- **Credit Insurance Cover to Banks**: Given the risk in international trade, banks are exposed to nonpayment risk by the exporters. So credit insurance also provides cover to banks to protect them against risks of default by exporters for all short-, medium- and long-term export orders.

- **Overseas Investment Insurance Cover**: ECGC also provides cover to protect Indian entrepreneurs investing in overseas ventures (equity/loans) against expropriation risks. This cover is known as overseas investment insurance cover.

The business profile of ECGC is given.

2.7.1 Business Profile

In terms of authorized and paid-up capital, ECGC performs really well. There are five regional offices and 59 branch offices. The working of ECGC is ISO 2001–08 certified and they are registered under Insurance Regulatory and Development Authority (IRDA). Also, ECGC is rated iAAA by the Investment Information and Credit Rating Agency Ltd (ICRA) for its highest claim paying ability.

The benefits of export credit insurance for banks (ECIB) cover are as follows.

- Flow of adequate credit to exporters—back up of insurance

- Competitive pricing of credit

- Lower margins/collateral securities

- Increased liquidity—claims payment

- Lower weights for risk on export credits covered by ECGC—capital adequacy

- Lower provisioning for nonperforming assets (NPAs) to the extent of ECGC coverage—RBI norms

- Better customer selection—specific approval list (SAL)

2.7.2 ECIB Overview

ECIB is issued to banks and financial institutions to cover the risk of nonpayment of advances by exporters due to insolvency or willful default. This ECIB cover can be obtained on individual or whole turnover (WT) basis. Also, this cover is available for export credits only (fund-based and nonfund-based). To mitigate the risks involved in export finance by banks, ECGC has introduced the following covers to banks as mentioned below:

1. Pre-shipment Stage: ECIB

2. Post-shipment Stage: ECIB

Figure 2.1   Structure of ECGC Cover

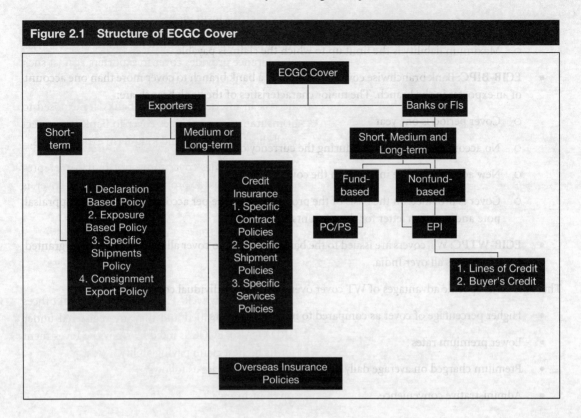

3. Surety Cover:

   a. ECIB—Surety cover (Export Performance Indemnity Cover)

   b. ECIB—Surety cover (Whole Turnover)

A.1 Pre-shipment Stage: Export Credit Insurance for Banks (ECIB–PC)

In detail, the short-term pre-shipment cover for banks includes:

- ECIB—Individual Packing Credit (INPC)

- ECIB—Bank Branchwise Individual PC (BIPC)

- ECIB—Whole Turnover Packing Credit (WTPC)

We describe each of the previously mentioned covers to understand the application of the cover in international trade:

- **ECIB-INPC:** Individual covers are issued to a bank branch to cover the specific account of an exporter.

   o Cover period is one year

- o   Rupee PC and Packing Credit in Foreign Currency (PCFC) (Rupee equivalent is covered)

  - o   Maximum liability is the limit up to which the claim is payable

- **ECIB-BIPC**: Bank branchwise covers are issued to a bank branch to cover more than one account of an exporter in the branch. The major characteristics of the bank branch are:

  - o   Cover period is one year

  - o   No account can be excluded during the currency of cover

  - o   New accounts can be included in the cover

  - o   Cover is provided on the basis of the proposal with a fee per account along with an appraisal note and sanction letter for the accounts to be covered

- **ECIB-WTPC**: WT covers are issued to the bank as a whole to cover all its export advances granted by its branches all over India.

There are some specific advantages of WT cover over and above individual cover.

- Higher percentage of cover as compared to individual covers

- Lower premium rates

- Premium charged on average daily product basis

- Administrative convenience

B.1 Post-shipment Stage: Export Credit Insurance for Banks

Post-shipment Credit–Post-shipment credit is offered to an exporter to finance export sales receivables after the date of shipment of goods till the date of realization of export proceeds. Cover for post-shipment credit can broadly be categorized as:

- Advances against negotiation of documents (LC)

- Advances against purchase of export bills

- Advances against discounting of export bills

- Advances against bills sent on collection

- Advances against undrawn balances of export bills

- Advances against receivables from Government (duty drawback)

Any bank or financial institution who is an AD in foreign exchange can obtain individual post-shipment export credit cover in respect of each of its exporter-clients who is holding the standard policy of ECGC without any exclusion. ECIB (WT-PS) protects the bank against losses that the bank may suffer while granting post-shipment advance to its exporter clients. The risks covered under the guarantee are (a) Insolvency of the exporter and (b) Protracted default by the exporter to pay post-shipment advance due to the bank. There are two types of cover:

1. ECIB-Individual post-shipment credit
    The major features of INPS are:

    - Cover period is one year.

    - Rupee PS advances and Post Shipment Credit in Foreign Currency (PSCFC) (Rupee equivalent is covered).

    - Percentage of cover and premium rate as stipulated in schedule based on type of cover opted.

    - Maximum liability is the limit up to which claim is payable.

    - Monthly declarations to be submitted by 10th of the succeeding month.

    - Advances against bills drawn on Restricted Cover Category (RCC) require prior approval.

2. ECIB-WT post-shipment credit (WTPS)

    The features are mostly the same as pre-shipment credit. The features are depicted as follows:

    - Cover issued to central office of the bank against a proposal with a fee along with statements of limits in force and defaults.

    - Only short-term export credits covered.

    - Cover period is normally July 1 to June 30.

    - Compliance to terms and conditions of cover lies with the respective bank branch where the account is conducted to the nearest office of ECGC.

    - Accounts in default as on commencement of cover not covered.

    - Advances against receivables such as duty draw back not covered under WT cover.

    - Advances for deferred term exports, turnkey projects, civil construction works and services not covered.

    - Interest and other debits not related to exports not covered.

Exclusions allowed at the time of obtaining fresh cover/renewal are:

- Advances to MSME.

- Advances to government companies (central and state PSUs). The definition of government companies is any company in which not less than 51% of the paid up share capital is held by the Central or by any state government(s).

- Advances to units by offshore banking accounts (OBUs). The OBUs means that the office of the bank is situated in a special economic zone or an export processing zone in India and is a deemed foreign branch of the bank and shall undertake international banking business involving foreign-currency-denominated assets and liabilities.

- Advances against LCs (For WTPS only).

Checklist for the bank

- Ensure that the exporter, management or guarantors are not in SAL of ECGC. If in SAL, obtain approval.

- Notify within 30 days from sanction, the limits that are:

  ○ Sanctioned up to discretionary limit for new accounts.

  ○ Enhanced/ad hocs sanctioned for standard assets.

  ○ Reduced/cancelled.

- Check ECGC circulars for covers on specific commodities—gold, gem and jewelry, and diamond and iron ore.

- Obtain prior approval of the corporation within 60 days of limits.

  ○ Sanctioned beyond DL for new accounts.

  ○ Sanctioned if the asset classification is other than standard or if the account has slipped from standard.

- Obtain prior approval of ECGC if the exporter, management and guarantors are in SAL of the corporation.

- Obtain specific approval of the corporation before granting advances against bills drawn on buyers in restricted cover countries (WTPS, if exporter has not obtained such approval under the policy).

- Submit the monthly declarations with due premium by the end of subsequent month.

- Remit premium for all accounts agreed to be covered by the bank (no other exclusion/waiver is allowed).

C.1 Surety Cover Export Credit Guarantee Corporation of India (ECGC)

Surety cover of ECGC is issued to make the exporters' process of obtaining a bond from a bank smooth. According to the definition of ECGC Ltd, Export Credit Insurance for Banks (ECIB) Surety Cover (SC) provides the bank an indemnity to protect the interest of the bank against losses that it may suffer on account of guarantees given by it on behalf of exporters. This protection is intended to encourage banks to give guarantees on a liberal basis for export purposes. As we know, bank may have to give guarantees, such as bid bond guarantee, performance guarantee and retention money guarantee, to the Indian exporters; banks may sometimes take extra safeguard if they foresee or assess any risk. As in these cases, providing guarantee becomes a mandatory criteria for exporters to carry out trade with the international partners; exporters may insists on issuance of guarantee to the banker with the protection provided by ECGC Ltd under surety cover.

Cover under ECIB (SC) can be considered to those banks whose exporter clients have standard asset classification with an acceptable credit rating weightage of 50% and above. The banks intending to seek ECIB (SC) cover for an exporter client should have sanctioned certain working capital limit facilities for export in favor of their exporter client. So, the new accounts of exporter clients and/or the export clients whose credit rating weightage is less than 50% are not eligible for ECIB (SC) covers.

The types of short-term guarantees which are entitled for our indemnity are:

1. Bid Bond Guarantee: When an exporter clients desire to bid for a foreign tender, he or she needs to submit a guarantee to the foreign tender. This guarantee is issued by a bank on behalf of its exporter clients to provide some assurance to the foreign tender.

2. Performance Guarantee: In case an exporter succeeds in getting an export contract, he or she may be required to provide a BG for his or her due performance. In this context, his or her bank may furnish the due performance guarantee to the foreign buyer.

3. Surety cover is also available for LCs transaction. If LC is opened for purchase or import of raw materials in respect of export transactions, ECGC Ltd provides surety cover to the bank.

4. Bank guarantees which are issued for the purpose of clearing goods without payment of duty or for exemption from tax for goods procured for export surety cover may be issued. These guarantees are provided by exporters to DGFT, Customs, central excise or sales tax authorities.

5. Surety cover is also available for the bank guarantees which is furnished in support of the EOs by the exporters to export promotion councils, commodity boards, the State Trading Corporation of India, the Metals and Minerals Trading Corporation of India (MMTC) or recognized export houses.

Note: The underlying contracts for issue of bid bond and performance guarantee should be purely for supply of goods for which payments due are to be received within a maximum period of 180 days.

2.8 International Chamber of Commerce

International Chamber of Commerce, popularly known as ICC, is an organization which promotes international trade and investment. In international trade there are many parties of different countries with different culture. Many a times parties in international trade faces some problem in interpreting the terms and conditions, rules and regulations. At the time, dispute either in the documents or in terms of order supplied parties gets confused as there was no dispute-solving mechanism which was acceptable to all the countries, to all the parties. Let us take an example. Suppose, in country M, XYZ has received an export order for supplying 2,000 rugby shirts to country N, ABC Ltd. ABC Ltd has put a condition that before the shipment of the goods one sample is to be sent to ABC Ltd by XYZ for a check on the quality of the product. As per the condition in the contract XYZ sent a shirt to ABC Ltd. ABC Ltd has cut the shirt at its elbow and checked the quality of the cotton and fiber. Being satisfied with the quality, ABC Ltd returned the shirt with a message saying "ok, send the goods as it is." He has got a customer while the goods were in transit. The company sold off the goods to the customer, Mr Wall, in country N. After a few days, ABC Ltd gets a call saying all shirts were delivered with a cut at the elbow.

To avoid this kind of scenario, ICC has come up with some guidelines which help the exporter, importer, or exporting bank and importing bank or the guarantors in the international trade transaction. It may be noted that documentary collection and documentary credit are bank intermediary transactions. ICC has given clear guidelines to operate under these two payment mechanisms. Also, it may be noted that in international trade, under documentary payment mechanism, many a times payment is not made due to documentary noncompliance. Even after having the guidelines set by ICC, at least more than 50% of the transactions may have documentary discrepancies. However, because of long-term trade relations, or just because some of them do not cause major damage to the product delivered, importer may not report the discrepancies; rather, they waive them. So, it is important that the parties in an international trade transaction must understand the application of such rules and regulations. To simplify the problem, ICC has come out with a few publications which help the banks and the other parties to understand the roles and responsibilities of the trade transactions.

1. Uniform Rules for Collection or URC 522: These rules are applicable for the payment mechanism of documentary collection. Under this rule banks are provided a clear idea about their roles and responsibilities as collecting agents. It provides clear guidelines for the bank if they take the responsibility as remitting bank, collecting bank, presenting bank etc. Banks do not hold any additional responsibilities or risk in terms of payment.

2. Uniform Rules for Documentary Credit or UCP 600: These rules are the governing rules for any trade transaction which involves documentary credit or LC mechanism. Under UCP 600, banks undertake the payment obligation of the importer, given that all documents submitted comply with the terms of the credit. Also, it may be noted that it is the safest payment mechanism for the exporters after the advance payment method.

3. International Standby Practices or ISP 98: In 1998, ICC has come out with a special publication, No. 590, which provides the guidelines to deal in standby LC. ISP 98 is effective from January 1, 1999. Earlier, up to 1999, issuing the standby LC, which is a nonpayment guarantee undertaken by the bank, was governed only by UCP 600. From 1999 onwards, a standby LC can be opened with reference to either UCP 600 or ISP 98.

4. International Standard Banking Practice or ISBP 745: This provides the guidelines to banks on the examination of documentary credit. This fills the gap in interpreting the rules examining documentary credit and the practice followed in banking domain. ISBP was first came in the form publication in the year 2002 when UCP 500 was prevailing. Later on, with the recommended changes in UCP 500, when UCP 600 came in practice, ISBP 681 was updated and ISBP 745 came into practice.

5. Uniform Rules for Demand Guarantee or URDG 758: This rule governs all the types of guarantees, such as bid bond guarantee, performance guarantee, retention money guarantee and so on, issued by banks to support international trade transaction. URDG 758 is effective from July 1, 2010.

6. INCOTERMS 2010: These are the terms which divide the cost and risk between the exporters and importers when the goods are in transit. Depending on the negotiating power, exporter or importer may insist on using INCOTERMS in his or her favor. For example, if Ex Work (EXW) is used as INCOTERMS, then the exporter passes all the risks to the importer at his or her own premises with the physical delivery of the goods. Including the custom clearance in exporter's country and in importer's country, all the costs in transit are borne only by the importer. If EXW is used along with the cost, the importer takes all risk of goods being lost or damaged in the transit.

References and Resources

https://www.ecgcltd.in/portal/productnservices/guarantees/packcredit/ecib-wtpc.asp

https://www.scribd.com/document/32658947/post-shipment-credit

http://www.unionbankofindia.co.in/pdf/HKB_08identiAssetPolicyECIBWTPS.pdf

http://agriexchange.apeda.gov.in/Ready%20Reckoner/ECGC.aspx

https://www.ecgcltd.in/portal/productnservices/ECIB-SC.asp

Project export memorandum (PEM), https://www.google.co.in/url?sa=t&rct=j&q=&esrc=s&source=web&cd=3&cad=rja&uact=8&ved=0ahUKEwiF9cS5y83RAhUGu48KHTRGCUcQFggjMAI&url=https%3A%2F%2Fwww.rbi.org.in%2Fupload%2Fnotification%2Fdocs%2F39814.doc&usg=AFQjCNH9IwiPtQnxIoo4wvQoG-ytX8JUuQ&sig2=o_9O0YRiU8NT-jSc3jepEg&bvm=bv.144224172,d.c2I

Export-Import Bank of India—Role, functions and facilities. iibf.org.in/documents/THE-EXPORT-IMPORT-Bank-of-India-IIBF.docx

Foreign Trade Policy, http://dgft.gov.in/exim/2000/highlight2015.pdf

QUESTIONS

Answer the Following Questions

1. Write the role and responsibilities of FEDAI in international trade finance.

2. What are the role of FTP and DGFT?

3. Write three different stages of regulatory compliance under FEMA.

4. Write the salient features of FEMA regulations?

5. How does FEMA applied to current and capital account transaction?

6. How does the enforcement of the panel provisions operate under FEMA?

7. Write important role and responsibilities of the RBI.

8. Write about SEIS and MEIS. Which all centers are entitled to get the benefit of SEIS and MEIS?

9. Write the main characteristics of freely transferable duty credit scrips.

10. Which all exporters are known as status holder? What are the classifications of status holder exporters?

11. What is self-certification? Which categories of exporters are entitled to this facility?

12. What are the main schemes of FTP to "boost India"?

13. What are the steps taken by DGFT for trade facilitation and ease of doing business?

14. What are the forthcoming e-governance initiatives to boost the export of Indian economy?

15. Write about the new initiatives for EOUs, EHTPs and STPs.

16. What is SCOMET? What are the facilities taken to encourage the export of dual items and FTP?

17. What are the initiatives taken for the export of Defense items under FTP?

18. What is DFTP scheme?

19. What are the roles and responsibilities of EXIM bank?

20. Describe the products under ECIB?

21. Write short notes on industrial turnkey projects, civil construction projects, technical and consultancy services contracts and supply contracts.

22. What is the export capability creation loan? What are the three broad categories of this loan?

23. Write a short note about the role and responsibilities of ECGC? What are the classifications of ECGC cover?

24. Classify different insurance cover under ECGC.

25. Write about the ECGC pre-shipment cover. Write short note on INPC, BIPC and WTPC.

26. Write about post-shipment credit cover.

27. What are the major features of INPS and WT-PS?

28. What is the check list for banks for insurance cover under ECGC?

29. Write a short note on surety cover.

30. What is the role of ICC in international trade finance? Write briefly about the URC 522, UCP 600, INCOTERMS, ISBP 745, ISP 98 and URDG 758.

Appendix

Foreign Trade Policy: Annexure-1

1. Country groups

Category A: Traditional Markets (30), European Union (28), the USA, Canada.

Category B: Emerging & Focus Markets (139), Africa (55), Latin America and Mexico (45), CIS countries (12), Turkey and West Asian countries (13), ASEAN countries (10), Japan, South Korea, China, Taiwan.

Category C: Other Markets (70).

2. Products supported under MEIS

a. **Level of Support:**

Higher rewards have been granted for the following category of products:

- Agricultural and village industry products, presently covered under VKGUY.

- Value-added and packaged products.

- Eco-friendly and green products that create wealth out of waste from agricultural and other waste products that generate additional income for the farmers, while improving the environment.

- Labor-intensive products with large employment potential and products with large number of producers and/or exporters.

- Industrial products from potential winning sectors.

- Hi-tech products with high export earning potential.

3. Markets supported

- Most agricultural products supported across the globe.

- Industrial and other products supported in traditional and/or emerging markets only.

4. High potential products not supported earlier

Support to 852 tariff lines that fit in the product criteria but not provided support in the earlier FTP. Includes lines from fruits, vegetables, dairy products, oils meals, Ayush & Herbal products, paper and paper board products.

5. Global support has been granted to the following category:

- Fruits, flowers, vegetables

- Tea, coffee, spices

- Cereals preparation, shellac, essential oils

- Processed foods,

- Eco-friendly products that add value to waste

- Marine products

- Handloom, coir, jute products and technical textiles, handmade carpets. Other textile and ready-made garments have been supported for European Union, the USA, Canada and Japan

- Handicraft, sports goods

- Furniture, wood articles

6. Support to major markets have been given to the following product categories:

- Pharmaceuticals, herbals, surgicals

- Industrial machinery, IC engine, machine tools, parts, auto components/parts

- Hand tools, pumps of all types

- Automobiles, two wheelers, bicycles, ships, planes

- Chemicals, plastics

- Rubber, ceramic and glass

- Leather garments, saddlery items, footwear

- Steel furniture, prefabs, lighters

- Wood, paper, stationary

- Iron, steel and base metal products

7. Other sectors supported under MEIS

- 352 defense-related products with export of US$ 17.7B consisting of core products (20), dual-use products (60), general purpose products (272).

- 283 pharmaceutical products of bulk drugs and drug intermediates, drug formulations biologicals, herbal, surgicals and vaccines.

- 96 lines of environment-related goods, machinery, equipment's.

- 49 lines where mandatory BIS standards are prescribed.

- Seven lines of technical textiles.

8. Participation in global value chain of the items falling under the scheme

- 1,725 lines of Intermediate Goods–These goods become inputs in the manufacturing of other countries and will strengthen backward manufacturing linkages which is vital for India's participation in global value chains.

- 1,109 lines of Capital Goods sector–Will also strengthen manufacturing base in India.

- 1,730 lines of Consumer Goods sector–We hope a quantum jump in export from this sector with strengthening of the Make in India brand in near future.

9. Technology-based analysis

- 572 lines–Low-skill Technology-intensive manufacturing.

- 1,010 lines-Medium-skill Technology-intensive manufacturing.

- 1,309 lines-High-Skill Technology-intensive manufacturing.

10. Women-centric products supported under MEIS

- Women workers constitute 52% of plantation workers—203 lines of tea, coffee, spices and cashew.

- 69% of the aggregate female employment is concentrated in the following sectors:

  o Manufacture of other food products—Jelly confectionery, tomato ketchup, cooked stuffed pasta, *pawa, mudi* and the like, gingerbread, *papad*, pastries and cakes.

  o Manufacture of wearing apparel—396 lines of readymade garments.

- Sectors that have a significant proportion of female employment (more than 25%):

  o Agricultural and animal husbandry service activities, except veterinary activities—263 lines of basic agriculture products.

  o Manufacture of footwear—28 Footwear and Leather products.

  o Consumer electronics and electronic components, watches and clocks—483 lines.

Foreign Trade Policy: Annexure-2

SL No	Sectors	Admissible Rate
1	BUSINESS SERVICES	
a	Professional services Legal services, Accounting, auditing and bookkeeping services, Taxation services, Architectural services, Engineering services, Integrated engineering services, Urban planning and landscape architectural services, Medical and dental services, Veterinary services, Services provided by midwives, nurses, physiotherapists and paramedical personnel	5%

b	Research and development services R&D services on natural sciences, R&D services on social sciences and humanities, Interdisciplinary R&D services	5%
c	Rental/Leasing services without operators Relating to ships, Relating to aircraft, Relating to other transport equipment, Relating to other machinery and equipment	5%
d	Other business services Advertising services, Market research and public opinion polling services Management consulting service, Services related to management consulting, Technical testing and analysis services, Services incidental to agricultural, hunting and forestry, Services incidental to fishing, Services incidental to mining, Services incidental to manufacturing, Services incidental to energy distribution, Placement and supply services of personnel, Investigation and security, Related scientific and technical consulting services, Maintenance and repair of equipment (not including maritime vessels, aircraft or other transport equipment), Building- cleaning services, Photographic services, Packaging services, Printing, publishing and Convention services	3%
2.	COMMUNICATION SERVICES Audiovisual services Motion picture and video tape production and distribution service, Motion picture projection service, Radio and television services, Radio and television transmission services, Sound recording	5%
3.	CONSTRUCTION AND RELATED ENGINEERING SERVICES General Construction work for building, General Construction work for Civil Engineering, Installation and assembly work, Building completion and finishing work	5%
4.	EDUCATIONAL SERVICES (Under education services, SEIS shall not be available on Capitation fee.) Primary education services, Secondary education services, Higher education services, Adult education	5%
5	ENVIRONMENTAL SERVICES Sewage services, Refuse disposal services, Sanitation and similar services	5%
6	HEALTH-RELATED AND SOCIAL SERVICES Hospital services	5%
7.	TOURISM AND TRAVEL-RELATED SERVICES	
a.	Hotels and Restaurants (including catering)	
i.	Hotel	3%
ii.	Restaurants (including catering)	3%
b.	Travel agencies and tour operators services	5%
c.	Tourist guides services	5%

(Continued)

(*Continued*)

8	RECREATIONAL, CULTURAL AND SPORTING SERVICES (other than audiovisual services) Entertainment services (including theatre, live bands and circus services), News agency services, Libraries, archives, museums and other cultural services, Sporting and other recreational services	5%
9.	TRANSPORT SERVICES (Operations from India by Indian Flag Carriers only is allowed under Maritime transport services.)	
a.	Maritime Transport Services Passenger transportation*, Freight transportation*, Rental of vessels with crew *, Maintenance and repair of vessels, Pushing and towing services, Supporting services for maritime transport	5%
b.	Air transport services Rental of aircraft with crew, Maintenance and repair of aircraft, Airport Operations and ground handling	5%
c.	Road Transport Services Passenger transportation, Freight transportation, Rental of Commercial vehicles with operator, Maintenance and repair of road transport equipment, Supporting services for road transport services 5%	5%
d.	Services Auxiliary To All Modes Of Transport. Cargo-handling services, Storage and warehouse services, Freight transport agency services	5%

Product Structure under Documentary Credit

3.1 Structured Documentary Credit

Day by day, international trade finance has become dynamic in nature with different types of risk associated with the transactions. To deal with the different types of demands and the conditions, trade financers have come out with a few new structured products of LCs. Under different circumstances, these products are invented with the objective to serve the traders of the international market.

In this chapter we discuss a few such products, such as (a) back-to-back LCs, (b) transferable LCs, (c) standby LCs (SBLCs), (d) red clause LCs, (e) green clause LCS, (f) revolving LCs, (g) instalment LCs, and (h) transit LCs.

3.2 Back-to-Back LC

When an LC is issued on the basis of the application by an ultimate buyer in favor of a particular beneficiary who may not be the actual supplier/manufacturer, he or she will apply for another LC with near identical terms in favor of the actual supplier/manufacturer offering the main LC issued in his or her favor as security.

This refers to the second set of credit that is issued on the basis of a parent credit. This second credit is termed as back-to-back credit or countervailing credit. The original credit which is offered as security for issuing a back-to-back credit is known as overriding credit/principal credit.

3.2.1 Flow Chart Under Back-to-Back LC

1. Sales contract must be open under back-to-back LC (see Figure 3.1). This contract may be under the Contract for International Sales of Goods (CISG), which provides a standard form of contract to the exporters and importers. The standardization of the contract mostly helps the small- and medium-scale exporters and importers to have all the necessary terms and conditions mentioned in the contract itself.

2. After having sales contract established, the trader or the agent gets one LC opened in his or her favor from Renuka Import. This LC is known as the principal LC. It must mention the country of origin.

3. Once the issuing bank (IOB India) advises the principal LC to the trader, the trader requests the issuing of another LC against the principal LC (from IOB, India). The advising bank of trader issues this back-to-back LC in favor of the sub-supplier (ABC Export, UK) keeping the first LC as collateral.

Figure 3.1   Transaction Flow of Back-to-Back LC

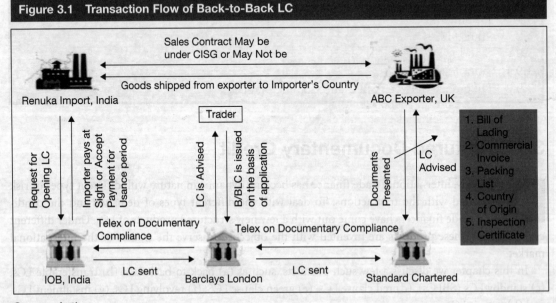

Source: Author.

4. Any bank other than the advising bank also may open the back-to-back LC. However, it requires efficiency to open a back-to-back LC with similar terms and conditions. It may be noted the second LC may be different from the first LC in terms of

   a. the amount of the credit

   b. the expiry date

   c. the period for presentation

   d. the latest shipment date or given period for shipment

5. The back-to-back LC is advised to the ultimate supplier.

6. The supplier supplies the goods with the country of origin mentioned and negotiates the document with the advising bank.

7. After the receipt of the documents by the issuing bank, the issuing bank pays on the compliance of the document.

Example of Back-to-Back Letter of Credit

11 September, 2006

Principal LC

To:	CREDIT BANQUE LONDON 15 The Archway London E1 4R, UK
From:	BANCO DO INDOCHINO Raffles House Singapore

We hereby issue our irrevocable documentary credit C 960535 dated 11 September 2006. Please advise beneficiary without adding your confirmation

Beneficiary:	ABC London, UK
Applicant:	Garments International Ltd 17 LEA Bridge Road Singapore 059413
Amount:	USD 1,000,000 (United States Dollar One Million Only)
Draft:	Sight Draft of 100 percent invoice value
Expiry Date:	29th November 2006
Place of Expiry:	United Kingdom

Available with advising bank by negotiation of beneficiary's

Documents Required

1. Beneficiary's manually signed commercial invoices certifying merchandise are of Iranian origin, mentioning contract number 102 DT 26.08.2006

(Continued)

(Continued)

2. Complete set of clean on board bill of lading, issued to order BANKCO DO INDOCHINO, Raffles house, Singapore, and marked
   Freight Collect,
   Notify
   Burmagent PTE Ltd
   Trafalgar Avenue
   King George Building
   Singapore

3. Certificate of Iran Origin issued by the Chamber of Commerce in Iran
4. Certificate of Quantity and quality issued at the time and place of shipment by SGS (Iran)
5. Certificate of Packing issued by Iran
6. Packing list

Additional Conditions

1. A tolerance ± 5 PCT in Cargo quantity is acceptable
2. Seaway, Forwarder, Blank back, stale, Lashed, Claused, and short form bill of lading are prohibited.
3. Documents must be presented within 15 days from the date of shipment, however, within L's validity whichever is earlier
4. LC is restricted to advising bank for negotiation
5. Third party documents are acceptable, except invoice, draft.
6. All documents must not be dated on or before 4th September 2006

Back to Back LC

London, 13 September 2006

From: Credit Banque
          15 The Archway
          London E1 4R, UK

To: Iran Export Development Bank
          129 Khalid Istanbul Avenue
          Tehran -15
          Iran

We hereby issue our following documentary credit

Number:	CSL – 100268
Form:	Irrevocable
Applicant:	(Benone)
Beneficiary:	(Bentwo)
Amount:	USD 10,000,000 (United States Dollars One Million One Hundred Thousand Only)
Tolerance in percent:	±5
Date and Place of Expiry:	20 November 1996, London
Available with:	Credit Banque UK By Negotiation at Sight

Documents Required

1. Beneficiary's manually signed commercial invoices certifying merchandise are of Iranian origin, mentioning contract number 102 DT 03.09.2006
2. Complete set of clean on board bill of lading, issued to order BANKCO DO INDOCHINO, Raffles house, Singapore, and marked
   Freight Collect,
   Notify
   Burmagent PTE Ltd
   Trafalgar Avenue
   King George Building
   Singapore
3. Certificate of Iran Origin issued by the Chamber of Commerce in Iran
4. Certificate of Quantity and quality issued at the time and place of shipment by SGS (Iran)
5. Certificate of Packing issued by Iran
6. Packing list

Additional Conditions

1. A tolerance ± 5 PCT in Cargo quantity is acceptable
2. Seaway, Forwarder, Blank back, stale, Lashed, Claused, and short form bill of lading are prohibited.
3. Documents must be presented within 15 days from the date of shipment, however, within L's validity whichever is earlier
4. LC is restricted to advising bank for negotiation
5. Third party documents are acceptable, except invoice, draft.
6. All documents must not be dated on or before 4th September 2016

SOURCE: International Trade and Pre-export Finance: a Practitioner's Guide, Howard Palmer.

3.3 Transferable LC

Transferable credit means a credit that specifically states it is "transferable." A transferable credit may be made available in whole or in part to another beneficiary (second beneficiary) at the request of the beneficiary (first beneficiary). It is used where an exporter or an agent plays the role of an intermediary between an ultimate supplier (one or several suppliers) and the importer (See Figure 3.2).

The exporter (first beneficiary) transfers all or a portion of its rights to a supplier beneficiary (known as the second beneficiary (ies) in the uniform customs and practices (UCP). This kind of LC is used for big projects where there may be different sub-suppliers delivering the parts for the production of final goods.

For example, say Tata Motors has to deliver a few cars to Bangladesh. It gets the confirmed order under transferable LC. Tata Motors gets some parts delivered from say beneficiary A and beneficiary B, for which it transfer a percentage of the total credit to these two second suppliers.

3.3.1 Some Important Points About the Transferable LC

1. Such credit can be transferred only once. A transferred credit cannot be transferred at the request of a second beneficiary to any subsequent beneficiaries. The first beneficiary is not considered as the second beneficiary.

Figure 3.2   Transaction Flow of Red Cause LC

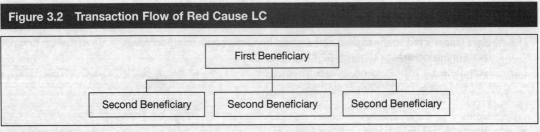

SOURCE: Author.

2. A bank is under no obligation to transfer a credit except to the extent and in the manner expressly consented to that bank.

3. The first beneficiary (the exporter) may request the paying, accepting or negotiating bank to make the credit available in whole or in part to one or more second beneficiaries.

4. The LC must designate the LC as transferable. If the words "transmissible, assignable, divisible, and fractionable" are used then the LC is not transferable.

5. The importer may accept the risk that the ultimate source of the contract goods remains unknown; thereof, it is difficult for the importer to be assured of the ultimate supplier's reputation and reliability.

6. A credit may be transferred in part to more than one second beneficiary provided partial drawings or shipments are allowed.

3.3.2 What is Transferred Credit and Which Bank is the Transferring Bank?

The LC that was transferred or made available to the second beneficiary is known as the transferred credit. The bank that makes the transfer to a second beneficiary is known as transferring bank.

Transferring bank is a nominated bank that transfers the credit. A bank that is specifically authorized by the issuing bank to transfer and that transfers the credit.

3.3.3 Terms and Conditions of Transferred LC

The transferred credit must accurately reflect the terms and conditions of the credit, including confirmation, if any, with the exception of:

1. The amount of the credit

2. The expiry date

3. The period for presentation

4. The latest shipment date or given period for shipment

Unless otherwise agreed at the time of transfer, all charges (such as commissions, fees, costs or expenses) incurred in respect of a transfer must be paid by the first beneficiary.

3.3.4 Conditions of Amendment of Transferable LC

If a credit is transferred to more than one second beneficiary, rejection of an amendment by one or more second beneficiary does not invalidate the acceptance by any other second beneficiary, with respect to which the transferred credit will be amended accordingly.

For any second beneficiary that rejected the amendment, the transferred credit will remain unamended.

3.3.5 Payment Conditions Under Discrepancies

The first beneficiary has the right to substitute its own invoice and draft, if any, for those of a second beneficiary for an amount not in excess of that stipulated in the credit, and upon such substitution the first beneficiary can draw under the credit for the difference, if any, between its invoice and the invoice of a second beneficiary.

If the first beneficiary is to present its own invoice and draft, if any, but fails to do so on first demand, or if the invoices presented by the first beneficiary creates discrepancies that did not exist in the presentation made by the second beneficiary and the first beneficiary fails to correct them on first demand, the transferring bank has the right to present the documents as received from the second beneficiary to the issuing bank without further responsibility to the first beneficiary.

3.3.6 Back-to-Back or Transferable LC: Which One is More Risky from Bank's Point of View

A back-to-back LC is not as safe as transferable credit, though they serve the same practical purpose.

- Payment is to be made against documents received under the back-to-back credit, whereas, the opener of the back-to-back LC may not be able to submit the same documents under the original credit to obtain reimbursement.

- In reality, the transaction can expand beyond the two LCs, if back-to-back LC is forwarded by the sub-supplier to the sub-sub-supplier and the circle continues.

3.4 Red Clause LC

It allows pre-shipment advances to be made to the exporter at the risk and expense of the applicant. Under a red clause credit, the bank would honor the exporter's sight drafts up to a specified percentage of the total credit agreement against production of certain preliminary documents.

- This credit is extended for purchasing raw materials/purchasing and/or packing the goods.

- The clause LCs are so named as they are originally written in red ink to draw the attention of the nominated bank.

Why is it important?

- Tapping the local source of funding for pre-shipment finance was costly.

Figure 3.3   Transaction Flow of Red Clause LC

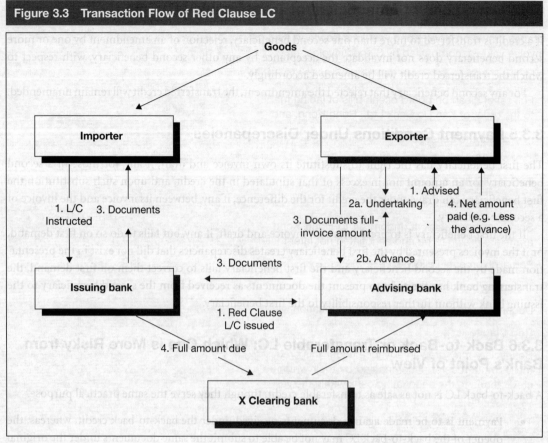

SOURCE: Palmer, 1996.

- Also, if the advance is coming from the applicant then there would be less cost associated with negotiation.

Figure 3.3 explains the risks associated with the red clause LC. They are as follows:

- The opener bears the risk to some extent as this LC draws the drafts on the issuing bank while the amount is immediately charged to applicant and then reimbursed to the buyer bank.

- The opener is directly financing the credit. However, the fund may be misused by the beneficiary. So, sometimes, this credit is restricted for the manufacturing purpose, rather to finance the process of shipment.

- In the above case, it may be disbursed against documents evidencing not only the existence of the goods but that they are in suitable pre-shipment state as required by the applicant. The existence and the quality may be evidenced by the inspection certificate on the quality check of the goods.

- It would be less risky if the amount offered is very less, may be 10%–20% of the invoice value. To mitigate the risk of advance payment, sometimes the advance payment guarantee issued by an acceptable bank is called for.

Please advise our irrevocable credit no. 220791 in favour of Jakarta Shirt Company, Jakarta, Indonesia for US$ 196,000.00 (United States Dollars one hundred ninety six thousands, only) available by their draft(s) drawn on Hong Kong Fashions Kowloon Ave, Kowloon, Hong Kong at sight of, 100 percent of invoice value accompanied by Signed invoice.

Documents Required

Full set of clean on board ocean bills of lading made out to order of negotiating bank and endorsed to the order of Kan Do Bank Ltd., Hong Kong, and marked:

> freight to collect and
>
> notify Hong Kong Fashions Ltd.

Packing list in 5 copies

FOB vessel Jakarta, Indonesia

Shipment from Jakarta, Indonesia to Hong Kong and must be made no later than 31 July 2015, drafts are drawn to be and negotiated not later than 21 August 2015.

Partial shipment is allowed

Transshipment is permitted

Documents must be presented for negotiation within 21 days from BL

Red Clause

Beneficiary may draw in advance under this credit for 80 pct of LC amount against presentation of their simple receipt accompanied by their written undertaking to effect shipment on or before the credit terms to the negotiating bank within the validity of the credit. The amount of such advances to be deducted from the proceeds of the draft drawn under this credit upon negotiation.

Therefore, the beneficiaries will only be paid for the amount negotiated after the advance made under the red clause is fully recovered.

Example 1: Red Clause LC

From: Merchants Bank of California
          1 Civic Plaza Dr # 100, Carson,
          CA 90745, United States

To: Indian Overseas Bank,
          763 Anna Salai,
          Chennai, 600002, India
          MT 700 Issue of Documentary Credit

FLD	Text	Contents
27	Sequence number	1/3
40A	Form of DC	Irrevocable letter of credit
20	DC number	ABC 239872
31C	Date of issue	15 12 31 [YY MM DD]
31D	Expiry date and place	16 05 31 [YY MM DD]

(Continued)

(Continued)

50	Applicant	ABC International, Civic Plaza Apartment, El Cerrito, Santa Clara, CA 95050
59	Beneficiary	XYZ manufacturer, Anna Salai, Rangoon Street
32B	DC amount	USD 250,000 CIF Chennai
41D	Available with/by	Indian Overseas Bank, 763 Anna Salai, Chennai, 600002, India
41E	Drafts at/drawn on	Drafts at sight for full invoice value, drawn on issuing bank
43P	Partial shipment	Allowed
43T	Transshipment	Prohibited
44A	Shipment from	Mumbai, India
44S	Latest shipment date	16 05 15 [YY MM DD]
44D	For transportation to	Any US seaport
45G	Goods	2,000 tons of wires of 25 m length piece

SOURCE: This idea has been taken from the book by Beedu (2010). However, the names of the parties have been changed.

Example 2: Red Clause LC

Field	Text	Content
46A	Documents required	1. Sight commercial invoice in five copies 2. Full set of original clean on board ocean bills of lading plus two nonnegotiable copies of bill of lading, marked freight prepaid 3. Packing list in duplicate 4. Certificate of quality issued by SGS 5. Additional Insurance will be covered by the applicant 6. US customs invoice in five copies
47A	Additional conditions	1. All banking charges outside US are for the account of beneficiary 2. All documents shall bear the number of DC 3. This DC is subject to UCP 600, 2007 revision
47B	Type of LC	This is a Red Clause letter of credit and the negotiating bank is authorized to make an advance to the beneficiary up to 50% of the documentary credit value against a draft signed by the beneficiary, accompanied by written undertaking that the advance is to be used to purchase and ship the merchandise covered by the documentary credit.
49	Confirmation instruction	Without

78	Information to paying and reimbursement bank	a.	Issuing bank undertakes to repay you on first demand any amount so advanced within the validity of the credit.
		b.	On receipt of documents at our counter confirming to the terms of this credit, we undertake to reimburse you in the currency of this credit.

SOURCE: This idea has been taken from the book by Beedu (2010). However, the names of the parties have been changed.

3.5 Green Clause LC

It is an extended version of red-clause credit in the sense that it not only provides for an advance towards purchase, processing, and packing but also for warehousing and insurance charges at port when the goods are stored pending availability of ships/shipping space.

Generally, money under this credit is advanced after the goods are put in bonded warehouses etc. up to the ships or shipping space.

In certain export transactions, the overseas buyer purchases various commodities in bulk from various parties. It is beneficial for an importer to get the shipment booked for all the goods or the same goods purchased from different suppliers from the same country. If there are multiple suppliers, they may not supply the goods on the same date. It is highly likely that the supply of the different goods or from the different suppliers take one or two month time span. Until entire purchase are kept ready for the shipment they engage warehouse.

This process normally take two/three months when goods are procured and offered for shipment.

Since the exporter's funds are locked for a longer period, they normally desire to have advances without paying any interest for the same.

3.6 Revolving LC

The basic principle of a revolving credit is that after a drawing is made the credit reverts to its original amount for reuse by beneficiary.

The amount of the credit is revived or reinstated without requiring specific amendment to the credit. The amount can revolve in relation to time or value.

Two types are:

- First, *reinstated immediately after a drawing is made* (for example if a credit is issued for USD 100,000 and the beneficiary draws a bill for USD 100,000, immediately after that drawing, the credit again reverts to its original amount.

- Second, *only after the documents are checked,* the credit reverts to its original amount only after it is confirmed by the issuing bank.

The risk exposure is an indefinite amount.

They may be issued with explicit stipulations on the ceiling for aggregate drawings and the total period for which the credit will be available.

Example of Revolving LC

Irrevocable Documentary Credit No	GLC $ 02398
Date and Place of Issue 30th November 2015 Incheon, South Korea	Date and Place of Expiry 28th February, 2016, India
Applicant B & S Global Trading, Daegu, South Korea	Beneficiary Hyphen Garment Private ltd P-46, Garden Reach, Kolkata, West Bengal 700088
Advising Bank Punjab National Bank Bangalore, India	Amount In Figures: US$ 35000 In Words: United States Dollars. Thirty Five Thousand Only, CIP Korea
Partial Shipment: Prohibited Transshipment: Prohibited Airfreight from: Kolkata Airfreight to: Daego, South Korea Latest date for Airfreight: 20th February, 2016	Credit available with any bank by negotiation of beneficiary's draft at sight drawn on Hana Bank, Daegu, South Korea for full invoice value, accompanied by the following documents in duplicate unless otherwise stipulates

Documents Instruction:

1. Clean on board airway bill made out to the order of Commercial bank Ltd., notifying opener and applicant with full address mentioning this letter of credit number ad date marked freight paid.
2. Signed Commercial invoice in quadruplicate
3. Packing list in triplicate showing colour, size assessment, gross weight, measurement, and net weight in each carton.
4. Air Insurance policy endorsed in blank for 110% of invoice value with claim payable at destination in the currency of draft covering Institute of Cargo Causes (A), Institute of War Causes (Cargo), Institute of Strike Clauses (Cargo).
5. Certificate of Origin issued by Chamber of Commerce and Industry, showing applicant as the consignor.
6. Beneficiary's certificate certifying that one full set of non-negotiable copies of shipping documents has been sent to applicant by courier after air freight
7. Insurance certificate issued and signed by Apparel Export council, mentioning that the fabric and performance of goods are in accordance with the samples.

Other terms and conditions:

1. This is a revolving letter of credit up to an agreement amount of $ 7,000, per month.
2. Each month maximum 5 drawings under this letter of credit is permitted
3. The amount of this documentary credit will be reinstated on receipt of our reinstatement instructions for the earlier drawings and subject to documentary compliance

We hereby, issue a documentary credit in your favour subject to UCP 600 of 2007 revision.

Hana Bank
Daegu, South Korea

3.7 Instalment LC

Instalment credit calls for the full value of the goods to be shipped but stipulates that the shipments be made in specific quantities at stated periods or intervals.

- This credit differs from simple credit, which may allow partial shipment, in the sense that part shipments under instalment credit are made in specific quantities and at specified intervals, whereas in case of simple-credit-permitting partial shipment, there would be no specific stipulation with regard to quantity and time.

- The credit also differs from revolving credit in the sense that the amount of credit does not revert to the original sum for reuse by the beneficiary.

- As per Article 32 of UCP, if the beneficiary has not shipped the goods or drawn under the credit any instalment within the period allowed for such shipment/drawing, the credit ceases to be available for that and subsequent instalments, unless otherwise stipulated in the credit.

3.8 Transit LC

- The services of a bank in a third country (neither the buyer country nor the seller's country) would be utilized.

- This generally happens when the issuing bank has no correspondent relations with any bank in the beneficiary's country.

- May be used by a small country whose credits may not be accepted in another country. In such case, the issuing bank may request a bank in a third country to issue the credit on its behalf.

3.9 Standby LC

Primary function of the SBLC is to provide guarantee against the nonpayment of the document. Standby credit practice is largely developed in the USA. Like the USA, Japan also did not recognize the guarantees because of legal restrictions on banks from issuing bonds and guarantees. Recent changes in the law, however, do not seem to have significantly altered bankers' reliance on the standby. Hence, SBLC is independent of the underlying contract and is issued to substitute the guarantees.

The first reference to SBLC in UCP was in Publication 400 in 1983. The ICC has adopted the International Standby Practices (ISP 98) as separate rules for SBLC and implemented them from January 1, 1999.

SBLCs can be opened either under UCP 600 or under ISP 98 where ISP 98 is applicable for both the inland SBLC and international SBLC.

SBLC is intended to cover a "nonperformance" (default) situation instead of a "performance" situation. SBLC can perform the functions of various guarantees such as advance payment guarantee, performance guarantee, and so on by suitably amending the wording.

It can also be used to secure payment for outstanding invoices under "account sales" or "open account" systems. They are particularly used in the international oil trade.

Transaction Flow under SBLC

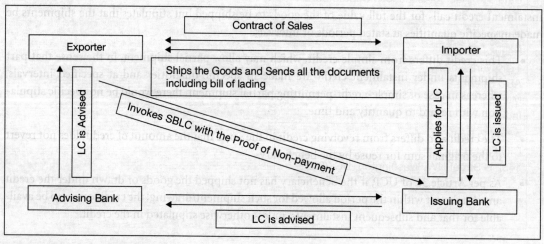

SOURCE: FEDAI Guidelines on SBLC.

3.9.1 Transaction Flows

1. Sales contract between the exporter (beneficiary) and the importer (principal).

2. The importer applies for an SBLC to his or her banker, that is, the issuing bank.

3. The issuing bank advises SBLC through an advising bank.

4. The advising bank advises the SBLC to the beneficiary/exporter.

5. The exporter ships the goods.

6. The exporter dispatches the documents to the importer.

7. The importer takes delivery of the goods.

8. The importer remits the invoice amount to the exporter.

9. *In case of default by the importer*, the beneficiary invokes payment under the SBLC through his or her banks.

10. On invocation, the issuing bank makes the payment to the beneficiary through his or her banks.

Example of SBLC   Swift Code:
Bank of Baroda,
ABC Street,
Mumbai – 400009
India.

We hereby issue our irrevocable Stand by Letter of Credit No: ADBC $ 0980

Date and Place of Issue: 30th September 2016, Mumbai	Date and Place of Expiry: 31st August, 2017 at Washington DC, USA
Applicant Renuka Textile, 17 Kuvera Colony ABC Street Mumbai – 400009 India	Beneficiary: Global Garments 1432 U Street NW Washington DC Pin 20009
Advising Bank City First Bank 1432 U Street NW, Washington, DC 20009	Amount: In Figures US$: 75,000.00 In Words: United States Dollars: Seventy Five Thousands Only
	Covering: Readymade Garments: T-Shirts

Available by your draft drawn on us at sight payable on or after 16th June 2017 and against surrender with this original credit along with the following documents:

1. Statement signed by an authorized official stating that invoice referred below was presented to Renuka Textile, 17 Kuvera Colony, ABC Street, Mumbai 400009 was not paid in accordance with the terms and contract no AB 537, dates 2nd February, 2016 and remains unpaid at the time of the claim under letter of credit No. ADBC $ 0980, dated 30th September, issued by Bank of Baroda, ABC Street, Mumbai 400009, India.
2. Copy of the Commercial invoice with the full description of goods supplied mentioning the details of the transport document.
3. Partial Shipments allowed.
4. The amount available for drawing under the credit will be reduced o the extent of payment made by us and will be to the extent of failure of the applicant to meet the commitments under the contract for agreed supply of goods
5. This credit available with the advising bank for payment.
6. We hereby undertake that all the drafts drawn hereunder will be duly honored by us if drawn and presented in accordance with the terms and conditions stated in this stand by letter of credit.

We hereby issue the Standby letter of credit in your favor. It is subject to the UCP 600.

Bank of Baroda
ABC Street, Mumbai India, 400009

3.9.2 Difference Between SBLC and Commercial LC

- In a commercial LC, the beneficiary is entitled for payment once he or she is able to submit the documents prescribed in the LC within the stipulated time. In SBLC, the beneficiary is eligible for payment from the issuing bank when the applicant fails to perform his or her obligation.

- A commercial LC performs as a simple payment mechanism for a trade transaction, whereas an SBLC acts as a backup available to the exporter.

- Commercial LC is a short-term payment instrument for trade finance, while SBLC can be a long-term instrument.

The RBI has permitted ADs to open SBLCs for their importer constituents for import into India any goods whose import is permissible under the Foreign Trade Policy (AP Dir 84, March 3, 2003).

Categories of Importers

- Where such standbys are required by applicants *who are independent power producers/importers of crude oil and petroleum products.*

- Special category of importers, namely, export houses, trading houses, star trading houses, super-star trading houses or 100% Export Oriented Unit (EOU).

- Public sector units/public limited companies with good track records.

- Request from private limited companies and noncorporate bodies for issuance of commercial standbys can be considered by the AD banks on the merits of each case (i.e., credit relationship/long standing relationships/regular submission of evidence of import etc.) subject to the usual credit drill. Banks may formulate their own internal policy guidelines in this regard.

Detailed guidelines for issuance of such SBLCs issued by the FEDAI. (SPL-16 / Standby LC / 2003 dated 01st April 2003 and further modifications).

Invocation of commercial standby by the beneficiary is to be supported by proper evidence.

- Beneficiary of the credit should furnish a declaration to the effect that the claim is made on account of the failure of the importer to abide by the contractual obligations and enclose.

- A copy of the invoice.
- Nonnegotiable set of documents including a copy of nonnegotiable B/L.
- A copy of inspection certificate wherever provided for as per the underlying contract.
- *Importer to ensure submission of evidence of import.*
- *When payment under a SBLC is effected, the issuing bank shall report invocation to the RBI.*

Undertaking to be obtained from the applicant.

- The applicant of a commercial SBLC (Indian importer) shall undertake to provide evidence of imports in respect of *all* payments made under standby.

- AD banks shall follow up evidence of imports as provided for under FEMA in *all* cases of payments made under standby covering imports into India.

Important provision under ISP 98 for SBLC.

- ISP 98 provides an opportunity to present documents within 30 days of a re-opening after a closure caused by "force majeure" or any other reason.

- UCP 500 Article 17 and UCP 600 Article 36 do not provide the beneficiary the opportunity to present documents once the bank has reopened.

Force Majeure.

- A bank assumes no liability or responsibility for the consequences arising out of the interruption of its business by acts of God, riots, civil commotions, insurrections, wars, acts of terrorism, or by any strikes or lockouts or any other causes beyond its control.

- A bank will not, upon resumption of its business, honor or negotiate under a credit that expired during such interruption of its business.

Example: Peter Beathered et al. Plaintiffs v. Chicago Football Club INC et al. Defendants, No 753339 (United States District Court, Aug 30, 1976)	
Domestic Letter of Credit No. 160	Date:15 August, 1975

- Peter was a member of American Football Club and was offered a SBLC based on his concern that the company backing the Chicago football club would get into financial trouble. Thereby, they would be unable to pay his wages for the number of games he was due to play in the following season.
- A standby was issued to him by the Mid-City National Bank of Chicago in his favour if the company get into difficulties.
- The amount could be claimed under the following declaration
- Drafts presented under this credit must be accompanied by a signed affidavit of Mr. Peter Beathard stating that the Chicago Football Club Inc General Partner of Chicago Winds Limited Partnership has not paid Mr. Beathard for a scheduled football game by Tuesday of the following week.
- As the company got into financial difficulties, Standby was presented by Peter.
- The claim was dishonored even though Peter had fulfilled all his obligations under the SBLC.
- The L/C was not under UCP 600. It was not mentioned that LC is irrevocable and in those days prior to ICC 500 publications, the LC could be deemed to be revocable.

SOURCE: International Trade and Pre-Export Finance: Second Edition, A Practitioner's Guide, Howard Palmer; Euro Money Book.

Case

An SBLC that provided for payment in the event of nonpayment for an oil shipment. The credit mentioned that loading was to occur between December 18 and 22, 2015, both the dates included. The unpaid commercial invoice of the beneficiary showed the BL date as December 23, 2015. The issuing bank refused the claim due to late shipment based on the commercial invoice information. The beneficiary presented a revised document showing BL date December 23, 2015 and loading date December 22, 2015. Again, the issuing bank refused the claim, this time for conflicting data. Is the issuing bank right?

This is a case of an SBLC that covered the value of goods delivered and services rendered. It is also a query where the wording of the credit could have been better drafted.

Any drawing under the credit was to consist of a draft, written declaration from the beneficiary, copy of beneficiary's unpaid invoice, and a copy of the transport document representing value of the goods only. The credit was confirmed.

A drawing was made under the credit in respect of services rendered but not paid for. The drawing did not include a copy of the transport document. The issuing bank refused the drawing due to the absence of a copy of the transport document. The confirming bank objected to the refusal stating that as only nonpayment for services was being claimed, no copy of a transport document was necessary.

Fraud under Standby Letter of Credit
Article in the South China Morning Post, 28th July 1993

Four men seized for HK $77 billion bank deal.

Four people, including two Chinese-Americans, have been arrested for issuing US$10 billion (about HK$77.54 billion) worth of fake letter of credit, the nationality televised evening news reported yesterday.

The report said Zhao Jingrong, manager of a Hebei province branch of the Agriculture Bank of China and Xu Shiguo, assistant manager, were arrested recently.

Francisco Hung Moy, president of the New York registered United Asia (Group) Corp and Raymond Lee, of the same company were also arrested in China.

The two are accused of issuing a false letter of credit on March 30 in the name of United National Bank of Russia for USD 10 billion in favour of Zhao's bank branch.

The next day, Zhao illegally issued 200 letters of credit ranging in value from US$ 25 to US$ 100 million and totalling US$ 10 billion to Sherwood Investments (Bahamas) Ltd in Canada, the report said.

The Agriculture Bank's main office later discovered that the Russian Bank did not exist, and last Saturday announced that all the letter of credits were void.

SOURCE: Extracted from International Trade and Pre-Export Finance: Second Edition, A Practitioner's Guide, Howard Palmer; Euro Money Book.

References and Resources

Beedu, R. R. (2010). *Documentary letter of credit*. Mumbai, India. Snow White Publications.

FEDAI (Foreign Exchange Dealers Association of India). (2009). *Documentary credits and standby credits*. FEDAI.

ICC Publication. (2013). *International standard banking practices (ISBP)* (ISBP Publication no 745). Geneva. ICC Publication.

Palmer, H. (1995). *International trade finance: A practitioner's guide*. London. Euromoney Publications PLC.

———. (1999). *International trade and Pre-export Finance: A Practitioner's Guide*, (2nd ed.) London. Euromoney Institutional Investor PLC.

Uniform Customs and Practices–UCP 600, *ICC guidelines to govern operation under letter of credit*. Retrieved February 23, 2016, from www.fd.unl.pt>mhb_MA_24705

Uniform Rules for Collection–URC 522, *ICC guidelines to govern operations under collection*. Retrieved February 23, 2016, from www.uef.fi

QUESTIONS

A. Multiple Choice Questions

1. SBLC
   a. Does work as guarantee and is implemented from January 1, 1999
   b. Mostly applicable in oil sale and open account transaction.
   c. SBLC can be issued subject to UCP 600 or ISP 98 of ICC
   d. Only (a), (c), (d)
   e. All (a), (b), (c), (d)

2. SBLC
   a. Is a payment instrument
   b. Is a nonpayment instrument
   c. None of the above

3. SBLC can be issued under
   a. UCP 600
   b. ISP 98
   c. Both the above

4. Green Clause LC
   a. Having clause written in green color
   b. Involves the warehouse and insurance paid by the importer in advance
   c. Both the above

5. Red Clause LC
   a. Requires advance payment from the importer
   b. Advance payment is used for purchasing raw-material and pre-shipment requirement
   c. Both the above

6. Back-to-back LC
   a. Requires a principal LC as a collateral
   b. Having terms and conditions almost same as principal LC

   c. It is same as transferable LC
   d. Only a and b
   e. All a, b, and c

7. Installment Credit
   a. Requires shipment of credit with the stipulated frequency
   b. Any value can be shipped in each shipment
   c. Both the above

8. Transit Credit
   a. Is opened by a country other than the exporter or importer's country
   b. Is opened when importer's country is having no reputation in the international market
   c. Both the above
   d. None of the above

9. Back-to-back LC
   a. Is more risky than transferable LC
   b. More than one advising bank is involved in the transaction
   c. Both the above
   d. Only b

10. In case of transferable LC
   a. LC should have the term "Transferable" and "Divisible"
   b. Importer request its bank for opening one LC in favor of the first beneficiary
   c. Unless otherwise specified transferring charge is paid by the first beneficiary
   d. a and b
   e. b and c
   f. a, b, and c

B. The Following Case is on Transferable LC. Answer the Questions Below:

A transferable LC for USD 200,000 was transferred by M in favor of X for USD 85,000 and in favor of Y for USD 85,000. Subsequently an amendment calling for inspection certificate was received. X accepted the amendment. Amendment was not acceptable to Y. He or she decided to transfer his or her portion to Z. This was not allowed by transferring bank. Hence he or she decided to retransfer it back to original beneficiary.

1. Can Y transfer his or her portion to Z?

2. Can Y transfer his or her portion to M?

3. Whether the rejection of amendment is binding on X?

4. Who would bear the cost of transfer?

5. In the above LC if the term "divisible" is mentioned and the negotiating bank refuses the transfer of the credit then which bank is at fault?

6. If the documents presented by M are not complied on first presentation while the documents presented by X are complied, then bank would not pay either of the parties involve. Is it correct?

7. In case of transferable LC what is the risk borne by the importer?

8. Back-to-back and transferable LC—which one is considered as more risky?

9. In the above example while making the transfer does issuing bank need to nominate the transferring bank?

10. How a transferred LC is different from the transferable LC?

C. Answer the Following Questions

1. Write the flow chart of SBLC. Which country was the first to invent SBLC?

2. Draw the flow chart of back-to-back LC. How many LCs are there in the back-to-back LC?

3. Which bank takes the maximum risk for a simple back-to-back LC and why?

4. In which terms back-to-back LC should be exactly similar to the principal LC and in which aspects they do differ?

5. What are the major difference between back-to-back LC and transferable LC.

6. How many LCs are involved in a transferable LC?

7. What is the roles and responsibility of a transferring bank? Is it mandatory that issuing bank nominates a transferring bank?

8. What is instalment credit? When is it considered to be ceased?

9. Write three important differences between red clause and green clause LC. What is the need for red clause LC in the international trade transaction?

10. Under transferable LC, if first beneficiary fails to make a complying presentation on first demand can payment be made to the second beneficiaries on their complying presentation?

Chapter	Documentary Collection and Documentary Credit: Caselets under URC 522 and UCP 600
4	

Highlights of the Chapter

4.1	International Chamber of Commerce
4.2	Documentary Collection and URC 522
4.2.1	Caselets in URC 522
4.3	LC Transaction
4.3.1	Uniform Customs and Practices (ICC Publication 600) in Connection to International Standard Banking Practice (ISBP)

4.1 International Chamber of Commerce

We already have discussed different payment methods involved in international trade transactions. In this chapter, we discuss a few caselets on documentary collections and documentary credits in connection to two ICC rules (a) URC 522 and (b) UCP 600. These two payment methods are together known as bank intermediary payment methods. Although these two payments methods are used popularly in international trade transaction, there is hardly any documentation on the practical aspects and application of the ICC guidelines governing the payment methods.

Traditionally, trade finance is considered to be the most convenient way to utilize the integrity of the international banking system to ensure the safety of any particular transaction. Although language and cultural differences are prevalent across countries, it is invariably true that an exporter would not wish to part with his or her goods prior to the payment reaching him or her and an importer would not wish to pay for goods prior to having inspected the goods and being assured that they were of the quality and specifications required. Given these risks, the exporter takes the least risk under advance payment, while for the importer, the risk is the least under open account. Out of all the four methods of payment (discussed in the Chapter 1), documentary credit is the only transaction which depends on documentary compliance and assures an exporter a timely payment if not opted for advance payment. This is the sole reason it is considered to be the costliest payment method. On the other side, under documentary collection, banks play the role only as a collecting agent and the cost of service is relatively lower. However, these two banks intermediary payment systems are required to go by the prescribed guidelines of ICC. A number of global surveys indicated that because of discrepancies, approximately 70% of documents presented under LCs were being rejected on first presentation. This obviously had, and continues to have, a negative implication in international trade transaction. Also, for documentary compliance, there exist certain rules prescribed by ICC which describes the division of risk and responsibility among different parties. In this context, it is important to know these two payment methods in the light of those rules of ICC.

4.2 Documentary Collection and URC 522

We have already understood that the banks are engaged only as a collecting agent for either obtaining payment or accepting the payment in future and, on the other hand, delivering the documents to the importer against payment or acceptance. Also, there are two types of documents in any documentary collection process; one a financial document and the second a commercial document. "Documents" means financial documents and/or commercial documents:

1. Financial documents are those which facilitates the financial transaction. For example bills of exchange, promissory notes, checks or other similar instruments can be considered as financial documents which are used for obtaining the payment of money.

2. Commercial documents are those which help in establishing the commerce between the two parties. For instance, invoices, transport documents, documents of title or other similar documents, or any other documents whatsoever, not being financial documents.

There may be another type of transaction which may consists collection of financial documents not accompanied by commercial documents. This type of transaction is popularly known as *clean collection*.

Compared to open account payment, a documentary collection shifts the balance of risks from the exporter towards the importer. Unlike documentary credit, under documentary collection, the importer takes control of the goods on presentation of an appropriate document of title, together with some form of commitment to pay (typically, a bill of exchange).

It may be noted that under documentary collection, banks do not take the risk of payment until the buyer's bank *Avals* an accepted bill of exchange or adds its name to guarantee payment on the due date. As a result, the most significant risk to the seller is that of nonpayment. In other words, *avalization* is the only way to shift payment risk from seller to bank under documentary collection. For instance, see Box 4.1.

Although documentary collection is not subject to documentary compliance, according to the Article 4(i) of URC, all documents sent for collection must be accompanied by a collection instruction indicating that the collection is subject to URC 522 and giving complete and precise instructions.

Through a few caselets, we discuss the application of some of the important rules of ICC for simplifying international trade transaction under documentary collection.

Box 4.1   An example of Avalization under Documentary Collection

For some reasons an Indian manufacturing company is asked by foreign supplier to accelerate payment. In this situation the supplier may draw a bill of exchange on the Indian company with a future date for payment and ask buyer's bank to avalize the paper. If Indian company's bank offer agrees to avalize and accelerates the payment to the supplier, then both the parties benefit from this transaction.

4.2.1 Caselets in URC 522

Case 1: Partial Payment in Case of Clean and Documentary Collection

Scenario 1: *Party A requests the presenting bank to release the documents against the partial payment under clean collection. Bank says financial document can be released only against full payment.*

According to Article 19 (a), the financial document(s) will be released to the drawee only when full payment thereof has been received. In respect of clean collections, partial payments may be accepted if, and to the extent to which and on the conditions on which, partial payments are authorized by the law in force in the place of payment.

Scenario 2: *Party A requests the presenting bank to release the document against the partial payment under documentary collection, while the bank refuses to do so as there is no such instruction mentioned for collection. Party A holds the bank responsible for the damage to the goods thereof. Is the bank's decision correct?*

The presenting bank's decision is correct without holding any further responsibility. According to Article 19(b), partial payments will only be accepted if specifically authorized in the collection instruction. However, unless otherwise instructed, the presenting bank will release the documents to the drawee only after full payment has been received. Also, in such circumstances the presenting bank will not be responsible for any consequences arising out of any delay in the delivery of documents.

Case 2: Interest Collection and Waiver

Collection instruction says that interest is to be collected, and the drawee refuses to pay such interest; however, the presenting bank delivers documents to drawee against payment. Remitting bank holds presenting bank responsible for the same and claims interest. Which bank is correct and why?

Even if there is an instruction for collection of interest, presenting bank may waive it unless until collection instruction expressly states that interest may not be waived, and in case the drawee refuses to pay such interest, the presenting bank will not deliver documents and will not be responsible for any consequences arising out of any delay in the delivery of document(s).

Case 3: Goods Directly Delivered to the Bank

B Bank sent a documentary collection to L Bank. The goods were consigned directly to the B Bank. The collection instructions were to deliver goods against payment.

L Bank initially refused to take delivery of goods and act as per instructions. However, later, L Bank cleared the goods, arranged for insurance, and stored the goods until paid by buyer.

In the process, L Bank incurred expenses on account of demurrage, clearance, storage, and insurance. The buyer paid only the bill amount. L Bank deducted these charges from the proceeds. The seller and B Bank insisted for full proceeds.

As per Article 10 URC 522, goods can be consigned to collecting bank, subject to their prior consent to such arrangement.

In the absence of such arrangement, the collecting bank has no obligations about the goods.

However, if the collecting bank takes any action about goods, it is entitled to recover its expenses from the remitting bank.

Case 4: Disclaimer for Acts of an Instructed Party

P Bank sent documents for collection to Q Bank. The instruction included:

- *Deliver documents against payment.*

- *Protest for nonpayment.*

The drawee did not honor the bill. Q Bank failed to comply with the instruction to protest. The drawer claimed damages from P Bank.

As per URC Article 11, the remitting bank is not responsible if their instructions are not complied with by the collecting bank, though they have chosen such collecting bank.

Case 5: Usance Bill of Exchange but Documents to be Delivered After Payment

ABC Bank sent a bill for USD 50,000 to XYZ Bank for collection. The documents included a bill of exchange payable on the 45th day from date of shipment.
   The documents were to be delivered against payment.

As per Article 7 of URC, if bill of exchange on usance terms includes a clear instruction that the documents are deliverable only after the payment, then issuing bank should release the document only after the payment. However, a clear instruction to that effect is expected from remitting bank.

Case 6: Partial Payment

A set of collection documents for USD 100,000, included two sets of BLs covering equal quantity of same material. The documents were to be delivered against payment.
   The drawee requested the collecting bank to deliver one BL against partial payment of USD 50,000. The collecting bank obliged.

- The action of collecting bank is not correct as per Article 19 of URC. They should have taken the approval of the remitting bank before initiating such action.

URC 19 (b) states that in respect of documentary collections, partial payments will only be accepted if specifically authorized in the collection instruction. However, unless otherwise instructed, the presenting bank will release the documents to the drawee only after full payment has been received, and the presenting bank will not be responsible for any consequences arising out of any delay in the delivery of documents.

Case 7: Interest Waiver

A collection instruction contained the following instructions among others.

- *Collect interest at 10% p.a. for 20 days.*

- *Collection charges are for the account of drawee.*

- *Interest not to be waived.*

The drawee refused to pay interest and charges. The collecting bank delivered DPs of bill amount only.

- As per Article 20 and 21 of URC 522, the collecting bank is not authorized to waive interest and commission when it is clearly mentioned in the "collection instruction" that these should not be waived.

- In the absence of such indication they can waive recovery of interest and charges.

- Thus the action of collecting bank is in order as far as commission is concerned, but it is not correct in respect of interest.

Case 8: Returning the Documents

On June 1, 2012, GHI Bank received a bill for collection from SMT Bank. The drawee refused to pay. GHI Bank immediately informed of the refusal to the remitting bank on June 5, 2012 and sought their instructions.

On June 20, 2012, GHI Bank returned the documents to SMT Bank since no instructions were received.

On June 21, 2012, GHI received a message from SMT Bank to deliver documents to another drawee against payment.

GHI informed that they have already returned the document. The documents were lost in transit and SMT Bank did not receive the same.

As per Article 26 of URC, documents can be returned by the collecting bank after 60 days from the date of nonpayment advice. Hence the action taken by the collecting bank in the given situation is incorrect.

4.3 LC Transaction

In the previous chapter, we have discussed the basic concepts of documentary credit and related parties to the credit. In this chapter, we would discuss the documentary requirement of *LC* transaction under the light of the application of *UCP 600*. First, we establish flow of the documentation and a check list in LC transaction. Having proper documentation is very important as it may cause noncompliance followed by nonpayment by the issuing bank. This is the most sensitive issue in international trade finance which is subject to many oddities and complications. Only an application-based discussion on a real life situation may provide a good understanding on the associated rules and regulations.

On the basis of the request for a quote from the importer, the exporter is likely to send a pro forma invoice, a document that specifies basic terms of sale including the price, delivery and payment terms to the importer. In this backdrop, it is noteworthy that United Nations Convention has a standard format of sale contract, popularly known as *Contract for International Sales of Goods,* having two different types of conditions: (a) specific (similar to pro forma invoice) and (b) general. As of September 2015, CISG has been consented by 83 countries, while India is not a part of it as of today. This CISG has become popular in many countries, especially among small and medium enterprises which did not have any standard to follow unlike the large corporate houses.

Once pro forma invoice is accepted by the importer, he or she provides a confirmed purchase order to the exporter. On the basis of this confirmed order, the exporter may request for the payment under LC, especially when the exporter does not know the importer or the importer is from a country where country risk is quite high. When payment has to be made under documentary credit, then the buyer is obliged to request its bank, that is, the issuing bank, to open an irrevocable LC before (or after, in special cases) the shipment of the goods.

4.3.1 Uniform Customs and Practices (ICC Publication 600) in Connection to International Standard Banking Practice (ISBP)

Case 9: Date of Shipment and Negotiation

One LC stipulates last date for shipment and negotiation as 31-8-2011 and 15-9-2011 respectively. The set of documents received by the LC opening bank indicated that the documents were negotiated on 10-9-2011 and those included a BL dated July 2, 2011 covering shipment from Bangkok to Mumbai India.

Documents must be presented not later than 21 calendar days after the date of shipment as per Article 14c. Hence, in the above case, the documents became discrepant. If LC itself permits presentation beyond 21 days, then only the above mentioned document not to be treated as discrepant.

Case 10: Stale Document

LC mentions that a stale document is accepted. Shipment date is January 1, 2014, and expiry date of LC is January 28. Documents presented on January 25, 2014. A) Is it a discrepancy? B) If in the above case credit expires on January 24, 2014, and LC allows stale document. Is it a discrepancy?

ISBP is another important ICC document which defines some rules to be implemented in connection to UCP 600. While UCP 600 does not define stale document or how to deal with this type of document, ISBP 681 Article 21(b) and ISBP 745 Article A19 (b) throws some light on this. It says that if any condition of LC states that a *stale document* is allowed, then documents presented later than 21 calendar days after the date of shipment are acceptable as long as they are presented no later than the expiry date for presentation as stated in the credit. As in case A, the document is presented on January 25 which is a date prior to the expiry date; it is not a discrepancy. However, according to case B, it would be considered as a discrepant document as documents have been presented after the expiry of LC.

Case 11: Third Party Documents

Credit includes the condition that "third party document is acceptable" Invoice is issued by a party other than the beneficiary. Issuing bank rejects the document saying that invoice is not considered as under "third party document"

Like stale documents, UCP 600 also does not define the third party document. As per the definition provided by ISBP 681 Article 21(c) and ISBP 745 Article A19(c), third party documents are all those documents, excluding drafts but including invoices, which may be issued by a party other than the beneficiary.

At the same time, it is recommended by the practitioners to avoid unnecessary complication that it is better not to use such a term or phrase that is not defined in UCP 600.

Case 12: Consignor or Shipper Other than the Beneficiary

The documents that are presented state the name of the beneficiary is K. Steve in the credit. Transport documents consists the name of the consignor/shipper as G. Wall. Is it a discrepancy?

According to UCP 600 [Article 14(k)], the shipper/consignor of the goods indicated on any document need not be the beneficiary of the credit. However, if in the above case the LC excludes the above mentioned clause as an additional clause, then it would be considered as a discrepant document. This is because LC always overrules UCP 600.

Case 13: Inspection Certificate

Issuing bank rejects the payment as the date of inspection certificate is January 20, 2014 while the date of shipment is January 19, 2014. Is the issuing bank's decision is correct?

No, it is not a discrepant document. According to ISBP 681 Article 14 and ISBP 745 Article A(12) (a), (b), any document, including a certificate of analysis, inspection certificate, and pre-shipment inspection certificate, may be dated after the date of shipment. The document must only, either by its title or content, indicate that the event (e.g., inspection) took place prior to or on the date of shipment.

Case 14: Typing Error

LC describes a product as "Model 123," while the transport document submitted by the exporter shows the product name is "Modle 132." Could this be treated as discrepant document?

Yes, it is a discrepant document, but not because Model is represented as Modle, which is nothing but a typographical error and does not alter any meaning thereby. Instead, it can be considered as discrepant document because the number of the products differs between the two documents.

ISBP 681 Article 25 and ISBP 745 Article A23 says that a misspelling or typing error that does not affect the meaning of a word or the sentence in which it occurs does not make a document discrepant. For example, a description of the merchandise as "mashine" instead of "machine," "fountan pen" instead of "pen" or "modle" instead of "model" would not make the document discrepant.

Case 15: Commercial Invoice

Scenario 1: Issuing bank rejects the payment for three reasons: (a) the document titled only "invoice" and the commercial term was not written, while credit specifically requires presentation of a commercial invoice, (b) credit describes two types of goods—10 trucks and 4 tractors—while invoice evidences shipment of only four trucks, and credit also prohibits partial shipment, and (c) the currency stated in credit and invoice does not match. Are the decisions of issuing bank right?

In case (a), the decision of issuing bank is not right. According to the definition of commercial terms, it is not mandatory to write the commercial term in the invoice. Any document titled invoice would be accepted as a commercial invoice ISBP 745 Article C1(b).

However, in case (b), issuing bank is right to reject the document. According to ISBP 681 Clause 58 and 59 and ISBP 745 Article C4, the description of the goods, services or performance in the invoice must correspond with the description in the credit and an invoice must reflect what has actually been shipped or provided. As the credit restricts partial shipment, the documents would be treated as discrepant documents. If partial shipment was allowed in the credit, then invoice could be drawn for four trucks first and then invoice can be drawn for the rest of the goods. However, as it is not allowed as the invoice is drawn only for four trucks exporter cannot draw the invoice further.

Issuing bank is also right in rejecting the document in case (c), because as per UCP 600 [Article 18(a-iii)], credit and invoice should state the amount in the same currency.

Scenario 2: An invoice is not signed and dated. The credit is not specific about it. Will it be considered as discrepancy?

No, it would not be considered as a discrepancy. According to UCP 600 [Article 18(d)], it need not be signed. However, it does not mention anything about the date of an invoice which is rather clarified by

ISBP 681 Clause 62 and ISBP 745 C 10. It clearly says, if credit does not specifically mention anything on the requirement of date and signature, invoice may be without sign and signature.

Scenario 3: *Documents for USD 210,000 were submitted for negotiation to UHN Bank. The face value of LC was USD 200,000. The negotiating bank refused to negotiate in view of the following discrepancy that LC is overdrawn.*

If the invoice amount exceeds the LC value and the negotiating bank decides to negotiate up to the face value of the LC, its decision will be binding upon all parties as per article UCP 600, Article 18b.

Case 16: Extension of Expiry or Last Day for Presentation

Beneficiary has presented the documents on July 2, 2014, for the reason that June 30, 2014, is a Saturday and July 1, 2014, is a Sunday. The negotiating bank refused to negotiate stating that the LC is expired. The exporter claims that he or she was ready with the set of documents but as Saturday and Sunday Forex market is closed, it is his or her right to have the documents negotiated on the next working day.

If the last date for presentation of documents is a holiday, then the LC shall be automatically treated as valid on the next working day. (UCP 600, Article 29a). In this case the last working day was a Saturday. Even though the forex markets are closed on Saturdays, the banks are open for presentation of documents. The presentation, therefore on Monday, will be treated as presentation after expiry of the credit.

Case 17: Force Majeure

The banks in Guwahati were closed for three consecutive days from August 8, 2012 to August, 10, 2012 due to riots. On August 13, 2012, an exporter client approached the bank with a request to negotiate export documents under LC, which was valid up to August 10, 2012. The negotiating bank refused to negotiate, stating that the LC was expired. The exporter claimed that he or she was ready with the set of documents on 9-Aug-2012 and since the banks were closed he or she could not submit the documents before August 10, 2012. Is the negotiating bank correct?

UCP 600 Article 36 clearly explains is the term known as force majeure. It says, a bank assumes no liability or responsibility for the consequences arising out of the interruption of its business by acts of God, riots, civil commotions, insurrections, wars, acts of terrorism, or by any strikes or lockouts or any other causes beyond its control. A bank will not, upon resumption of its business, honor or negotiate under a credit that expired during such interruption of its business.

So, in the above case, LC expired during the period of interruption in the business of bank for reasons stated in Article 36 and cannot be acted upon when the banks reopen.

Case 18: Amendment of LC

On April 1, 2015, the bank received an amendment to the credit whereby the shipment date has been brought back. The amendment states that if there is no communication from beneficiary rejecting the amendment within seven days, it will be presumed to have been accepted. The beneficiary submits documents showing shipment within original validity and insists for payment. Is the beneficiary right? This LC does not include the term "irrevocable," so the importer party argues that he or she has every right to bring back the dates even without beneficiary's consent.

The beneficiary of the credit has right to accept or reject any amendment to the credit. There is no specified time limit. The LC opening bank cannot restrict this right or specify time [Article 10f UCP 600]. The beneficiary is within his or her rights to demand payment for submission of documents that are compliant with the LC without the amendment.

Case 19: Date in Packing List

A set of documents was submitted for negotiation on June 30, 2014. It indicates the packing date as January 1, 2014, prior to LC opening date. The issuance date of the LC was January 13, 2014. Is it a discrepancy? If the BL is dated January 11, 2014, is it a discrepancy? If the above LC allows stale documents, then is it a discrepancy?

According to UCP 600 [Article 14 (i)], a document may be dated prior to the issuance date of the credit, but must not be dated later than its date of presentation. If the LC specifically mentions that the documents prior to the issuance of the LC are not acceptable, then it is a discrepancy. If the BL date shows that the shipment has happened on January 11, then presentation on January 30 would be considered as discrepant as the documents may be considered as stale after 25 days from the shipment date. In the above case, if the LC allows the stale document, then it is not a discrepant document.

Case 20: Tolerance Limit

LC was opened for approximately USD 100,000. A bill was submitted for USD 108,000. Are the documents discrepant?

As per UCP 600, Article 30a, the words "about" or "approx" mean 10% more or 10% less than the amount, quantity or unit price stated in the credit in relation to which such words are used. So, in this case, the document cannot be treated as a discrepant document. It may be noted that using words like "approximately" actually may adversely affect the interest of the importing party.

Instead, LC may add a supplementary clause that +/- 5% tolerance is accepted. By the rule of UCP 600, Article 30b, 5% more or less than the quantity stated in the LC is acceptable and in this case the amount cannot surpass the LC value. It may be noteworthy to mention that the previously mentioned tolerance is accepted provided the quantity is not in terms of stipulated number of packing units or individual items (e.g. no of machineries, boxes, and so on).

Case 21: Transshipment

LC prohibits transshipment. It requires the presentation of single BL while BL shows transshipment happened. Payment was rejected. Is it a correct decision? What additional condition should be added in this circumstance?

A credit requiring the presentation of a BL and containing a prohibition on transshipment will, in most cases, have to exclude UCP 600 Sub-article 20(c) to make the prohibition against transshipment effective. Otherwise, a transport bill indicating that transshipment may or will take place is acceptable even if LC prohibits transshipment under two conditions: (a) the entire carriage may be under the same transport document and (b) the shipment is a container shipment.

UCP 600, Article 19 (b) defines transshipment as unloading from one means of conveyance and reloading in another means of conveyance (whether or not in different modes of transport) during the carriage from the place of dispatch, taking in charge or shipment to the place of final destination stated in the credit.

Case 22: Partial Shipment

Documents submitted include two sets of BL dated May 10 and May 15, 2011, showing shipment by SS Jal Vidya, port of loading being Mumbai (JNPT) and Kochi and port of destination being Colombo.

The Sri Lankan bank refuses to reimburse your bank stating that documents indicate partial shipment while LC prohibits partial shipments.

Even though the ports of loading and dates of loading are different, the two BLs are for the same voyage of the same vessel. Hence this is not a case of part shipment provided the total quantity of these BLs matches with the quantity specified in the credit (Article 31b).

The definition of partial shipment, according to UCP 600, Article 31(b), is a presentation consisting of more than one set of transport documents evidencing shipment commencing on the same means of conveyance and for the same journey, provided they indicate the same destination, will not be regarded as covering a partial shipment, even if they indicate different dates of shipment or different ports of loading, places of taking in charge or dispatch.

If the presentation consists of more than one set of transport documents, the latest date of shipment as evidenced on any of the sets of transport documents will be regarded as the date of shipment. A presentation consisting of more than one set of transport documents evidencing shipment on more than one means of conveyance within the same mode of transport will be regarded as covering a partial shipment, even if the means of conveyance leaves on the same day for the same destination.

Case 23: Advising and Pre-advising LC

Scenario 1: LK Bank was approached by their importer client on August 2, 2016, stating that the supplier has not received the LC opened by the bank on August 7, 2016. LK Bank immediately contacted the advising bank, which admitted the nonadvising of the LC, and the same was now being advised.

Now, the beneficiary is not ready to ship the goods unless the price is increased by USD 1,000. The importer complained that the opening bank is responsible for the delay and loss.

If the advising bank is not in a position to advise the LC for any reason, it should inform accordingly to the opening bank immediately (Article 9f). In this case, the opening bank is not responsible for failure of the advising bank in carrying out their instructions though it has chosen such bank (Article 37).

Scenario 2: Bank has received sanction for opening of an LC for USD 1.0 MIO on behalf of bank's importer customer. One of the terms of sanction is the importer to arrange for mortgage of collateral security.

The importer requests the issuance of a short message to beneficiary for pre-advising the credit. Will bank agree? If so, under what conditions?

As per Article 11(b), pre-advising the LC is advisable only if bank is completely ready to establish the credit. Because, once preadvised, the bank has to transfer the full amount of LC, irrespective of whether its sanctioned terms are complied with or not!

Case 24: Insurance Cover

An LC for USD 200,000 called for an insurance policy (among other documents) covering all the risks of loss and damage. A set of documents was submitted for negotiation which included an insurance policy for USD 200,000 dated September 29, 2011. The date of shipment was September 27, 2011. The policy covered institute cargo clauses (A). Is this policy acceptable?

Insurance policy dated subsequent to the shipment date is acceptable only if it indicates that the risk cover is effective from at least the date of shipment (Article 28e).

If the LC does not specify the extent of cover, it should be at least 110% of the invoice value. [Article 28f(ii)].

LC should stipulate the type of insurance required and should not use imprecise terms about risk coverage (Article 28g).

Case 25: Instalment Shipment

An LC was opened for USD 1,000,000 for 500 tons of goods. 100 tons were to be shipped each month from July 2016 to November 2016 and the bills for USD 200,000 were to be drawn for each month's shipment.

The bills for the first two months were duly paid. There was no shipment and bill in the month of September 2016. In the month of October 2016, the bill for USD 200,000 was received by the opening bank, covering 100 tons of goods. The opening bank refused to pay.

If the LC permits installment drawings/shipments and any installment is not drawn, the LC ceases to be valid for that and subsequent installments as per UCP 600, Article 32.

Case 26: Received for Shipment BL

A BL indicated that goods were received for shipment on September 14, 2011. The last date for shipment was September 15, 2011. Documents were refused for negotiation.

As per Article 20a(ii) UCP 600, the BL must indicate that the goods have been shipped onboard a named vessel. Hence, a BL indicating that goods are received for shipment is unacceptable.

Case 27: Clean and Charter Party BL

Scenario 1: *The LC asked for a clean on board BL. The issuing bank rejects the payment stating that clean term is missing in the BL submitted by the party. Is the issuing bank's decision right?*

A clean transport document is one bearing no clause or notation expressly declaring a defective condition of the goods or their packaging (UCP 600 Article 27). The word "clean" need not appear on a transport document, even if a credit has a requirement for that transport document to be "clean on board."

Scenario 2: *The LC stipulated submission of BL (among other documents). The documents presented under the LC included a BL indicating that (a) it is a charter party BL and (b) out of 500 drums shipped, 50 drums were found leaking.*

As per Article 20a(vi) UCP 600, a BL containing indication that it is charter party BL is unacceptable.

As per article 27, BL bearing clause indicating that the defective condition of goods/packages is unacceptable since LCs stipulate requirement of clean BL.

Case 28: Credit prohibits partial shipment and more than one set of BL is presented BL with a Usance Bill of Exchange

The credit requires shipment from a European port, and there are more than one BL evidences on board vessel "A" from Dublin on August 16 and on board vessel "B" from Rotterdam on August 18. The credit has usance of 60 days after BL. Which date should be considered for counting the maturity date of the credit?

According to ISBP 745 E 19 (b) if a credit prohibits partial shipment and if there are more than one set of original bills of lading presented then the latest of these dates is to be used for the calculation of any presentation period and must fall on or before the latest shipment date stated in the credit.

Case 29: Partial shipment is allowed and more than one set of original BL are presented as part of a single presentation with a Usance Bill of Exchange

If partial shipment is allowed and more than one original BL is presented as a part of the single presentation under one covering schedule of letter and incorporate different dates of shipment, on different vessels or the same vessel for a different journey, then the earliest of these dates is to be used for the calculation of any presentation period, and each of these dates must fall on or before the latest shipment dates.

References and Resources

Uniform Customs and Practices–UCP 600. *ICC guidelines to govern operation under letter of credit.* Retrieved on February 23, 2016, from www.fd.unl.pt>/mhb_MA_24705

Uniform Rules for Collection–URC 522. *ICC guidelines to govern operations under collection.* Retrieved on February 23, 16, from www.uef.fi

International chamber of Commerce. (ICC). (2013). *International Standard Banking Practices (ISBP).* ICC Publication No. 745, International Chamber of Commerce, Geneva.

Standby letter of credit. Sample format, Retrieved on January 31, 2017, from https://wred-lwrd.countyofdane.com/documents/Forms/exampleLOC.pdf

Sample text standby letter of credit. Retrieved on January 31, 2017, from http://allianceinvestmentcapital.com/images/SampleSBLCText.pdf

Transferable letter of credit. Sample, Retrieved on January 31, 2017, from http://www.lorianmarketing.co.uk/images/doc/150610-004.LC%20TEMPLATE.pdf

QUESTIONS

Answer the Following Questions

1. If one ship is going to go to Colombo with loading happening at two different ports, say A and B on different dates, say October 18 and October, 19 2016, is it considered to be partial shipment? Which date would be considered for the calculation of 45 days usance credit?

2. Suppose a container shipment is going from Cochin to Colombo and LC says transshipment is prohibited, is it an effective prohibition? Explain.

3. Suppose Renuka export gets an order from Netherland for six instalment shipment of 2,000 T-shirts, each shirt costing USD 100 and each

shipment staring from January 2016. In April, Renuka export does not ship the goods with the stipulated amount. It sends the double of the amount in May. Issuing bank refuses the payment. Is the issuing bank correct?

4. If an issuing bank finds discrepancies in the documents, within how many days must the issuing bank notify the advising bank about these discrepancies?

5. Can the packing date show that packaging has happened prior to the LC opening date?

6. If the insurance cover date is October 21, 2016 and shipment date is 19ᵗʰ October, 2016 is it a discrepancy? Explain

7. What is tolerance limit? How and when is it applied to an LC?

8. An LC is opened for the amount USD 500,000/ approximately and an issuing bank refuses to pay stating that the bill is drawn for USD 510,000/, which is more than the face value of the credit. Is it a discrepancy?

9. An issuing bank refuses the payment for the following two reasons: (a) two documents, packing list and insurance documents, are having dates prior to LC opening date and (b) inspection certificate is having date after the presentation date. Is the issuing bank right?

10. Exporter goes to bank for negotiation under an LC immediately after the expiry date of the credit and bank refuses to negotiate the document stating that LC is already expired. Exporter argues that the on the last date of the credit bank was closed for the causes other than force majeure. So he or she has the right to get the negotiation of the credit on the next working date. Is the exporter correct? What is force majeure?

11. Is typing error to be treated as discrepancy under an LC? Explain.

12. Issuing bank refuses to pay stating that the invoice is not signed and dated. Exporter argues that it was not stated in the LC that invoice must be signed and dated. Is the issuing bank correct? Why?

13. An LC amount EUR 300,000 is opened. However, the advising bank draws the bill with EUR 310,000 under the same credit. Issuing bank pays for the face value of the credit. Is issuing bank correct?

14. What is third party document? Is it safe to have third party document allowed under an LC? If LC

allows third party document and exporter submits an invoice issued by another person is it considered to be a discrepant document?

15. What is stale document? If LC, which expires on December 16, 2016, allows stale document and documents are presented on December 17 whereas BL date is November 20, 2016, is it a discrepancy?

16. Can goods be consigned to the issuing bank? If the bank adds its consent to take the delivery and arrange for insurance and warehouse and goods are damaged in the process, who held responsible for the damage?

17. How does a bank make the transshipment prohibition effective?

18. What are clean and damaged BLs? Is the clean term mandatory to appear in the ocean BL?

19. Can a collecting bank waive interest rate when there is a specific instruction that interest rate should not be waived? Explain with an example.

20. What is the use of documentary collection with usance bill of exchange, containing an instruction that "documents can be released only after the payment"? What happens if collecting bank releases the document immediately after the acceptance of the credit?

21. In international trade, SBLC is governed by which ICC publication?

22. What are the major differences between SBLC and a commercial LC?

23. Suppose a SBLC is opened under ISP 98 and if SBLC expires because exporter is not able to present the document on the last date of presentation due to "force majeure." Is it possible for the exporter to get the payment?

24. Exporter submits a bill of exchange in the following format

---

Bill of Exchange

London, 31 January 2016
US$ 500,000

Amount

At 60 days after sight

pay against this sole Bill of Exchange

To the order of   Ourselves

The sum of   US Dollars Five Hundred Thousand

For value   Received

To:

For and on behalf of:

Thailand Import Banking Company
Bank Street
Thailand

UK Export Company Ltd.

Drawn under UK Export Banking
Company Ltd, Documentary Credit
No. 32345, Dated 29 September 2015

Signature
Saritha Smith, Director

The LC has called for an usance draft. Importer rejects the payment stating that bill of exchange is not a usance bill. Is the importer right? Who are the drawer and drawee in this example?

25. Party A requests the presenting bank to release the document against the partial payment under documentary collection while bank refuses to do so despite of a clear instruction mentioned for collection that document can be released after partial payment. Party A holds the bank responsible for the damage to the goods thereof. If the banks decision is correct?

26. Collection instruction says that interest is to be collected and the drawee refuses to pay such interest; however, presenting bank delivers documents to drawee against payment. Remitting bank holds presenting bank responsible for the same and claims interest on her. Which bank is correct and why?

27. LK Bank was approached by their importer client on August 2, 2016 stating that his or her supplier has not received the LC opened by the bank on July

2, 2016. LK Bank immediately contacted the advising bank, which admitted the nonadvising of the LC and the same was now being advised.

Now, the beneficiary is not ready to ship the goods unless the price is increased by USD 1,000. The importer complained that the opening bank is responsible for the delay and loss.

28. An LC was opened for USD 2,000,000 for 1,000 tons of goods. 200 tons were to be shipped each month from July 2016 to November 2016 and the bills for USD 10,000 were to be drawn for each month's shipment.

The bills for first two months were duly paid. There was no shipment and bill in the month of September 2016. In the month of October 2016, the bill for USD 10,000 was received by the opening bank, covering 200 tons of goods. The opening bank refused to pay. Is the opening bank correct?

29. An LC for EUR 400,000 called for an insurance policy (among other documents) covering all the risks of loss and damage. A set of documents was submitted for negotiation which included an

insurance policy for USD 400,000 dated September 29, 2016. The date of shipment was September 27, 2016. The policy covered institute cargo clauses (A). Is this policy is acceptable? If the insurance policy was for EUR 400,000, is it an acceptable policy.

30. A bank has received sanction for opening of an LC for USD1.0 MIO on behalf of the bank's importer customer. One of the terms of sanction is the importer to arrange for mortgage of collateral security.

    The importer requests to issue a short message to beneficiary for pre-advising the credit. Will the bank agree? If so, under what conditions?

31. A set of documents was submitted for negotiation on June 30, 2016. It indicates the packing date as January 1, 2016 prior to LC opening date. If the issuance date of LC was January 13, 2016, is it a discrepancy? If the BL is dated January 11, 2016, is it a discrepancy? If the above LC allows stale document, then is it a discrepancy?

32. On April 1, 2015, a bank received an amendment to the credit whereby the shipment date has been brought back. The amendment states that if there is no communication from beneficiary reject- ing the amendment, within seven days, it will be presumed to have been accepted. The beneficiary submits documents showing shipment within orig- inal validity and insists for payment. Is the ben- eficiary right? This LC does not include the term "irrevocable," so importer party argues that he or she has every right to bring back the dates even without beneficiary's consent.

33. Issuing bank rejects the payment for three rea- sons: (a) the document titled only "invoice" and the commercial term was not written, while credit specifically requires presentation of a commer- cial invoice and (b) credit describes two types of goods—10 trucks and 4 tractors—while invoice evidences shipment of only four trucks and credit also prohibits partial shipment, and (c) the cur- rency stated in credit and invoice does not match. Are the decisions of issuing bank right?

34. B Bank sent a documentary collection to L Bank. The goods were consigned directly to the B Bank. The collection instructions were to deliver goods against payment. L Bank initially refused to take delivery of goods and act as per instructions. However, later, L Bank cleared the goods, arranged for insurance and stored until paid by buyer. In the process, L Bank incurred expenses on account of demurrage, clearance, storage, and insurance. The buyer paid only the bill amount. L Bank deducted these charges from proceeds. The seller and B Bank insisted for full proceeds.

Chapter

5

Documents in International Trade

5.1 Transport Document: Bill of Lading

The main transport document in international trade is the BL. It can be classified into two different types.

1.   Order BL: "Order to" and transferable by delivery. Order BL is a negotiable instrument. A negotiable instrument helps in transferring the control over the goods. Once the goods arrive at their destination, they will be released to the bearer of one original BL. Normally BLs are made out to order and endorsed by the exporter.

     •   Advantage

         o   It allows the buyer to sell goods in transit by transferring the BL via endorsement.

         o   The seller can get paid as soon as the goods are properly shipped, by presenting the BL to an authorized bank.

         o   It provides the buyer the right to file case against the carrier for loss or damage of the goods.

- Disadvantage

  o In case of perishable goods, it may be loss making for the importer if the ship reaches the port before the BL reaches the bank. The importer would not be having any right to claim the goods from the port.

  o In case of oil trade, it is particularly common for the cargo to arrive before the documents. So the importer may have to bear the additional cost for holding the goods at the port.

2. Straight BL: As an alternative to the order BL, the name and the address of the importer may appear as the consignee. In such case, only the importer can obtain the goods, once the goods have arrived at their destination, by presenting the original BL, together with identification. This BL is known as the straight BL.

BL Sample

Shipper :	ABC International		
Consignee :			
Notify Party :			
Place of receipt :			
Vessel :		Port of Loading :	
Port of discharge :		Place of Delivery :	

Marks & Nos.	Description of goods :		Gross/Net Weight/CBM.

Freight & Charges	Pre-paid or collect	Number of Originals :	
Origin Inland haulage charges			
Origin THC/LCL Charges Ocean Freight		Place & Date of issue :	
Destination THC/LCL Charges			
Destination inland haulage			

5.2 Types of BL

The Ocean or Marine BL: In the class of all types of order BL, the ocean or marine BL is the most popular one. It is issued by the transport carrier or its agent, for example, a freight forwarder. The main three functions of marine BL are as follows:

1. The Right to Physical Delivery of the Goods: The legal holder of the BL is solely entitled to take the delivery of the goods. As the BL is a negotiable document, the goods can be sold in transit, even repeatedly, by mere transfer of BL. This also provides a security to the bank that wants to extend an advance to exporter.

2. BL Evidences the Contract of Carriage: BL must contain the terms of the contract of carriage, either explicitly or by reference to another document.

3. A Receipt: BL evidences the shipment of the goods.

The ocean or marine BL may be of two types—clean and damaged BL.

Clean BL: It indicates that goods are received in apparent good order and collection. It contains no notation of defect, damage or loss. However, "clean" term does not need to appear explicitly in the BL. No mention of damage or loss itself certifies that a BL is clean. Also, it requires the carrier to deliver the goods in the same good order and condition as received from the exporter or the agents.

Dirty/Foul/Claused: A notation to the effect that the goods have been partially/wholly damaged or partially lost. When a claused BL is issued, the ship owner or their agents can disclaim their liability to deliver the goods in good order and condition.

OnBoard BL: BL acknowledges that the goods having been put onboard of a ship for shipment. This is a safer document for an exporter as evidencing that the goods are delivered in the same order.

Difference Between Received for Shipment BL and the Onboard BL

Carrier may issue a BL as soon as the goods are received. This is a "received for shipment" BL and not be acceptable for negotiation until, after the loading it is converted by the carrier into a "onboard" BL by inscribing the term "onboard."

Received for shipment BL is also known as the "lash BL" as it is issued by the lash operator.

Clean Onboard BL: BL acknowledges the goods having been put onboard of a ship for shipment without any damage clause. Shipper is responsible for delivering the goods in the same good order.

Multimodal/Combined Transport BL: Involves more than one mode of transport.

- The carrier, called Multimodal Transport Operator, takes the liability for safe conduct of transport of goods.

- UCP 600, ICC's revised rules on Documentary Credit (DC), no longer entitle an article as "Multimodal Transport Documents," but rather "Transport Document Covering at least Two Different Modes of Transport."

Through BL: When cargo is to be transshipped at an intermediate port by another vessel, the first carrier issues this kind of BL and collects freight for the entire journey. This BL, issued for the entire voyage covering several modes of transport and/or transshipment, is called a through BL. It is used if at least one part of the journey is covered by a sea voyage.

Under through BL, the cargo is released by the second carrier at the final port of discharge, against the surrender of the through BL issued by the first carrier.

Example: BL covering journey from Bombay to Lagos with transshipment at Geneo.

- Combined transport BL are sometimes used in place of a through BL.

- Multi-modal transport document is safer than a through BL, as it guarantees the safe conduct of goods right through.

Liner BL: Indicates that goods are being transported on a ship that travels on a schedule route, so exporter can reasonably assume that his or her goods will reach the buyer's country by a set date.

Freight Forwarder BL: A freight forwarder is an indispensable member of the international trade community; it acts as an agent/principal between exporter and importer. FIATA BL or FBL is a standard form of BL issued by a freight forwarder; along with other forwarder bills in which the agent accept full responsibility as a carrier.

FBL is governed by the guidelines conducted by International Federation of Freight Forwarders Associations (or FIATA; French: Fédération Internationale des Associations de Transitaires et Assimilés).

FBL is a negotiable multimodal transport document. Acceptable as the clean onboard BL issued by a carrier.

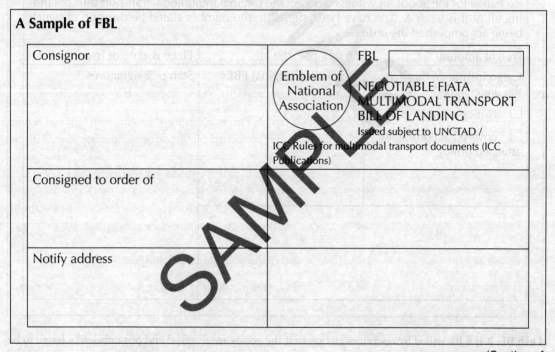

(Continued)

(*Continued*)

Place of receipt	
Ocean vessel	Place of loading
Port of discharge	Place of delivery

Marks and numbers	Number and kind of packages	Description of goods	Gross weight	Measurement

According to the declaration of the consignor

Declaration of the interest of the consignor in timely delivery (Clause 6.2)	Declared value for ad valorem rate according to the declaration of the consignor (Clauses 7 and 8)

The goods and the instructions are accepted and dealt with subject to the standard conditions printed overleaf.

Taken in charge in apparent good order and condition, unless otherwise noted herein, at the place receipt for transport and delivery as mentioned above.

One of these multimodal transport bills of landing must be surrendered duly endorsed in exchange for the goods. In witness whereof the original multimodal transport bills of landing all of this tenor & date have been signed in the number stated below, one of which being accomplished the order.

Freight amount	Freight payable at	Place & date of issue
Cargo insurance through the undersigned ☐ Not covered ☐ covered according to attached policy	Number of original FBL's	Stamp & signatures

Lash BL: It is a BL issued by operators stating that the goods are received and put onboard a barge to be carried and put on a parent vessel.

Thus, a BL issued by a lash operator is the same as a BL received for shipment BL until it bears a clause stating that the barge is put onboard the parent vessel (then it becomes an onboard BL).

Short form BL: One of the functions of a BL is that it evidences underlying contract of carriage. Thus, a BL should have the terms and conditions of carriage printed on it. However, the characteristics of short form BL are as follows:

- Do not contain the full details of the contract of carriage which is a major risk for the exporter. However, short-form BL are considered as the documents of title.

- It provides the minimum information—name of the shipper, name of the ship, date of shipment and so on. If any other details are stated, then it may be by reference to the other documents.

- Most often this type of BL is restricted in international trade, for example, LC specifically prohibit the acceptance of "short form BL" or blank back.

- Generally charter party BL are of this nature as they are governed by the terms and conditions of the charter party.

Charter Party BL: This type of BL is issued to the charter party. Charter party is the agent who has hired the space in the vessel either in full or in part. The terms of the BL are subject to the contract of hire between the ship owner and the hirer and is generally marked as "subject to charter party terms and conditions."

Like short-form BL, it is not a very secure deal for the exporter as the ship owner may exercise ban over the goods in case charterers do not pay the hire charge. Mostly importantly, charter party BL is only an evidence of contract of carriage.

There are three types of charter.

- Time Charter (for specified time)

- Voyage Charter (for specified voyage)

- Mixed Charter (for specified time and voyage)

5.3 Waybill

This kind of transport document can be issued by the shipping or airways companies to the named consignee against the identification. The major difference between the waybill and BL are the following:

- Waybills are nonnegotiable, as goods can be claimed only against the identification.

- Waybills are not a document of title. The importer can collect the goods without the need to produce the waybill to the shipper or consigner.

The Sea Waybills: This kind of waybill mostly goes with an open account arrangement. Under open account payment method, a transport document is called for that can be issued by the shipping company to the named consignee against identification. On arrival at the destination, the goods will be released to the named consignee against the identification.

The FIATA Waybill (FWL): This waybill is issued by the freight forwarder. Like other waybills, this is also a nonnegotiable document. However, it may be issued in case of involvement of multimodal transport. Also, freight forwarder takes the responsibility for the safe delivery of the goods.

The Road Waybill: It is a document containing the details of the international transportation of goods by road. The rules are set out by the Convention for the Contract of the International Carriage of Goods by Road in 1956 (the CMR Convention). Usually, a CMR is issued for each vehicle. However, the CMR is not a document of title and also nonnegotiable.

The Rail Waybill: The rail waybill is a document required for the transportation of goods by rail. It is regulated by the Convention concerning International Carriage by Rail 1980 (COTIF). It is considered as the rail transport contract.

Postal Receipt/Courier Receipt: Issued by postal or courier company. It can be a sea mail receipt or air mail receipt, depending upon the mode by which it is sent. However, this is not a negotiable document. It also does not carry a document of title goods; instead, it works as a receipt. Identification is not must for taking delivery of goods, most often it is required for customs purposes.

5.4 Caselets on Transport Documents

Case 1

The issuing bank rejects the payment as the BL does not show the name of the carrier and the signature also is missing. Is the issuing bank correct?

A BL, however named, must appear to indicate the name of the carrier and be signed by the carrier or a named agent for/on behalf of the carrier. So, as per UCP 600 Article 20 a(i), the issuing bank is correct in rejecting the payment.

Case 2

Payment is refused on the ground that the BL is signed by an agent, not by the carrier, without a mention on behalf of which carrier the agent has signed. Is the issuing bank correct?

The issuing bank is correct as per UCP 600, Article 20 (i). If a BL is signed by an agent, it is necessary that the agent must indicate whether he or she has signed for/on behalf of the carrier or for/on behalf of the master.

Case 3

LC requires the BL date should be no later than November 11. When the BL was submitted, the issuing bank rejects the document stating the BL is discrepant.

The exporter argues that the date of issue of BL was November 11. He or she has shipped the goods as per the LC terms. However, the issuing bank argues that the BL contains onboard notation indicating that the date of shipment is November 12. In such case, issuance date of BL would be disregarded as the date of shipment.

The issuing bank is right. As per UCP 600, Clause 20 (ii), the date of issuance of the BL will be the date of shipment only if the BL contains no onboard notation indicating the date of shipment. If the BL indicates any notation then the date stated in the onboard notation will be deemed to be the date of shipment.

Case 4

The BL does not specify any name of the vessel. Instead, it indicates "intended vessel." There is no onboard notation mentioned. Issuing bank rejects the documents. The issuance date of BL is January 5, 2016.

The negotiating bank states that if onboard notation is not mentioned, then the issuance of BL needs to be treated as the date of shipment.

This is true in the case where the name of the vessel appears on the BL. However, instead of any name of the vessel, if the BL indicates "intended vessel," an onboard notation indicating the date of the shipment and the name of the actual vessel becomes mandatory. This is as per the article 20 (ii) UCP 600.

Case 5

The BL does not indicate the port of loading stated in the credit as the port of loading; instead, it contains the indication "intended." The document was rejected as there was no onboard notation indicating the port of loading as stated in the credit.

The issuing bank is right. As per Article 20 a(iii), if the BL does not indicate the port of loading stated in the credit as the port of loading, or if it contains the indication "intended" or a similar qualification in relation to the port of loading, an onboard notation indicating the port of loading as stated in the credit, the date of shipment and the name of the vessel is required.

Case 6

The issuing bank rejects the documents stating that the conditions of carriage is not examined and no document is submitted regarding this.

The contents of terms and conditions of carriage will not be examined, according to UCP 600 Article 20 a (v). This is applicable for short form BL or blank back BL.

Case 7

The exporter submits more than one BL evidencing transshipment at two different ports. The issuing bank refuses the payment stating that transshipment will or may happen if the entire carriage is covered by one and the same BL.

A BL may indicate that the goods will or may be transshipped, provided that the entire carriage is covered by one and the same BL. This is as per Article 20 c (i), UCP (600).

Case 8

Transshipment is prohibited by LC. The shipment is a container shipment and the BL evidences that transshipment has happened.

Issuing bank rejects the document.

A BL indicating that transshipment will or may take place is acceptable, even if the credit prohibits transshipment, if the goods have been shipped in a container, trailer or lash barge as evidenced by the BL. This is as per the article c(ii) UCP 600.

Case 9

BL indicates a clause stating that the carrier reserves the right to transship. The goods are carried under more than one BL evidencing transshipment.

Issuing bank refuses the payment stating that LC prohibits the transshipment.

Issuing bank is right as per the Article no 20 (d) UCP 600. Any clauses in a BL stating that the carrier reserves the right to transship will be disregarded.

Case 10

The issuing bank rejects the payment saying that transshipment cannot happen if LC calls for a nonnegotiable sea waybill. The negotiating bank argues that transshipment will or may happen if the entire carriage is covered under one and the same sea waybill. Is the negotiating bank correct?

The negotiating bank is correct under the provision of UCP 600 Article 21 c(i), which states that a nonnegotiable sea waybill may indicate that the goods will or may be transshipped provided that the entire carriage is covered by one and the same nonnegotiable sea waybill.

Case 11

The issuing bank refuses the payment stating that sea waybill evidences transshipment whereas LC has restricted transshipment. The sea waybill also evidences that the shipment has happened through a lash barge. Is the issuing bank correct?

A nonnegotiable sea waybill indicating that transshipment will or may take place is acceptable, even if the credit prohibits transshipment, if the goods have been shipped in a container, trailer or lash barge as evidenced by the nonnegotiable sea waybill. This is as per the article 21 c(ii).

Case 12

An LC accepts the charter party BL and it was required to be presented by the terms of the credit.
    Negotiating bank refuses to examine the charter party contract. Issuing bank argues that as the presentation required the terms of the credit to be maintained, negotiating bank is likely to examine the contract.
    Which bank is right?

Negotiating bank is right as per article 22 (b). It says that bank is not liable to examine charter party contract even if they are required to be presented by the terms of the credit.

Case 13

An air transport carriage has not mentioned that the goods have been accepted for carriage. Issuing bank refused the payment on this account. If the issuing bank correct?

Issuing bank is correct as per the article 23 a (ii). It states that an air transport document, however named, must appear to indicate the goods have been accepted for carriage.

Case 14

An issuing bank rejects the payment stating that it is not signed by the owner or the charter. Agent signing a charter party BL is not acceptable.
    Negotiating bank argues that the agent has signed the transport document and also there is a mention about the name of the charter on whose behalf the agent has signed. So it can't be treated as discrepancy.
    Which bank is correct?

Negotiating bank is correct as per Article 22 (i). Any signature by an agent must indicate whether the agent has signed for or on behalf of the master, owner or charterer.

An agent signing for or on behalf of the owner or charterer must indicate the name of the owner or charterer.

5.5 Pro Forma Invoice

It is one of the important documents to establish the international trade transaction. Other than mentioning the address of the importer and the beneficiary party, it also describes about the terms of trade such as FOB, free carrier (FCA), EXW etc, notifying party and so on.

SHIPPER / EXPORTER Renuka Garments Exporting Ltd 92 Acharya Jagadish Chandra Bose Road. Kolkata 700009	PROFORMA INVOICE NO. 34		DATE: 31-01-2017
	CUSTOMER PURCHASE ORDER NO: 210	B/L AWS NO. 16790	
	COUNTRY OF ORIGIN: India	DATE OF EXPORT 31-03-2017	
CONSIGNEE Harish Mehta Silk Emporium Ltd 34 ABC Street Frankfurt, Germany	TERMS Sale: FCA Kolkata (Netaji Subhash Chandra International Airport) Payment : 30 days Usance		
NOTIFY James Wall 23 XYZ Street Frakfurt, Germany	Export References Currency: EUR		
	AIR/ OCEAN PORT OF LOADING Kolkata		
FORWARDING AGENT ABC Ltd, 123320 Goddard Rd. Romulus, MI 48174	EXPORTING CARRIER/ROUTE Air India Flt A1345 Frankfurt		

Terms of sale and terms of payment are governed by INCOTERMS 2010, UCP 600 for letters of credit, and URC 522 for documentary collections.

PKGS.	Quantity	Net Weight	Gross Weight	Description of Merchandise	Unit Price	Total Value
10	500	423	2115	Baluchari Silk	50	25000
PACKAGE MARKS: Harish Mehta Silk Emporium Ltd 34 ABC Street, Frankfurt, Germany Pride of Bengali Silk			MISC. CHARGES (Packaging, Insurance etc)		34	
			Pre- Carriage			
			FCA Kolkata, INVOICE TOTAL			25034

(Continued)

(Continued)

CERTIFICATIONS

We certify that this invoice is true and correct, and that the origin of these goods India. These goods licensed by India for ultimate destination Germany. Diversion contrary to Indian Law is prohibited.

AUTHORIZED SIGNATURE

5.6 Packing List

Packing list contains the description of the packaging of goods without any reference to the amount of the goods or the unit price or the payment terms.

However, packing list must mention the following:

- The name of the importer and the exporter

- The number of packing list

- Date of packing list

- Description of the goods

- Quantity of the goods

- Documentary credit number

- Container number

- Port of loading and port of discharge

- The international commercial terms or the INCOTERMS

PACKING LIST

PACKING LIST NO.: PL- 14072014
DATE : 12 SEP 2014

Consignee:
NJ TOUCH SCREEN MONITORS CO. LTD
400 Sylvan Avenue
Englewood Cliffs NJ 07600
T. 001.880.880.3010
F. 001.410.550.5300

DESCRIPTION OF GOODS	QUANTITY	NET WEIGHT (KGS)	GROSS WEIGHT (KGS)
Touch Screen LED Monitors	1000 PCS	12.500 KGS	15.000 KGS
TOTAL	1000 PCS	12.500 KGS	15.000 KGS

Delivery Terms : FOB Port of Tokyo, Japan INCOTERMS 2010

DOCUMENTARY CREDIT NUMBER : LC142252
METHOD OF LOADING : 1X40 HQ CNTR (S)
CONTAINER NUMBER : MRKU 844444-7
PORT OF LOADING : PORT OF Tokyo, Japan
PORT OF DISCHARGE : Nawaseva

CERTIFICATE OF ORIGIN SHOWS:
NET WEIGHT   : 12.500 KGS
GROSS WEIGHT   : 15.000 KGS

5.7 Insurance Certificate

It is one of the important documents in the international trade transactions. Insurance is taken to cover any type of damage or loss when goods are in the main carriage. It gives the coverage for waterways, railways, and air shipment. There are three types of insurance which cover the waterway and road movement: (a) Institute Cargo Clauses (A),[1] (b) Institute Cargo Clauses (B),[2] and (c) Institute Cargo Clauses (C).[3] Clauses A covers all the risk whereas Clauses C covers minimum risk. If shipment is through airway, then Institute Cargo Causes (Air) is applicable.

5.7.1 Case Studies Related to LC Transaction and Insurance Cargo Clause

Under LC, transaction insurance document is governed by UCP 600 Article 28. We learn the specification of this article through the following caselets.

Case 15

Under LC, payment is refused by the issuing bank stating that the exporter submitted only three original copies of the insurance document out of the four issued as mentioned in the insurance document. Is the issuing bank correct?

Yes, the issuing bank is correct. As per UCP 600 Article 28 (b), all originals must be presented when the document has been issued in more than one original.

---

[1] The details are available at http://www.ms-ins.com/pdf/cargo/ICCA010109.PDF, retrieved on December 21, 2016. Refer to Appendix.

[2] The details are available at http://www.ms-ins.com/pdf/cargo/ICCB010109.PDF, retrieved on December 21, 2016. Refer Appendix.

[3] The details are available at http://www.ms-ins.com/pdf/cargo/ICCC010109.PDF retrieved on December 21, 2016. Refer to Appendix.

Case 16

The issuing bank rejects the payment saying that the date of shipment is June 5, 2017 whereas the date of insurance is July 6, 2017. The negotiating bank argues that this cannot be treated as discrepant document as the insurance document clearly mentions that the insurance cover is effective from the date of the shipment.
Which bank is right and for what reason?

The negotiating bank is right. As per UCP 600 Article 28 (e), although it is mandatory that the date of the insurance document must be no later than the date of shipment, however, it may have a date later than the shipment date with a clause that the cover is effective from a date no later than the date of shipment.

Case 17

The value of the LC transaction is $1 MIO. However, the insurance document shows that the value of the insurance is mentioned as €1.1 MIO. The issuing bank rejects the payment stating it as a discrepancy. Is the issuing bank correct?

The issuing bank is correct in its decision as per Article 28 f(i). It says that the insurance amount should be mentioned in the same currency as the credit. Insurance document must also indicate the amount of insurance coverage.

Case 18

The LC indicates that it operates under international commercial terms, cost, insurance, and freight (CIF). There is no indication of the amount of insurance in the credit. The CIF value is $10 MIO. The issuing bank refuses the document stating that the insurance amount does not cover minimum 110% of the CIF value. Is the issuing bank correct?

The issuing bank is correct. As per Article 28 f(ii), if there is no indication in the credit of the insurance coverage required, the amount of insurance coverage must be at least 110% of the CIF or the carriage and insurance paid (CIP) value of the goods.

Case 19

The issuing bank rejects the payment stating that the CIF or CIP value cannot be calculated from the document submitted. As the credit is under insurance cover, the bank cannot examine if the amount stated in the insurance document is correct. The invoice value under this credit is $1MIO. However, the negotiating bank negotiates up to $0.8MIO. Is the issuing bank correct?
The issuing bank is incorrect in its decision as per UCO 600 Article 28 (ii). It states that when the CIF or CIP value cannot be determined from the documents, the minimum insurance coverage must be calculated on the basis of the amount for which honor or negotiation is requested or the gross value of the goods as shown in the invoice, whichever is greater.

Case 20

Insurance document did not indicate till which port the insurance coverage is effective. Although, it mentions the destination port name as A in the insurance document whereas credit states that the destination port is B. Issuing bank rejects the document. Is the issuing bank correct?

The issuing bank is correct in its decision as per UCP 600 Article f(iii). First, the insurance document must indicate that the name of the ports, that is, shipment port and the final destination port or the place of discharge within which risks are covered. Second, in the insurance document, the place of taking in charge or shipment and the place of discharge or final destination have to be as stated in the credit.

Case 21

The LC does not mention the type of insurance coverage. Instead, in the credit it is mentioned that insurance must cover the "usual risk." The issuing bank argues that credit has to be clear about the type of the coverage. Is the issuing bank correct?

The issuing bank is correct as per the UCP 600 Article 28 (g). It states that a credit should state the type of insurance required and the additional risks to be covered, if any. Imprecise terms such as "usual risks" or "customary risks" shall be disregarded, and an insurance document will be accepted without regard to any risks that are not covered.

Case 22

Credit requires insurance coverage for all risk. Issuing bank rejects the insurance document as it is not mentioned in any of the documents headings, however, all risk coverage appears by a notation in the insurance document. Is the issuing bank correct?

No, the issuing bank is not correct. As per the UCP 600 Article 28 (h), the insurance document containing all risk clause or notation is considered to have coverage for all risk. It does not depend if all risk coverage is mentioned in any of the headings or not.

5.8 Certificate of Origin

International trade transactions requires a certificate depicting the origin of the goods. Many a time, many counties are restricted from doing trade transaction with some other countries. This kind of restriction in international trade is known as "sanction." For example, the USA imposed a sanction on Iran in which Iran was not allowed to do trade transactions with the other countries in the world. As USD is the "primary" currency in international trade settlement, this kind of restriction created a severe problem in converting the USD to Iranian Rial. During this period, as India continued to import oil from Iran, the payment had to be settled through INR only. So, we understand that certificate of origin plays a role to indicate *nonpreferential trade transactions.*

On the contrary, it plays a substantial role in *indicating preferential customs policy* in import transactions. However, to get preferential treatment in terms of tariff concession, a *preferential certificate of origin* is to be submitted to Customs at the time when goods enter the importer's country. It may be noted that an *ordinary certificate of origin* does not qualify for any such preferential treatment. An ordinary certificate of origin is just an indicator of the origin of goods. It may be issued by the chambers of commerce, chambers of industry and chambers of commerce and industry.

If an LC transaction requires a certificate of origin to be submitted, it may ask for any of the following types of certificate of origin:

Generalized System of Preferences (GSP): This type of preferential tariff is extended by developed countries or the donor countries to developing countries or the beneficiary countries. It involves reduced

most favored nation (MFN) tariffs or duty-free entry of eligible products exported by beneficiary countries to the markets of donor countries.[4] This kind of certificate requires GSP Form A to be submitted.[5]

North American Free Trade Agreement (NAFTA): Certificate of origin is applicable only if the shipment is from Canada, Mexico, Puerto Rico or the USA. If the goods qualify for reduced duty, then in order to receive the benefits the LC must attach the NAFTA certificate of origin to the Commercial Invoice if:

- The shipment is a USA, Puerto Rico, or Canada origin and a Mexico destination with a value of US$1,000 or greater (or local equivalent).

- The shipment is a USA, Puerto NAFTA CO Rico, or Mexico origin and a Canada destination with a value of $1,600 in Canadian dollars or greater (or local equivalent).

- The shipment is a USA, Puerto Rico, or Mexico origin and a United States destination with a value of US$2,500 or greater (or local equivalent).

Shipments valued less than the above amounts only require a statement on the commercial invoice requesting NAFTA preferential tariff treatment.[6]

5.8.1 EUR1 Form Movement Certificate

An EUR1, also known as a "movement certificate," enables importers in certain countries to import goods at a reduced or nil rate of import duty under trade agreements between the EU and beneficiary countries. Chamber International is authorized to issue EUR1 certificates on behalf of HM Revenue & Customs.[7]

5.8.2 ATR Movement Certificate

The ATR certificate entitles goods, which are in "free circulation" in the EU (i.e., the goods are EU-originating, or on importation into the EU all the relevant duties and taxes have been paid) to receive preferential import duty treatment when shipped to Turkey. This applies to all eligible goods except agricultural goods, minerals, and steel which require an EUR1 movement certificate.[8]

5.9 Quality Certificate

Quality certificate is an important document to check the quality of the product for the importer. It is always advisable that importers call for a quality certificate irrespective of whether they are under LC

---

[4] The details may be read from the following website http://www.eicindia.gov.in/knowledge-repository/Certification/Generalised-System-of-Preferences.aspx, retrieved on December 20, 2016.

[5] A copy of the form can be seen in http://unctad.org/Sections/gsp/docs/gsp_form_a_new_en.pdf retrieved on December 20, 2016.

[6] For details see https://www.ups.com/worldshiphelp/WS15/ENU/AppHelp/GlossPopup/NAFTA.htm, retrieved on December 20, 2016.

[7] See http://www.chamber-international.com/exporting-chamber-international/documentation-for-export-and-import/eur-1-certificates/ retrieved on December 20, 2016.

[8] See http://www.londonchamber.co.uk/lcc_public/article.asp?aid=4457 retrieved on December 20, 2016.

transaction or not. However, if an importer calls for the quality certificate, then it must be mentioned who should be authorized to provide the quality certificate. If there is no mention about the issuing authority, then whoever issues it would be accepted by the bank and it cannot be treated as a discrepant document.

QUALITY CERTIFICATE	
Cargo:	Lames Long 'Poland'
Port of loading:	Poland
Bills of landing:	
Quantity:	500 Unit
Shipper:	Devidoff Caffe, Poland
Consignee	Dorabjee, India
Notify address:	D'mart, Pune
Destination:	Pune Airport

XYZ Full Member Superintendent & Analyst

L/C NO, 89234C DATED 31 January 2017

In pursuance of an order received from shipper, requesting us to carry out the sampling & determine the quality of the aforementioned parcel, we certify the following:

SAMPLING: Sets of samples were drawn uniformly and systematically, concurrently with loading, at the nearest and best practicable point to the vessel in accordance with the method laid down by XYZ 124.

QUALITY/ANALYSIS According to instructions one average sample of the total shipped quantity was served to our laboratory for the determination of the quality. The Laboratory reported.

Product Details	**Devidoff Café Grande Cuvee, Espresso 57**
Content Finest Arabica Beans Perfect Temperature is maintained Balanced composition and time for Roasting	
Signed at Tax On 31/01/2017	For and on behalf of Pride of Colombia

QUESTIONS

Answer the Following Questions

1. What is a BL? How many types of BLs are there in international trade? Give examples.

2. Differentiate between a straight BL and a negotiable BL.

3. What is a clean BL? Is the term clean required to be mentioned in the BL

4. What is the lash BL? When is it issued?

5. What is short form BL? Is it a safe document in international trade? Why?

6. What is charter party BL? Does this kind of BL contains title of the goods? Is this a negotiable instrument?

7. Write some differences between short form and the charter party BL.

8. What is multimodal or combined BL? Is FBL a multimodal? Is it safe and negotiable?

9. Compare through and multimodal BLs.

10. What is container BL? If transshipment is not allowed by documentary credit, under which conditions does this restriction not hold?

11. What is the difference between BL and waybill?

12. An air transport carriage has not mentioned that the goods have been accepted for carriage. The issuing bank refused the payment on this account. Is the issuing bank correct?

13. The BL does not indicate the port of loading stated in the credit as the port of loading, instead it contains the indication "intended." The document was rejected as there was no onboard notation indicating the port of loading as stated in the credit. Is this rejection correct?

14. What is certificate of origin? What are the objectives of using a certificate of origin in international trade? Is there any special tariff concession for developing countries exporting to the developed countries? If so, it is applicable under which certificate of origin?

15. How many types of insurance documents are there in the international trade? Does LC require the mention of a specific insurance certificate?

16. How much is the insurance cover under CIP and CIF?

17. How does a bank calculate the minimum insurance cover when the value of CIP and CIF cannot be calculated from the document?

18. What is a packing list? What are the contents that a packing list must and must not mention?

19. What are the differences between EUR1 and ATR movement certificate of origin?

20. Describe the certificate of origin applicable for NAFTA.

21. Credit requires insurance coverage for all risk. The issuing bank rejects the insurance document as it is not mentioned in any of the documents headings; however, all risk coverage appears by a notation in the insurance document. Is the issuing bank correct?

22. LC requires the BL date should be no later than November 11. When the BL was submitted, issuing bank rejects the document stating the BL is discrepant.

    The exporter argues that the date of issue of BL was November 11. He or she has shipped the goods as per the LC terms. However, the issuing bank argues that the BL contains onboard notation indicating that the date of shipment is November 12. In such case issuance date of BL would be disregarded as the date of shipment. Is the bank correct in rejecting the payment? Explain.

23. Payment is refused on the ground that BL is signed by an agent, not by the carrier, without a mention on behalf of which carrier the agent has signed. Is the issuing bank correct?

24. LC accepts the charter party BL and it was required to be presented by the terms of the credit.

    Negotiating bank refuses to examine the charter party contract. Issuing bank argues that as the presentation required the terms of the credit to be maintained, negotiating bank is likely to examine the contract.

25. Under LC payment is refused by the issuing bank stating that exporter did submit only three original copies of insurance document out of the four issued as mentioned in the insurance document. Is the issuing bank correct?

26. The value of the LC transaction is $1 MIO. However, insurance document shows that the value of the insurance is mentioned in $1.1 MIO. Issuing bank rejects the payment stating it as a discrepancy. Is the issuing bank correct?

27. Insurance document did not indicate the insurance coverage is effective till which port. Although, it mentions the destination port name as A in the insurance document whereas credit states that the destination port is B. Issuing bank rejects the document. Is the issuing bank correct?

28. BL does not specify any name of the vessel. Instead, it indicates "intended vessel." There is no onboard notation mentioned? Issuing bank rejects the documents. The issuance date of BL is 5th January 2016.

Appendix

Institute Cargo Clauses (A)

RISKS COVERED

Risks

1. This insurance covers, except as excluded by the provisions of Clauses 4, 5, 6 and 7 below:

General Average

2. This insurance covers general average and salvage charges, adjusted or determined according to the contract of carriage and/or the governing law and practice, incurred to avoid or in connection with the avoidance of loss from any cause except those excluded in Clauses 4, 5, 6 and 7 below.

"Both to Blame Collision Clause"

3. This insurance indemnifies the Assured, in respect of any risk insured herein, against liability incurred under any **Both to Blame Collision Clause** in the contract of carriage. In the event of any claim by carriers under the said Clause, the Assured agree to notify the Insurers who shall have the right, at their own cost and expense, to defend the Assured against such claim.

EXCLUSIONS

4. In no case shall this insurance cover

    4.1. loss damage or expense attributable to willful misconduct of the Assured

4.2. ordinary leakage, ordinary loss in weight or volume, or ordinary wear and tear of the subject-matter insured

4.3. loss damage or expense caused by insufficiency or unsuitability of packing or preparation of the subject-matter insured to withstand the ordinary incidents of the insured transit where such packing or preparation is carried out by the Assured or their employees or prior to the attachment of this insurance (for the purpose of these Clauses "packing" shall be deemed to include stowage in a container and "employees" shall not include independent contractors)

4.4. loss damage or expense caused by inherent vice or nature of the subject-matter insured

4.5. loss damage or expense caused by delay, even though the delay be caused by a risk insured against (except expenses payable under Clause 2 above)

4.6. loss damage or expense caused by insolvency or financial default of the owners managers charterers or operators of the vessel where, at the time of loading of the subject-matter insured on board the vessel, the Assured are aware, or in the ordinary course of business should be aware, that such insolvency or financial default could prevent the normal prosecution of the voyage This exclusion shall not apply where the contract of insurance has been assigned to the party claiming hereunder who has bought or agreed to buy the subject-matter insured in good faith under a binding contract

4.7. loss damage or expense directly or indirectly caused by or arising from the use of any weapon or device employing atomic or nuclear fission and/or fusion or other like reaction or radioactive force or matter.

5. 5.1. In no case shall this insurance cover loss damage or expense arising from

5.1.1. unseaworthiness of vessel or craft or unfitness of vessel or craft for the safe carriage of the subject-matter insured, where the Assured are privy to such unseaworthiness or unfitness, at the time the subject-matter insured is loaded therein

5.1.2. unfitness of container or conveyance for the safe carriage of the subject-matter insured, where loading therein or thereon is carried out prior to attachment of this insurance or by the Assured or their employees and they are privy to such unfitness at the time of loading.

5.2. Exclusion 5.1.1 above shall not apply where the contract of insurance has been assigned to the party claiming hereunder who has bought or agreed to buy the subject-matter insured in good faith under a binding contract

5.3. The Insurers waive any breach of the implied warranties of seaworthiness of the ship and fitness of the ship to carry the subject-matter insured to destination.

6. In no case shall this insurance cover loss damage or expense caused by

6.1. war civil war revolution rebellion insurrection, or civil strife arising therefrom, or any hostile act by or against a belligerent power

6.2. capture seizure arrest restraint or detainment (piracy excepted), and the consequences thereof or any attempt thereat

6.3. Derelict mines, torpedoes, bombs or other derelict weapons of war.

7. In no case shall this insurance cover loss damage or expense

    7.1. caused by strikers, locked-out workmen, or persons taking part in labour disturbances, riots or civil commotions

    7.2. resulting from strikes, lock-outs, labour disturbances, riots or civil commotions

    7.3. caused by any act of terrorism being an act of any person acting on behalf of, or in connection with, any organization which carries out activities directed towards the overthrowing or influencing, by force or violence, of any government whether or not legally constituted

    7.4. caused by any person acting from a political, ideological or religious motive.

DURATION

Transit Clause

8. 8.1. Subject to Clause 11 below, this insurance attaches from the time the subject-matter insured is first moved in the warehouse or at the place of storage (at the place named in the contract of insurance) for the purpose of the immediate loading into or onto the carrying vehicle or other conveyance for the commencement of transit, continues during the ordinary course of transit and terminates either

    8.1.1. on completion of unloading from the carrying vehicle or other conveyance in or at the final warehouse or place of storage at the destination named in the contract of insurance,

    8.1.2. on completion of unloading from the carrying vehicle or other conveyance in or at any other warehouse or place of storage, whether prior to or at the destination named in the contract of insurance, which the Assured or their employees elect to use either for storage other than in the ordinary course of transit or for allocation or distribution, or

    8.1.3. when the Assured or their employees elect to use any carrying vehicle or other conveyance or any container for storage other than in the ordinary course of transit or

    8.1.4. on the expiry of 60 days after completion of discharge overside of the subject-matter insured from the oversea vessel at the final port of discharge, whichever shall first occur.

    8.2. If, after discharge overside from the oversea vessel at the final port of discharge, but prior to termination of this insurance, the subject-matter insured is to be forwarded to a destination other than that to which it is insured, this insurance, whilst remaining subject to termination as provided in Clauses 8.1.1 to 8.1.4, shall not extend beyond the time the subject-matter insured is first moved for the purpose of the commencement of transit to such other destination.

8.3. This insurance shall remain in force (subject to termination as provided for in Clauses 8.1.1 to 8.1.4 above and to the provisions of Clause 9 below) during delay beyond the control of the Assured, any deviation, forced discharge, reshipment or transshipment and during any variation of the adventure arising from the exercise of a liberty granted to carriers under the contract of carriage.

Termination of Contract of Carriage

9. If owing to circumstances beyond the control of the Assured either the contract of carriage is terminated at a port or place other than the destination named therein or the transit is otherwise terminated before unloading of the subject-matter insured as provided for in Clause 8 above, then this insurance shall also terminate *unless prompt notice is given to the Insurers and continuation of cover is requested when this insurance shall remain in force, subject to an additional premium if required by the Insurers,* either

9.1. until the subject-matter insured is sold and delivered at such port or place, or, unless otherwise specially agreed. until the expiry of 60 days after arrival of the subject-matter insured at such port or place, whichever shall first occur,

    or

9.2. if the subject-matter insured is forwarded within the said period of 60 days (or any agreed extension thereof) to the destination named in the contract of insurance or to any other destination, until terminated in accordance with the provisions of Clause 8 above.

Change of Voyage

10. 10.1. Where, after attachment of this insurance, the destination is changed by the Assured, *this must be notified promptly to Insurers for rates and terms to be agreed. Should a loss occur prior to such agreement being obtained cover may be provided but only if cover would have been available at a reasonable commercial market rate on reasonable market terms.*

10.2. Where the subject-matter insured commences the transit contemplated by this insurance (in accordance with Clause 8.1), but, without the knowledge of the Assured or their employees the ship sails for another destination, this insurance will nevertheless be deemed to have attached at commencement of such transit.

CLAIMS
Insurable Interest

11. 11.1. In order to recover under this insurance the Assured must have an insurable interest in the subject-matter insured at the time of the loss.

11.2. Subject to Clause 11.1 above, the Assured shall be entitled to recover for insured loss occurring during the period covered by this insurance, notwithstanding that the loss occurred before the contract of insurance was concluded, unless the Assured were aware of the loss and the Insurers were not.

Forwarding Charges

12. Where, as a result of the operation of a risk covered by this insurance, the insured transit is terminated at a port or place other than that to which the subject-matter insured is covered under this insurance, the Insurers will reimburse the Assured for any extra charges properly and reasonably incurred in unloading storing and forwarding the subject-matter insured to the destination to which it is insured.

    This Clause 12, which does not apply to general average or salvage charges, shall be subject to the exclusions contained in Clauses 4, 5, 6 and 7 above, and shall not include charges arising from the fault negligence insolvency or financial default of the Assured or their employees.

Constructive Total Loss

13. No claim for Constructive Total Loss shall be recoverable hereunder unless the subject-matter insured is reasonably abandoned either on account of its actual total loss appearing to be unavoidable or because the cost of recovering, reconditioning, and forwarding the subject-matter insured to the destination to which it is insured would exceed its value on arrival.

Increased Value

14. 14.1. If any Increased Value insurance is effected by the Assured on the subject-matter insured under this insurance the agreed value of the subject-matter insured shall be deemed to be increased to the total amount insured under this insurance and all Increased Value insurances covering the loss, and liability under this insurance shall be in such proportion as the sum insured under this insurance bears to such total amount insured.

    In the event of claim the Assured shall provide the Insurers with evidence of the amounts insured under all other insurances.

    14.2. **Where this insurance Is on Increased Value the following clause shall apply**:
    The agreed value of the subject-matter insured shall be deemed to be equal to the total amount insured under the primary insurance and all Increased Value insurances covering the loss and effected on the subject-matter insured by the Assured, and liability under this insurance shall be in such proportion as the sum insured under this insurance bears to such total amount insured.

    In the event of claim the Assured shall provide the Insurers with evidence of the amounts insured under all other insurances.

BENEFIT OF INSURANCE

15. This insurance

    15.1. covers the Assured which includes the person claiming indemnity either as the person by or on whose behalf the contract of insurance was effected or as an assignee,

    15.2. shall not extend to or otherwise benefit the carrier or other bailee.

MINIMISING LOSSES

Duty or Assured

16. It is the duty of the Assured and their employees and agents in respect of loss recoverable hereunder

    16.1. to take such measures as may be reasonable for the purpose of averting or minimizing such loss, and

    16.2. to ensure that all rights against carriers, bailees or other third parties are properly preserved and exercised and the Insurers will, in addition to any loss recoverable hereunder, reimburse the Assured for any charges properly and reasonably incurred in pursuance of these duties.

Waiver

17. Measures taken by the Assured or the Insurers with the object of saving, protecting or recovering the subject-matter insured shall not be considered as a waiver or acceptance of abandonment or otherwise prejudice the rights of either party.

AVOIDANCE OF DELAY

18. It is a condition of this insurance that the Assured shall act with reasonable despatch in all circumstances within their control.

LAW AND PRACTICE

19. This insurance is subject to English law and practice.

NOTE: *Where a continuation of cover is requested under Clause 9 or a change of destination is notified under Clause 10, there is an obligation to give prompt notice to the Insurers and the right to such cover is dependent upon compliance with this obligation.*

Institute Cargo Clauses (B)

RISKS COVERED

Risks

1. This insurance covers, except as excluded by the provisions of Clauses 4, 5, 6 and 1 below,

    1.1. loss of or damage to the subject-matter insured reasonably attributable to

        1.1.1. fire or explosion

        1.1.2. vessel or craft being stranded grounded sunk or capsized

        1.1.3. overturning or derailment of land conveyance

    1.1.4. collision or contact of vessel craft or conveyance with any external object other than water

    1.1.5. discharge of cargo at a port of distress

    1.1.6. earthquake volcanic eruption or lightning,

  1.2. loss of or damage to the subject-matter insured caused by

    1.2.1. general average sacrifice

    1.2.2. jettison or washing overboard

    1.2.3. entry of sea lake or river water into vessel craft hold conveyance container or place of storage,

  1.3. total loss of any package lost overboard or dropped whilst loading on to, or unloading from, vessel or craft.

General Average

2. This insurance covers general average and salvages, charges, adjusted or determined according to the contract of carriage and/or the governing law and practice, incurred to avoid or in connection with the avoidance of loss from any cause except those excluded in Clauses 4, 5, 6 and 7 below.

"Both to Blame Collision Clause"

3. This insurance indemnifies the Assured, in respect of any risk insured herein, against liability incurred under any Both to Blame Collision Clause in the contract of carriage. In the event of any claim by carriers under the said Clause, the Assured agree to notify the Insurers who shall have the right, at their own cost and expense, to defend the Assured against such claim.

EXCLUSIONS

4. In no case shall this insurance cover

  4.1. loss damage or expense attributable to willful misconduct of the Assured

  4.2. ordinary leakage, ordinary loss in weight or volume, or ordinary wear and tear of the subject-matter insured

  4.3. loss damage or expense caused by insufficiency or unsuitability of packing or preparation of the subject-matter insured to withstand the ordinary incidents of the insured transit where such packing or preparation is carried out by the Assured or their employees or prior to the attachment of this insurance (for the purpose of these Clauses "packing" shall be deemed to include stowage in a container and "employees" shall not include independent contractors)

  4.4. loss damage or expense caused by inherent vice or nature of the subject-matter insured

  4.5. loss damage or expense caused by delay, even though the delay be caused by a risk insured against (except expenses payable under Clause 2 above)

4.6. loss damage or expense caused by insolvency or financial default of the owners managers charterers or operators of the vessel where, at the time of loading of the subject-matter insured on board the vessel, the Assured are aware, or in the ordinary course of business should be aware, that such insolvency or financial default could prevent the normal prosecution of the voyage.

This exclusion shall not apply where the contract of insurance has been assigned to the party claiming hereunder who has bought or agreed to buy the subject-matter insured in good faith under a binding contract

4.7. deliberate damage to or deliberate destruction of the subject-matter insured or any part thereof by the wrongful act of any person or persons

4.8. loss damage or expense directly or indirectly caused by or arising from the use of any weapon or device employing atomic or nuclear fission and/or fusion or other like reaction or radioactive force or matter.

5.

5.1. In no case shall this insurance cover loss damage or expense arising from

5.1.1. unseaworthiness of vessel or craft or unfitness of vessel or craft for the safe carriage of the subject-matter insured, where the Assured are privy to such unseaworthiness or unfitness, at the time the subject-matter insured is loaded therein

5.1.2. unfitness of container or conveyance for the safe carriage of the subject-matter insured, where loading therein or thereon is carried out prior to attachment of this insurance or by the Assured or their employees and they are privy to such unfitness at the time of loading.

5.2. Exclusion 5.1.1 above shall not apply where the contract of insurance has been assigned to the party claiming hereunder who has bought or agreed to buy the subject-matter insured in good faith under a binding contract.

5.3. The Insurers waive any breach of the implied warranties of seaworthiness of the ship and fitness of the ship to carry the subject-matter insured to destination.

6. In no case shall this insurance cover loss damage or expense caused by

6.1. war civil war revolution rebellion insurrection, or civil strife arising therefrom, or any hostile act by or against a belligerent power

6.2. capture seizure arrest restraint or detainment, and the consequences thereof or any attempt threat

6.3. derelict mines, torpedoes, bombs or other derelict weapons of war.

7. In no case shall this insurance cover loss damage or expense

7.1. caused by strikers, locked-out workmen, or persons taking part in labour disturbances, riots or civil commotions

7.2. resulting from strikes, lock-outs, labour disturbances, riots or civil commotions

7.3. caused by any act of terrorism being an act of any person acting on behalf of or in connection with, any organization which carries out activities directed towards the overthrowing or influencing, by force or violence, of any government whether or not legally constituted

7.4. caused by any person acting from a political, ideological or religious motive.

DURATION

Transit Clause

8.   8.1. Subject to Clause 11 below, this insurance attaches from the time the subject-matter insured is first moved in the warehouse or at the place of storage (at the place named in the contract of insurance) for the purpose of the immediate loading into or onto the carrying vehicle or other conveyance for the commencement of transit, continues during the ordinary course of transit and terminates either

8.1.1. on completion of unloading from the carrying vehicle or other conveyance in or at the final warehouse or place of storage at the destination named in the contract of insurance.

8.1.2. on completion of unloading from the carrying vehicle or other conveyance in or at any other warehouse or place of storage, whether prior to or at the destination named in the contract of insurance. which the Assured or their employees elect to use either for storage other than in the ordinary course of transit or for allocation or distribution, or

8.1.3. when the Assured or their employees elect to use any carrying vehicle or other conveyance or any container for storage other than in the ordinary course of transit or

8.1.4. on the expiry of 60 days after completion of discharge overside of the subject-matter insured from the oversea vessel at the final port of discharge, whichever shall first occur.

8.2. If, after discharge overside from the oversea vessel at the final port of discharge, but prior to termination of this insurance, the subject-matter insured is to be forwarded to a destination other than that to which it is insured, this insurance, whilst remaining subject to termination as provided in Clauses 8.1.1 to 8.1.4, shall not extend beyond the time the subject-matter insured is first moved for the purpose of the commencement of transit to such other destination.

8.3. This insurance shall remain in force (subject to termination as provided for in Clauses 8.1.1 to 8.1.4 above and to the provisions of Clause 9 below) during delay beyond the control of the Assured, any deviation, forced discharge, reshipment or transshipment and during any variation of the adventure arising from the exercise of a liberty granted to carriers under the contract of carriage.

Termination of Contract of Carriage

9. If owing to circumstances beyond the control of the Assured either the contract of carriage is terminated at a port or place other than the destination named therein or the transit is otherwise terminated before unloading of the subject-matter insured as provided for in Clause 8 above, then this insurance shall also terminate *unless prompt notice is given to the Insurers and continuation of cover is requested when this insurance shall remain in force, subject to an additional premium if required by the Insurers*, either

    9.1. until the subject-matter insured is sold and delivered at such port or place, or, unless otherwise specially agreed, until the expiry of 60 days after arrival of the subject-matter insured at such port or place, whichever shall first occur,

        or

    9.2. if the subject-matter insured is forwarded within the said period of 60 days (or any agreed extension thereof) to the destination named in the contract of insurance or to any other destination, until terminated in accordance with the provisions of Clause 8 above.

Change of Voyage

10. 10.1. Where, after attachment of this insurance, the destination is changed by the Assured, *this must be notified promptly to Insurers for rates and terms to be agreed. Should a loss occur prior to such agreement being obtained cover may be provided but only if cover would have been available at a reasonable commercial market rate on reasonable market terms.*

     10.2. Where the subject-matter insured commences the transit contemplated by this insurance (in accordance with Clause 8.1), but, without the knowledge of the Assured or their employees the ship sails for another destination, this insurance will nevertheless be deemed to have attached at commencement of such transit

CLAIMS

Insurable Interest

11. 11.1. In order to recover under this insurance the Assured must have an insurable interest in the subject-matter insured at the time of the loss.

     11.2. Subject to Clause 11.1 above, the Assured shall be entitled to recover for insured loss occurring during the period covered by this insurance, notwithstanding that the loss occurred before the contract of insurance was concluded, unless the Assured were aware of the loss and the Insurers were not.

Forwarding Charges

12. Where, as a result of the operation of a risk covered by this insurance, the insured transit is terminated at a port or place other than that to which the subject-matter insured is covered under this insurance, the Insurers will reimburse the Assured for any extra charges properly and reasonably

incurred in unloading storing and forwarding the subject-matter insured to the destination to which it is insured.

This Clause 12, which does not apply to general average or salvage charges, shall be subject to the exclusions contained in Clauses 4, 5, 6 and 7 above, and shall not include charges arising from the fault negligence insolvency or financial default of the Assured or their employees.

Constructive Total Loss

13. No claim for Constructive Total Loss shall be recoverable hereunder unless the subject matter insured is reasonably abandoned either on account of its actual total loss appearing to be unavoidable or because the cost of recovering, reconditioning, and forwarding the subject-matter insured to the destination to which it is insured would exceed its value on arrival.

Increased Value

14. 14.1. If any Increased Value insurance is effected by the Assured on the subject-matter insured under this insurance the agreed value of the subject-matter insured shall be deemed to be increased to the total amount insured under this insurance and all Increased Value insurances covering the loss, and liability under this insurance shall be in such proportion as the sum insured under this insurance bears to such total amount insured.

    In the event of claim the Assured shall provide the Insurers with evidence of the amounts insured under all other insurances.

    14.2. **Where this insurance is on Increased Value the following clause shall apply:**

    The agreed value of the subject-matter insured shall be deemed to be equal to the total amount insured under the primary insurance and all Increased Value insurances covering the loss and effected on the subject-matter insured by the Assured, and liability under this insurance shall be in such proportion as the sum insured under this insurance bears to such total amount insured.

    In the event of claim the Assured shall provide the Insurers with evidence of the amounts insured under all other insurances.

BENEFIT OF INSURANCE

15. This insurance

    15.1. covers the Assured which includes the person claiming indemnity either as the person by or on whose behalf the contract of insurance was effected or as an assignee,

    15.2. shall not extend to or otherwise benefit the carrier or other bailee.

MINIMISING LOSSES

Duty of Assured

16. It is the duty of the Assured and their employees and agents in respect of loss recoverable hereunder

16.1. to take such measures as may be reasonable for the purpose of averting or minimizing such loss, and

16.2. to ensure that all rights against carriers, bailees or other third parties are properly preserved and exercised and the Insurers will, in addition to any loss Recoverable hereunder, reimburse the Assured for any charges properly and reasonably incurred in pursuance of these duties.

Waiver

17. Measures taken by the Assured or the Insurers with the object of saving, protecting or recovering the subject-matter insured shall not be considered as a waiver or acceptance of abandonment or otherwise prejudice the rights of either party.

AVOIDANCE OF DELAY

18. It is a condition of this insurance that the Assured shall act with reasonable dispatch in all circumstances within their control.

LAW AND PRACTICE

19. This insurance is subject to English law and practice.

NOTE: -Where a continuation of cover is requested under Clause 9 or a change of destination is notified under Clause 10, there is an obligation to give prompt notice to the Insurers and the right to such cover is dependent upon compliance with this obligation.

Institute Cargo Clauses (C)

RISKS COVERED:

Risks

1. This insurance covers, except as excluded by the provisions of Clauses 4,5, 6 and 7 below:

1.1. Loss of damage to the subject matter insured reasonably attributable to

1.1.1. Fire or explosion

1.1.2. Vessel or craft being stranded, grounded, sunk or capsized

1.1.3. Over turning or derailment of land conveyance

1.1.4. Collision or contact of vessel craft or conveyance with any external object other than water

1.1.5. Discharge of cargo at a port of distress

1.2. Loss of or damage to the subject matter insured caused by

1.2.1. General average sacrifice

1.2.2. Jettison

General Average

2. This insurance covers general average and salvage charges, adjusted or determined according to the contract of carriage and/or the governing law and practice, incurred to avoid or in connection with the avoidance of loss from any cause except those excluded in Clauses 4, 5, 6 and 7.

"Both to Blame Collision Clause"

3. This insurance indemnifies the assured, in respect of any risk insured herein, against liability incurred under any **Both to Blame Collision Clause** in the contract of carriage. In the event of any claim by carriers under the said clause, the Assured agree to notify the Insurers who shall have the right, at their own cost and expense, to defend the Assured against such claim.

Exclusions

4. In no case shall this Insurance cover

   4.1. Loss, damage or expense attributable to willful misconduct of the Assured

   4.2. Ordinary leakage, ordinary loss in weight or volume or ordinary wear and tear of the subject-matter insured

   4.3. Loss, damage or expense caused by insufficiency or instability of packing or preparation of the subject-matter insured to withstand the ordinary incidents of the insured transit where such packing or preparation is carried out by the Assured or their employees prior to the attachment of this insurance (for the purpose of these Clauses "packing" shall be deemed to include stowage in a container and "employees" shall not include independent contractors.)

   4.4. Loss, damage or expense caused by inherent vice or nature of the subject matter insured.

   4.5. Loss, damage or expense caused by delay, even though the delay be caused by a risk insured against (except expenses payable under Clause 2 above)

   4.6. Loss, damage or expense caused by insolvency or financial default of the owners, managers, charterers or operators of the vessel where, at the time of loading of the subject-matter insured on board the vessel, the Assured are aware, or in the ordinary course of the business should be aware, that such insolvency or financial default could prevent the normal prosecution of the voyage.

   This exclusion shall not apply where the contract of insurance has been assigned to the party claiming hereunder who has bought or agreed to buy the subject-matter insured in good faith under a binding contract.

   4.7. Deliberate damage to or deliberate destruction of the subject-matter insured or any part thereof by the wrongful act of any person or persons.

   4.8. Loss, damage or expense directly or indirectly caused by or arising from the use of any weapon or device employing atomic or nuclear fission and/or fusion or other like reaction or radioactive force or matter.

5. 5.1. In no case shall this Insurance cover loss, damage or expense arising from

    5.1.1. Unseaworthiness of vessel or craft or unfitness of vessel or craft for safe carriage of the subject-matter insured where the Assured are privy to such unseaworthiness or unfitness at the time subject-matter insured is loaded therein

    5.1.2. Unfitness of container or conveyance for the safe carriage of the subject-matter insured, where loading therein or thereon is carried out prior to attachment of this insurance or by the Assured or their employees and they are privy to such fitness at the time of loading.

    5.2. Exclusion 5.1.1. above shall not apply where the contract of insurance has been assigned to the party claiming hereunder who has bought or agreed to buy the subject-matter insured in good faith under a binding contract

    5.3. The Insurers waive any breach of the implied warranties of seaworthiness of the ship and fitness of the ship to carry the subject matter insured to destination.

6. In no case shall this Insurance cover loss, damage or expense caused by

    6.1. War, civil war, revolution, rebellion, insurrection or civil strife arising therefrom, or any hostile act by or against a belligerent power

    6.2. Capture, seizure, arrest, restraint or detainment and the consequences thereof or any attempt threat

    6.3. Derelict mines, torpedoes, bombs or other derelict weapons of war

7. In no case shall this Insurance cover loss, damage or expense

    7.1. Caused by strikers, locked-out workmen or persons taking part in labour disturbances, riots or civil commotions

    7.2. Resulting from strikes, lock-outs, labour disturbances, riots or civil commotions

    7.3. Caused by any act of terrorism being an act of any person acting on behalf of, or in connection with any organization which carries out activities directed towards over-throwing or influencing, by force of violence, of any government whether or not legally constituted.

    7.4. Caused by any person acting from a political, ideological or religious motive.

DURATION

Transit Clause

8. 8.1. Subject to Clause 11 below, this insurance attaches from the time the subject-matter insured is first moved in the warehouse or at the place of storage (at the place named in the contract of insurance) for the purpose of the immediate loading into or onto the carrying vehicle or

other conveyance for the commencement of transit, continues during the ordinary course of transit and terminates either

8.1.1. on completion of unloading from the carrying vehicle or other conveyance in or at the final warehouse or place of storage at the destination named in the contract of insurance,

8.1.2. on completion of unloading from the carrying vehicle or other conveyance in or at any other warehouse or place of storage, whether prior to or at the destination named in the contract of insurance, which the Assured or their employees elect to use either for storage other than in the ordinary course of transit or for allocation or distribution, or

8.1.3. when the Assured or their employees elect to use any carrying vehicle or other conveyance or any container for storage other than in the ordinary course of transit or

8.1.4. on the expiry of 60 days after completion of discharge overside of the subject-matter insured from the oversea vessel at the final port of discharge, whichever shall first occur.

8.2. If, after discharge overside from the oversea vessel at the final port of discharge, but prior to termination of this insurance, the subject-matter insured is to be forwarded to a destination other than that to which it is insured, this insurance, whilst remaining subject to termination as provided in Clauses 8.1.1 to 8.1.4, shall not extend beyond the time the subject-matter insured is first moved for the purpose of the commencement of transit to such other destination.

8.3. This insurance shall remain in force (subject to termination as provided for in Clauses 8.1.1 to 8.1.4 above and to the provisions of Clause 9 below) during delay beyond the control of the Assured, any deviation, forced discharge, reshipment or transshipment and during any variation of the adventure arising from the exercise of a liberty granted to carriers under the contract of carriage.

Termination of Contract of Carriage

9. If owing to circumstances beyond the control of the Assured either the contract of carriage is terminated at a port or place other than the destination named therein or the transit is otherwise terminated before unloading of the subject-matter insured as provided for in Clause 8 above, then this insurance shall also terminate *unless prompt notice is given to the Insurers and continuation of cover is requested when this insurance shall remain in force, subject to an additional premium if required by the Insurers,* either

9.1. until the subject-matter insured is sold and delivered at such port or place, or, unless otherwise specially agreed, until the expiry of 60 days after arrival of the subject-matter insured at such port or place, whichever shall first occur,

or

    9.2. if the subject-matter insured is forwarded within the said period of 60 days (or any agreed extension thereof) to the destination named in the contract of insurance or to any other destination, until terminated in accordance with the provisions of Clause 8 above.

Change of Voyage

10. 10.1. Where, after attachment of this insurance, the destination is changed by the Assured, *this must be notified promptly to Insurers for rates and terms to be agreed. Should a loss occur prior to such agreement being obtained cover may be provided but only if cover would have been available at a reasonable commercial market rate on reasonable market terms.*

      10.2. Where the subject-matter insured commences the transit contemplated by this insurance (in accordance with Clause 8.1), but, without the knowledge of the Assured or their employees the ship sails for another destination, this insurance will nevertheless be deemed to have attached at commencement of such transit.

CLAIMS

Insurable Interest

11. 11.1. In order to recover under this insurance the Assured must have an insurable interest in the subject-matter insured at the time of the loss.

      11.2. Subject to Clause 11.1 above, the Assured shall be entitled to recover for insured loss occurring during the period covered by this insurance, notwithstanding that the loss occurred before the contract of insurance was concluded, unless the Assured were aware of the loss and the Insurers were not.

Forwarding Charges

12. Where, as a result of the operation of a risk covered by this insurance, the insured transit is terminated at a port or place other than that to which the subject-matter insured is covered under this insurance, the Insurers will reimburse the Assured for any extra charges properly and reasonably incurred in unloading storing and forwarding the subject-matter insured to the destination to which it is insured.

      This Clause 12, which does not apply to general average or salvage charges, shall be subject to the exclusions contained in Clauses 4, 5, 6 and 7 above, and shall not include charges arising from the fault negligence insolvency or financial default of the Assured or their employees.

Constructive Total Loss

13. No claim for Constructive Total Loss shall be recoverable hereunder unless the subject-matter insured is reasonably abandoned either on account of its actual total loss appearing to be unavoidable or because the cost of recovering, reconditioning, and forwarding the subject-matter insured to the destination to which it is insured would exceed its value on arrival.

Increased Value

14. 14.1. If any Increased Value insurance is effected by the Assured on the subject-matter insured under this insurance the agreed value of the subject-matter insured shall be deemed to be increased to the total amount insured under this insurance and all Increased Value insurances covering the loss, and liability under this insurance shall be in such proportion as the sum insured under this insurance bears to such total amount insured.

In the event of claim the Assured shall provide the Insurers with evidence of the amounts insured under all other insurances.

14.2. Where this insurance is on Increased Value the following clause shall apply:

The agreed value of the subject-matter insured shall be deemed to be equal to the total amount insured under the primary insurance and all Increased Value insurances covering the loss and effected on the subject-matter insured by the Assured, and liability under this insurance shall be in such proportion as the sum insured under this insurance bears to such total amount insured.

In the event of claim the Assured shall provide the Insurers with evidence of the amounts insured under all other insurances.

BENEFIT OF INSURANCE

15. This insurance

15.1. covers the Assured which includes the person claiming indemnity either as the person by or on whose behalf the contract of insurance was effected or as an assignee,

15.2. shall not extend to or otherwise benefit the carrier or other bailee.

MINIMISING LOSSES

Duty of Assured

16. It is the duty of the Assured and their employees and agents in respect of loss recoverable hereunder

16.1. to take such measures as may be reasonable for the purpose of averting or minimizing such loss, and

16.2. to ensure that all rights against carriers, bailees or other third parties are properly preserved and exercised and the Insurers will, in addition to any loss recoverable hereunder, reimburse the Assured for any charges properly and reasonably incurred in pursuance of these duties.

Waiver

17. Measures taken by the Assured or the Insurers with the object of saving, protecting or recovering the subject-matter insured shall not be considered as a waiver or acceptance of abandonment or otherwise prejudice the rights of either party.

AVOIDANCE OF DELAY

18.   It is a condition of this insurance that the Assured shall act with reasonable despatch in all circumstances within their control.

LAW AND PRACTICE

19.   This insurance is subject to English law and practice.

NOTE: -Where a continuation of cover is requested under Clause 9 or a change of destination is notified under Clause JO, there is an obligation to give prompt notice to the Insurers and the right to such cover is dependent upon compliance with this obligation.

Trade Terms or International Commercial Terms (INCOTERMS) and Their Application

Highlights of the Chapter

6.1 International Commercial Terms (2011)

In international trade, businesses use the standard trade definitions to resolve the dispute regarding the risk and cost of delivery of the goods. As different countries have different laws and practices determined and applicable only within that specific country's territory, standardization on account of division of risk between the seller and the buyer was required. For this reason, ICC came out with a publication which gives a clear direction in this context. It which defines the terms of sale which is popularly known as international commercial terms. Terms of sale is different from terms of payment, say 60 days at sight.

At present, we have INCOTERMS 2010. INCOTERMS 2010 is effective since January 1, 2011, containing 11 different commercial terms. Every 10 years ICC comes out with publication related to INCOTERMS. The previous publication is known as INCOTERMS 2000 and contained 13 INCOTERMS. The following table provides a detail description of INCOTERMS 2000 and INCOTERMS 2010.

INCOTERMS 2000	INCOTERMS 2010
• EXW or Ex works	• EXW or Ex works
• FCA or Free carrier	• FCA or Free carrier
• FAS or Free alongside ship…	• FAS or Free alongside ship…
• FOB or Free on board…	• FOB or Free on board…
• CPT or Carriage paid to….	• CPT or Carriage paid to….
• CIP or Carriage and insurance paid to…	• CIP or Carriage and insurance paid to…
• CFR or Cost and freight	• CFR or Cost and freight

INCOTERMS 2000	INCOTERMS 2010
• CIF or Cost, insurance and freight… • DDP or Delivered duty paid… • DAF or Delivered at Frontier • DEQ or Delivered Ex Quay • DES or Delivered Ex Ship • DDU or Delivered Duty Unpaid	• CIF or Cost, insurance and freight… • DAT or Delivered at Terminal… • DAP or Delivered at Place… • DDP or Delivered duty paid…

Each of these terms describe the risks, responsibilities, and obligations being divided between buyers and sellers.

6.2 Application of INCOTERMS in International Trade

With regard to INCOTERMS, we first need to understand the following.

Are INCOTERMS 2010 Applicable for both Domestic and International Sale?

INCOTERMS rules have traditionally been used in international sale contract where goods pass across national borders. In various areas of the world, however, trade blocs, like the European Union, have made border formalities between different countries less significant. Consequently, the subtitle of the INCOTERMS 2010 rules formally recognizes that they are available for application both to international and domestic sale contracts. In INCOTERMS 2010, the deleted terms are listed as:

- DAF: Delivered at Frontier

- DEQ: Delivered Ex Quay

- DES: Delivered Ex Ship

- DDU: Delivered Duty Unpaid

The four term are replaced by two new terms.

- DAT: Delivered at Terminal

- DAP: Delivered at Place

How to Incorporate the INCOTERMS 2010 Rules into Your Contract of Sale?

The exporter or importer must opt for an appropriate INCOTERM and it must be mentioned in the contract. Also, it may be noted that sometimes selection of appropriate INCOTERMS depends on the market power or the negotiating power of the exporter and the importer. For example, an exporter having good control over the international market would select an INCOTERM which is of maximum beneficial to him or her and vice versa. To use an INCOTERM in the sales contract and thereafter in other documents, the exporter/importer needs to specify it through such words as:

- "EXW Nariman Point, Mumbai, India, INCOTERMS 2010". It means that physical deliveries of the goods happen at the exporter's own premises or at it his or her warehouse. The location of the warehouse is Nariman Point.

- "FOB Nhava Sheva Port, Mumbai, India INCOTERMS 2010". In the example, FOB at Nhava Sheva Port, Mumbai, indicates the delivery would happen in exporter's country, that is, in India, and given that it is a seaway shipment, the shipment would start from Nhava Sheva port in Mumbai.

- "FAS Nhava Sheva Port, Mumbai, India, INCOTERMS 2010". In this example, free alongside ship (FAS) indicates that the physical delivery of the goods from the exporter to importer happens at a place alongside the ship.

- CPT Port of Singapore, Singapore, INCOTERMS 2010. In this example, the physical delivery of the goods happens when the exporter or any carrier of the exporter hands over the goods to the importer or his or her agent. Suppose goods are being exported from India to Singapore. Under carriage paid to (CPT), Port of Singapore, the physical delivery of the goods happen in India. So, the risk gets transferred from the exporter to the importer at the point where goods gets transferred from exporter to importer. However, cost is paid till Port of Singapore, that is, the importer's country, and it is paid by the exporter. So, under CPT, Port of Singapore, one additional place name in the exporter's country where goods gets physically delivered from the exporter to importer needs to be mentioned specifically in the INCOTERMS.

We would learn more about each of the INCOTERMS in the following section. However, it may be noted that the chosen INCOTERMS rule can work only if the exporters or importers mention the name of the place or port, and works best if the parties specify the place or port as precisely as possible. A good example of such precision would be: "FCA NIBM Junction, Pune, Maharashtra, India, INCOTERMS 2010."

Is the Name of Place Mentioned in INCOTERMS Always the Place of Delivery?

No, it is not. As mentioned to the above example, under the INCOTERMS rules, for EXW, FCA, DAT, DAP, Delivered Duty Paid (DDP), FAS, and FOB, the named place is the place where physical delivery takes place and where risk passes from the seller to the buyer. Also, the named place with all these terms refers to the point till where the cost is paid by the exporter. After that named place, the importer has to bear the cost of delivery. So, we can say that for the INCOTERM, the risk and the cost are passed from the exporter to the importer at the same named place. For example, if the trade happens under the INCOTERM "DAT," then the named place is a place at the bus, rail or air terminal of the importer's country. Till that name place, the exporter bears the risk and the cost of carriage.

However, under C terms the situation is different. For example, Carriage paid to (CPT), Carriage and Insurance Paid To (CIP), Cost and Freight (CFR), and Cost, Insurance and Freight (CIF), the place of delivery differs from the named place. Under these four INCOTERMS rules, the named place is the place of destination to which carriage is paid by the exporter. For example, if trade happens under CIP and the named place is Tokyo port Japan, if the shipment is going from Nhava Sheva, Mumbai, then the exporter from India pays the cost of carriage till Tokyo port Japan. However, delivery happens somewhere in India. With the physical delivery of the goods from the exporter/exporter's agent to the importer/importer's agent, risk is passed from the Indian exporter to the Japanese importer. So, it is advisable that under the above four INCOTERMS, in addition to the named place, there must be a mention about the name of the place or a precise point which to be considered as the delivery point. In case of any dispute, the settlement becomes easy between the exporter and the importer and it also becomes helpful in order to avoid doubt or argument.

6.2.1 The Mode of Transport and the Application of INCOTERMS

Also, it may be mentioned that all INCOTERMS are not applicable for all the mode of transport. There are four INCOTERMS which are applicable for only sea way or waterway transport. These four INCOTERMS are:

1. FAS or Free alongside ship…

2. FOB or Free onboard…

3. CFR or Cost and freight

4. CIF or Cost, insurance and freight…

On the other hand, the following seven INCOTERMS are applicable regardless of any mode of transport and even for more than one mode of transport. Importantly, it may be noted that even if the maritime transport is not involved at all, in the overall transport, these seven INCOTERMS are applicable. Also, they are applicable if ship transportation is involved for the part of the entire carriage. The seven INCOTERMS are:

1. EXW or Ex works

2. FCA or Free carrier

3. CPT or Carriage paid to….

4. CIP or Carriage and insurance paid to…

5. DAT or Delivered at Terminal…

6. DAP or Delivered at Place…

7. DDP or Delivered duty paid…

Terms and Definitions: As Defined by INCOTERMS 2010

For an appropriate application of trade terms, INCOTERMS have been made standardized across the border. To have a standardized approach, INCOTERMS define the following:

- **Carrier:** According to INCOTERMS 2010 rules, the carrier is defined as the party with whom carriage is contracted.

- **Customs formalities:** It is obvious to meet the requirement and comply with the different norms of customs regulations of different countries. The customs formalities mostly include documentary, security, information or physical inspection obligations.

- **Delivery:** In trade law and practice, the delivery of goods has several meanings. However, in the INCOTERMS 2010 rules, the term delivery is used to indicate where the risk of loss or damage to the goods passes from the seller to the buyer.

- **Delivery Documents:** This phrase is now used to provide that delivery of a particular goods have actually happened as per the instruction given in the contract. Any such document which is related to the event that delivery has occurred is known as a delivery document. The delivery documents are mostly the transport documents such as a BL or a corresponding electronic record. However, for a few INCOTERMS such as EXW, FCA, FAS, and FOB, the physical delivery of the goods takes place to a carrier selected by the importer or to a freight forwarder. So, for these INCOTERMS, the receipt or FBL is treated as the transport document. This delivery document plays a very important role in the payment mechanism. This is because, besides evidencing the physical delivery of the goods, the delivery document also provides the terms and conditions of the carriage.

- **Packaging:** INCOTERMS do not say anything on the packaging or how the seller should transport the goods to the agreed delivery point. According to INCOTERMS, packaging should ensure that the goods are fit for transportation and the packaging of goods must be in accordance to the contract of sale. So, if the transportation of the goods require a specific type of packaging, then it needs to be mentioned in the contract of sale. For example, if a chemical product is shipped and if packaging requires to have a storage with the temperature of 10–15°C, then it has to have a clear mention in the contract of sale itself. Otherwise, mere specification of such transportation conditions in the INCOTERMS do not assure that the goods are likely to be shipped with the similar condition.

  The definition of packaging given in INCOTERMS does not say anything specific about the "stowage of the packaged goods within a container or other means of transport. INCOTERMS 2010 rules do not deal with the parties' obligations for stowage within a container and therefore where relevant the parties should deal with this in the sale of contract" (INCOTERMS 2010, ICC Publication, p. 8).

For Example:

"In FOB Nhava Sheva, Mumbai, INCOTERMS 2010" the buyers has no control under INCOTERMS over how the seller transports the goods to Singapore. If it is important that the goods to be transported in refrigerated containers then it needs to be mentioned in a separate contract along with the terms and the conditions of the contract.

Factors Implicit in INCOTERMS

INCOTERMS rules do say which party to the sales contract has the obligation to make carriage or insurance arrangements, when the seller delivers the goods to the buyer, and which costs each party is responsible for. The obligations can be carried out personally by the seller or the buyer, or sometimes there may be intermediaries, such as carriers, freight forwarder or other persons nominated by the seller or the buyer.

What Do INCOTERMS Not Include?

1. INCOTERMS are not law; they must be specified in order to apply in international or domestic trade. If, suppose, a trade contract does not specify about the application of INCOTERMS and remain completely silent about the applicability, then exporter and importer would carry a huge risk in case of any dispute settlement and the division of cost.

2. In an international contract of sale or purchase, there are numerous related issues to the INCOTERMS that are not specifically an INCOTERMS element.

3. INCOTERMS are not all inclusive. They do not address government regulations, local customs operations of ports, carriers, and trades.

4. INCOTERMS do not have any connection to the title of the goods.

5. INCOTERMS have no reference to revenue recognition in international trade.

6. INCOTERMS do not refer to roles and responsibilities of banks. They do not cover all aspects of international trade business.

7. INCOTERMS do not address any Dispute related to the sales contract or the consequences of a breach of contract.

8. INCOTERMS do not provide any Intellectual Property Rights (IPRs).

9. INCOTERMS refer to only a minimum insurance of 110% of invoice value with reference to CIP and CIF terms. INCOTERMS do not say about any insurance on and above this minimum.

10. INCOTERMS do not refer to any other terms and conditions to maintain trade compliance with customs of the countries.

11. Packing detail, marking, and labeling concerns.

What is String Sale? Are INCOTERMS Applicable for the String Sale?

In international trade transaction, many a times the goods are sold in the transit. This kind of trade is quite frequent for commodities, as opposed to the sale of manufactured goods. Also, for commodity trade, the cargo is frequently sold several times during transit "down a string." When this happens, a seller in the middle of the string does not "ship" the goods because these have already been shipped by the first seller in the string. For clarification purposes, INCOTERMS 2010 rules include the obligation to "procure goods shipped" as an alternative to the obligation to ship goods in the relevant INCOTERMS rules. Procurement of goods which is already shipped is obvious for a seller who buys the goods in the transit and sells it off in the middle of the string. Therefore, in the chain of the string, the seller always performs his or her obligations towards its buyer, not by shipping the goods but by "procuring" goods that have been shipped.

What Happens if One Does not Refer to the Current or Any Edition of INCOTERMS?

If contract of sale refers only to INCOTERMS but not to a particular year or edition, then it is advisable that the INCOTERMS version in operation at that time of establishment of contract would apply in the event of dispute. However, the best practice for the benefit of the exporter and the importer may be to apply the current one.

Do INCOTERMS Decide on Property Right or Title of the Goods?

It does not decide the transfer of property right or title of goods. Since the law on transfer of property rights differs from country to country, the parties to a contract of sale may wish to specially provide for this matter in the contract.

EXW: Ex Works

This is one of the extreme INCOTERMS to apply in international trade. If this term is negotiated between the exporter and the importer, the importer bears all the risk and cost in transit. If the negotiating power of the exporter is high in international trade then he or she can very well establish the trade under this term for his or her own benefit. Under this INCOTERM, the physical delivery of the goods happens when the seller places the goods at the disposal of the buyer at the seller's premises or at another named place (i.e., works, factory, warehouse and so on). If suppose a seller whose factory is located at Kondwa Khurd, Pune, India, produces chemical products and wants to use EXW then the appropriate way of applying this INCOTERM is "EXW KONDWA KHURD, Pune, India, INCOTERMS 2010." So, the seller does not need to load the goods on any collecting vehicle, nor does he or she need to clear the goods for export, where such clearance is applicable. Even the responsibility of custom clearance in both the countries is borne by the importer.

The parties are well advised to specify as clearly as possible the point within the named place of delivery, as the costs and risks to that point are for the account of the seller. The buyer has to bear all the costs and risks involved in taking the goods from the agreed point, if any, to the destination point.

The seller has no obligation to the buyer to load the goods, even though in practice the seller may be in a better position to do so. If the seller does load the goods, he or she does so at the buyer's risk and expense.

Buyers are, therefore, well advised not to use EXW if they cannot directly or indirectly obtain export clearance.

FCA: Free Carrier

This is the second best policy for the exporter. The seller makes the physical delivery of the goods to a carrier or another person nominated by the buyer at the seller's premises or another named place. FCA means the goods are freed to the agent or carrier of the buyer. Many a time the freight forwarder does offer this service. Under this trade term, the seller is responsible for loading the goods on the transport vehicle. The parties are well advised to specify as clearly as possible the point within the named place of delivery, as the risk passes to the buyer at that point. For example, if a seller sells handicraft items from Kolkata, India, then he or she must specify exact name of the place in Kolkata where he or she wants the physical delivery of the goods to happen. So, an appropriate way of using the INCOTERMS is "FCA, Taratala, Kolkata 700032, India, INCOTERMS 2010."

In this example, FCA requires the seller from Kolkata to make all the arrangement to get customs clearance for the goods for export. However, the seller has no obligation to clear the goods for import, or to pay any import duty or for any import or customs formalities. Getting customs clearance for import of goods is the customers' responsibility.

CPT: Carriage Paid To

We have already discussed that C terms are the terms for which the physical delivery of the goods happen in the exporter's country, whereas the named place along with the INCOTERMS refer to the place till where carriage is paid to by the seller. Along with the named place in INCOTERMS, it is advisable that the buyer and the seller negotiate a named place where the physical delivery of the goods is expected to happen. If the delivery place is mentioned under CPT, then the seller delivers the goods to the carrier or another person nominated by the seller at that agreed place. For example, if an Indian exporter from Kolkata wants to sell goods to Tokyo and the trade is under CPT, then the appropriate way to apply the INCOTERM is

"CPT Tokyo Bay, Tokyo, Japan, INCOTERMS 2010". In this case, the seller from Kolkata pays for the carriage till Tokyo Bay. However, in this there is no mention of the exact place where the physical delivery of the goods happen. So, there should be a specific mention about the place where the risk gets transferred from the exporter to the importer.

According to the INCOTERMS 2010, it is defined that if CPT is used,

> [T]he seller fulfills its obligation to deliver when the seller hands the goods over to the carrier and not when they reach the buyer at the place of destination. This rule has two critical points because risk passes and costs are transferred at different places.

However, the parties are well advised to identify as precisely as possible in the contract both the place of delivery, where the risk passes to the buyer, and the named place of destination to which place the seller must contract for the carriage. If several carriers are used in the transaction and if no named place is mentioned where the goods to be delivered, then by default it would be taken as the first carrier to whom the exporter delivers the goods.

CIP: Carriage and Insurance Paid To

The term CIP is more like the term CPT. Additionally, it says that exporter pays for the insurance cost along with the carriage till the named point of destination. However, like CPT, there should be a separate mention about the place of delivery where the seller delivers the goods to the carrier or another person nominated by the seller at an agreed place (if any such place is agreed between the parties). The named place along with the INCOTERMS states that the seller must contract for and pay the cost of carriage necessary to bring the goods to the named place of destination. For example, "CIP Tokyo Bay, Tokyo, INCOTERMS 2010" means that the exporter pays the insurance and cost of carriage till Tokyo Bay. If the delivery place name, say Taratala Kolkata, is used in addition, then the exporter from Kolkata delivers the goods at Taratala, Kolkata.

However, this INCOTERM covers only minimum insurance, that is, 110% against the buyer's risk of loss of or damage to the goods during the carriage. The buyer should note that under CIP many of the risks in transit are not covered.

Like CPT, when CIP is used, the seller fulfills his or her obligation to deliver when the seller hands the goods over to the carrier and not when they reach the buyer at the place of destination. This rule has two critical points because the risk passes and the costs are transferred at different places. The parties are well advised to identify as precisely as possible in the contract both the place of delivery, where the risk passes to the buyer, and the named place of destination to which place the seller must contract for carriage. Failing so, the risk would transfer from the exporter to the importer at the first carrier to whom the exporter delivers the goods.

DAT: Delivered at Terminal

The D term indicates that the risk and cost get transferred from the exporter to the importer at the importer's country. If anything goes wrong in the transit, then the exporter has to bear the risk till the named point. The delivery of the goods happens once it is unloaded from the arriving means of transport and placed at the disposal of the buyer at a named terminal at the named port or place of destination. For example, "DAT Tokyo Bay, Tokyo INCOTERMS 2010" means the seller from Kolkata, India, has to bear all risks involved in bringing the goods to Tokyo Bay and unloading them at the terminal at Tokyo Bay.

DAT requires the seller to clear the goods for export along with the customs clearance. However, the seller has no obligation to clear the goods for import or to pay any import duty or for any customs formalities.

Moreover, if the parties intend the seller to bear the risks and costs involved in transporting and handling the goods from the terminal to another place, then the DAP or DDP rules should be used.

DAP: Delivered at Place

In case of DAP, "DAP ABC Plantation Unit, 23rd Rainbow Street, Tokyo, INCOTERMS 2010," the seller or exporter from Kolkata delivers the goods when the goods are placed at the disposal of the buyer, say, at the warehouse of ABC plantation unit in 23rd Rainbow Street. The goods are delivered on the arriving means of transport and ready for unloading at the named place of destination, here in this example, it is the warehouse of ABC plantation unit at 23rd Rainbow Street, Tokyo. The seller from Kolkata has to bear all the risks and costs involved in bringing the goods to the named place.

If the seller incurs costs under its contract of carriage related to unloading at the place of destination, the seller is not entitled to recover such costs from the buyer unless otherwise agreed between the parties. So, most often the seller is requested to bear the cost of unloading the goods from the arriving means.

DAP requires the seller to clear the goods for export and arrange for the custom clearance at exporters country. However, the seller has no obligation to clear the goods for import or to pay any import duty or for any customs formalities.

DDP: Delivered Duty Paid

This is extremely beneficial for the importer to use because for this INCOTERM all the cost and risk in the transit is borne by the seller or the exporter. The delivery of the goods happen when the goods are placed at the disposal of the buyer in the importer's country. The goods are considered to be delivered for import on the arriving means of transport, ready for unloading at the named place of destination. If the INCOTERM is "DDP ABC Plantation Unit, 23rd Rainbow Street, Tokyo, INCOTERM 2010," the exporter has to bear all the costs and risks involved in bringing the goods to 23rd Rainbow Street, Tokyo, has an obligation to clear the goods for export and import and is also responsible to have customs clearance in both the exporter and the importer's country. The exporter is also responsible to pay any import duty and for any customs formalities.

DDP represents the maximum obligation for the seller. The parties are well advised to specify as clearly as possible the point within the agreed place of destination, as the costs and risks to that point are for the account of the seller. The seller is advised to procure contracts of carriage that match that choice precisely. If the seller incurs costs under its contract of carriage related to unloading at the place of destination, the seller is not entitled to recover such costs from the buyer unless otherwise agreed between the parties.

6.2.2 Rules for Sea and Inland Waterway Transport

Free Alongside Ship

This is the INCOTERM used for waterway shipment. The seller delivers when the goods are placed alongside the vessel (e.g., on a dock or a barge) to a carrier nominated by the buyer at the named port of shipment. For example, "FAS Howrah Dock, Howrah Port, India INCOTERMS 2010." The risk of loss or damage to the goods passes when the goods are alongside the ship with the physical delivery of the goods. However, the buyer, say from Tokyo, has to bear all costs from that moment.

The seller is required either to deliver the goods alongside the ship or to procure goods already so delivered for shipment to the destination agreed in the sale contract. The reference to "procure" here caters to multiple sales down a chain (string sales), particularly common among the commodity trades.

FAS requires the seller to clear the goods for export, along with the customs clearance in the exporter's country. However, the seller has no obligation to clear the goods for import or to pay any import duty or for any customs formalities.

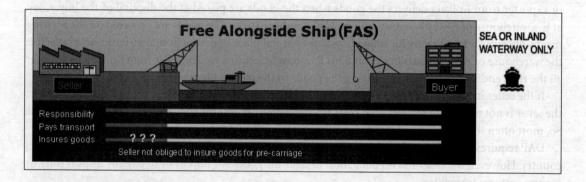

This is the most used and known INCOTERM for the waterway transaction. "FOB Howrah Port, Howrah, India, INCOTERMS 2010." The seller from India delivers the goods onboard the vessel at Howrah Port to a carrier nominated by the buyer at the named port of shipment or procures the goods already so delivered. The risk of loss or damage to the goods passes when the goods are on board the vessel and the buyer has to bear all costs from that moment.

The seller is required either to deliver the goods on board the vessel or to procure goods already so delivered for shipment to the destination agreed in the sale contract. The reference to "procure" here caters to multiple sales down a chain ("string sales"), particularly common in the commodity trades.

CFR: Cost and Freight

"CFR" means that the seller delivers the goods on board the vessel or procures the goods already so delivered. Suppose a seller or exporter wants to ship some garment items from Kolkata to Tokyo. "CFR Tokyo Bay, Tokyo, INCOTERM 2010" means the risk of loss of or damage to the goods passes when the goods are on board the vessel at Howrah Port as selected by the importer. However, the seller from Kolkata must contract for and pay the costs and freight necessary to bring the goods to the named port of destination, that is, till Tokyo Bay in this example.

Like CPT and CIP, INCOTERM CFR also makes the seller fulfills his or her obligation to deliver when the seller hands the goods over to the carrier in the manner specified in the chosen rule and not when they reach the buyer at the place of destination.

This rule has two critical points because risk passes and costs are transferred at different places. While the contract will always specify a destination port, it might not specify the port of shipment, and that is the place at which risk passes to the buyer. If the shipment port is of particular interest to the buyer, the parties are well advised to identify it as precisely as possible in the contract, like in this example where the place of delivery is well defined.

CIF: Cost Insurance and Freight

This rule is to be used only for sea or inland waterway transport. "CIF" means that the seller delivers the goods onboard the vessel or procures the goods already so delivered. This INCOTERM is same as CFR. The only difference is that the exporter bears the cost of insurance till the named place or destination. Suppose Renuka Silk Kolkata gets an export order to deliver silk saris in Tokyo to ABC importer. The exporter and the importer gets into a sale contract with CIF INCOTERM. Also, they agree to mention that the INCOTERM must state the place of delivery as Howrah Port where the exporter gives physical delivery of the goods to the carrier or agent of the importer's choice. In this case, the use of "CIF Tokyo Bay, Tokyo INCOTERMS 2010" means that the risk of loss of or damage to the goods passes when the goods are onboard the vessel, say in this example at Howrah Port, India, from Renuka Export to the ABC importer. However, the Renuka export must contract for and pay the costs and freight and insurance of 110% of the invoice value necessary to bring the goods to the named port of destination.

This insurance cover provides protection against the risk of loss of or damage to the goods during the carriage; however, it does not cover risk arising out of different causes. The buyer should note that if risk is more taking insurance cover only under CIF is not sufficient. Should the buyer wish to have more insurance protection, he or she would need either to agree as much expressly with the seller or to make their own extra insurance arrangements.

Common Dispute Under CIF

Often the dispute is related to unloading or discharge costs. So an *experienced exporter may choose to specify in the pro forma invoice or contract of sale that all unloading charges are for the importer*. In our example, Renuka export must make the arrangement to mention that all unloading charges are to be borne by ABC importer. Also, Renuka export should make a clear instruction to their freight forwarder about this. When the goods are delivered to the carrier, the exporter receives the BL from the carrier.

Some Important Points about INCOTERMS

- While the EXW term represents the minimum obligation for the seller, DDP represents the maximum obligation.

- Arrival Contracts: Only the D terms make for arrival contracts.

- Shipment Contracts: "F" and C terms: The seller fulfills his or her delivery obligation at the point of shipment, hence shipment contracts.

- Difference between C and D terms are important when goods are damaged in transit, as with C terms seller has already fulfilled the delivery obligations, while with D terms seller may be liable for breach of contract.

- INCOTERMS deal with the division of cost and also of risk between the parties but they do not deal with the transfer of property rights.

6.3 Caselets in INCOTERMS

Case Example 1: Cargo Insurance Company v. National Medical System

A seller from country A, Gareth, sold a mobile magnetic resonance imagining (MRI) system to an Indian buyer under the following terms: "CIF Howrah Seaport INCOTERMS 2010. When the goods were damaged in transit, the buyer's insurance, that is, Cargo Insurance Company, filed a claim against the manufacturer. Under the INCOTERMS CIF rule, the risk of loss transfers to buyer upon shipment, and since MRI had been loaded in good order, the buyer from India had to bore the risk of loss.

Case Example 2: German Seller v. American Buyer About the Applicability of INCOTERMS when Contract is under CISG

In this example, a German seller has got into a contract with an American buyer. In the initial contract, there was a mention of CIF New York Port INCOTERMS 2010. However, with reference to initial contract both the parties signed CISG. Conversely, a specific INCOTERM was not chosen by the parties in CISG. When the goods were in transit the goods were damaged. So, the exporter from Germany has refused to take the responsibility of the goods being damaged in the transit. Consequently, the buyer's insurance sought to avoid application of the INCOTERMS rule by pointing out that INCOTERMS had not been incorporated explicitly into the contract. The contract was governed by German law and, therefore, by the UN convention on CISG.

The judge held that INCOTERMS applied even in the absence of a specific mention. The court reasoned that as it was under CISG which incorporates INCOTERMS through article 9(2), reference to "usages" which are "widely known."

Case Example 3: Iranian Oil International Ltd. v. ABC Oil Company Ltd

ABC oil company ltd from India has contracted to purchase 100,000 barrels of gasoline from Iranian Oil International Ltd. The gasoline was sold on CFR terms and was to be loaded in Iran and shipped to India. Under the contract terms, the gasoline was required to have gum content less than two milligrams per one hundred milliliters.

When the gasoline was loaded in Iran, it was tested by an independent inspector and determined to comply with the contract terms. However, when the gasoline arrived in India the gum content was found to exceed the contractual limit and ABC oil company ltd had filed the case. The court choose to apply INCOTERMS finds that as the trade happened under CFR INCOTERM, the buyer has to bear the cost of damage of the goods. Under the INCOTERMS CFR rule, the risk of loss is transferred from seller to the buyer when the goods are loaded.

Since the gasoline was found by the inspector to be compliant with the contract upon loading, it was held that Iranian Oil International had fulfilled its delivery obligation.

Case Example 4: Inappropriate use of INCOTERMS

Amongst other documents, the credit required presentation of "full set 'clean on board' air transport documents" and evidenced the trade term as FOB Singapore. The presented air waybill was not marked "clean" and the invoice showed the trade terms as FCA Singapore. However, the air transport document did show the actual flight details and date.

Without seeking an amendment, the beneficiary had requested the bank to correct the INCOTERM and to change it to FCA as FOB was not the appropriate trade term.

The issuing bank refused the documents due to the absence of an onboard statement and the use of the trade term FCA instead of FOB, the justification of the issuing bank being that banks should strictly follow the terms and conditions of the credit.

The conclusion of the Banking Commission was that the discrepancy concerning absence of the word clean statement was not valid.

But the discrepancy concerning the different trade term was valid. It was not for banks to determine whether the stated trade term was accurate or appropriate. Banks are only required to examine documents on their face to determine compliance. So, if any banker finds any wrong application of INCOTERMS then he or she should request for an amendment.

Case Example 5: The Interpretation of Terminology should be Contextual

This request demonstrates how the use of different terminology, even if not intended for use in the same context, can cause disputes between banks.

The BL showed a shipped onboard date of September 14, 2016, and the packing list stated "shipping date September 13, 2016." The issuing bank refused the documents due to the packing list showing an inconsistent shipping date to the BLs.

The argument of the nominated bank was that the wording might have different meanings depending on the context in which it is used in each document.

The analysis and conclusion of the ICC Banking Commission agreed (DOCDEX cases 2009–12) with the nominated bank. In this case, the use of shipping date, in the packing list, could refer to the movement of the goods out of the warehouse of the beneficiary for the delivery to the carrier or their agent and should not be seen as an indication of the date of shipment (as is the case with the date appearing in a shipped onboard notation on a BL).

QUESTIONS

A. Multiple Choice Questions

1. Goods are handed over to the carrier before they are onboard the vessel, for example goods in containers, which are typically delivered at a terminal. In such situations, which of the following terms are used?

   a. FOB

   b. FCA

   c. CPT

   d. CIF

   e. FCA

2. Where the goods are packed in containers, it is typical for the seller to hand the goods over to the carrier at a terminal and not alongside the vessel. In this case the appropriate term is

   a. FOB

   b. FCA

   c. FAS

   d. 1 or 2

   e. 2 or 3

   f. 1 or 3

3. The seller delivers when the goods are placed at the disposal of the buyer on the arriving means of transport ready for unloading at the named place of destination. Which term is to be used?

   a. EXW

   b. DAP

   c. DAT

   d. DDP

4. The seller fulfills its obligation to deliver when the seller hands the goods over to the carrier and not when they reach the buyer at the place of destination.

   a. CPT, CIP, CFR or CIF

   b. DAT, DAP or DDP

5. If several carriers are used for the carriage to the agreed destination and the parties do not agree on a specific point of delivery, the default position is that risk passes

   a. when the goods have been delivered to the first carrier.

   b. a point entirely of the buyer's choosing and over which the buyer has no control.

   c. when the goods have been delivered to the last carrier.

6. The value of the goods under credit is $10,000. The INCOTERMS is under CIF. Insurance document indicates that under the minimum coverage, the value of the insurance is £11,000. Is it a discrepancy?

7. Which of the followings is the arrival contract?

   a. F term

   b. C term

   c. D term

   d. Both 2 and 3

8. A point to which the exporter should pay the transport costs must necessarily be indicated after the respective C-term. This point of the division of cost is referring a point in

   a. Exporter's country

   b. Importer's country

   c. Either 1 or 2

9. If CFR is to be paid by the exporter to the named port of destination then which of the followings will be correct INCOTERMS?

   a. C&F

   b. CFR

   c. C and F

   d. C+F

   e. C&F or CFR

   f. C and F or CFR

10. Suppose, CPT is used if several carriers are used for the carriage to the agreed destination and the parties do not agree on a specific point of delivery, the default position is that risk passes when the goods have been delivered

   a. To the first carrier, a point entirely of the seller's choice and over which the buyer has no control.

   b. To the first carrier, a point entirely of the buyer's choice and over which the seller has no control.

   c. To the last carrier, a point entirely of the buyer's choice and over which the seller has no control.

B. Answer the Following Questions

1. What are INCOTERMS? Explain the use of INCOTERMS in international trade.

2. Is the application of INCOTERMS country specific? Currently which version of INCOTERMS are in use? Prior to the current version which version of INCOTERMS were in use in international trade transaction?

3. Does INCOTERMS apply to domestic sale as well?

4. If the version or the publication number is not mentioned then which publication is applied?

5. What are the clauses INCOTERMS do not refer to?

6. What are the rules of Packaging under INCOTERMS?

7. How many INCOTERMS are there? Which all INCOTERMS are applicable only for waterway trade transaction and which for any mode of transaction?

8. What are the major differences between C terms and D terms?

9. What are the differences between CIP and CIF?

10. Explain FOB, CIF, and DDT

11. Why is EXW considered to be beneficial for the exporter?

12. Why is DDP considered to be beneficial for the importer?

13. Who takes the responsibility of customs clearance for EXW, DDP, FCA, CIF, and DAP?

C. Read the Following Case and Answer the Questions

ABC textile company ltd from India has contracted to purchase 10,000 silk saris from Bangladesh Tant. The Tant saris were sold on DAT terms and was to be loaded in Dhaka and shipped to India. Under the contract terms, the sari was required to have quality fiber content.

When the saris were loaded in Dhaka it was tested by an independent inspector and determined to comply with the contract terms. However, when the saris arrived in India some of the saris were found damaged. ABC textile company ltd had filed the case.

1. How do we mention INCOTERM in the sale contract? Write the appropriate way to apply. INCOTERM in the example explained in the case.

2. Who takes the responsibility of goods being lost in the transit?

3. If the INCOTERM was mentioned as any of the C terms, then who is likely to bear the risk of loss or damage in the transit?

Chapter 7

Export Trade and Export Credit or Pre- and Post-shipment Credit

7.1 Export Trade: Basics

The DGFT and its regional offices, functioning under the Ministry of Commerce and Industry, Department of Commerce, Government of India, regulates export trade. Any AD or AD Category–I banks may conduct export transactions in conformity with the FTP in practice and the rules framed by the Government of India and the directions issued by the RBI from time to time. Export contract can be invoiced in Indian rupees. According to FTP,

All export contracts and invoices shall be denominated either in freely convertible currency or Indian rupees but export proceeds shall be realized in freely convertible currency. However, export proceeds against specific exports may also be realized in rupees, provided it is through a freely convertible Vostro account of a nonresident bank situated in any country other than a member country of Asian Clearing Union (ACU) or Nepal or Bhutan.

It may be noted that Indian Rupee is not a freely convertible currency, as yet.

7.1.1 Transaction with Nepal or Bhutan

All trade dealings between a person resident in Nepal or Bhutan and a person resident in India may be settled in Indian rupees. However, if India exports goods to Nepal and if the importer from Nepal is permitted by the Nepal Rastra Bank to make payment in free foreign exchange, then such payments needs to be routed through the ACU mechanism.

7.1.2 Asian Monetary Unit (AMU)

In order to enable the transactions/settlements, members in the Asian Clearing Union (ACU) have the option to settle their transactions either in ACU Dollar or in ACU Euro, effective from January 1, 2009. Accordingly, the AMU which is denominated as "ACU Dollar" and "ACU Euro" are considered to be equivalent in value to one US dollar and one Euro, respectively.

Also, ACU Dollar and ACU Euro accounts can be opened and maintained by the AD Category–I banks with their correspondent banks in other participating countries. All eligible payments are required to be settled by the concerned banks through these accounts.

7.1.3 Relaxation from ACU Mechanism

Earlier Indo-Myanmar trade was likely to happen through only ACU settlement. However, this restriction is not there anymore. Trade transactions with Myanmar are allowed to be settled in any freely convertible currency in addition to the ACU mechanism.

7.1.4 Restricted Cover Country

According to the definition of the RBI, the country which experiences chronic political and economic problems as well as balance of payment difficulties is known as a restricted cover group II country. It may be noted that if the shipments goes to such type of country, for example, Sudan, Somalia and so on, then payments for the same may be received from an open cover country.

7.2 Some Important Concepts Related to Export

There are different accounts maintained by the exporters. We discuss some of those as the following:

7.2.1 Exchange Earner's Foreign Currency Account or EEFC Account

An account in foreign currency opened and maintained by a person resident in India with an AD Category–I bank in India, called the Exchange Earners' Foreign Currency (EEFC) account. This is a non-interest bearing current account and there is no fund-based or nonfund-based credit facility available against this account. As defined in the Companies Act 1956, a resident individuals can include resident close relative(s) as a joint holder(s) in their EEFC bank accounts on former or survivor basis.

All categories of foreign exchange earners can credit 100% of their foreign exchange earnings to their EEFC accounts, subject to the conditions that the sum total in the account during a calendar month should be converted into rupees on or before the last day of the succeeding calendar month. This conversion is applicable only after adjusting for utilization of the balances for approved purposes or forward commitments.

In EEFC account, the eligible credits are:

1. Inward remittances from normal channel: The inward remittance for foreign currency loan raised or investment received from outside India or those received for meeting specific obligations by the account holder are not considered to be eligible.

2. A unit in a domestic tariff area (DTA) that supplies goods to a unit in SEZs can receive payments in foreign currency from SEZs foreign currency account.

3. Exporters are permitted by AD Category–I banks to repay packing credit advances either availed in Rupee or in foreign currency from balances in their EEFC account and/or Rupee resources to the extent exports have actually taken place.

7.2.2 Diamond Dollar Account

Under the scheme of Government of India, diamond dollar account can be opened and maintained by the firms and companies (a) having track records of at least two years in import/export of diamonds/colored gemstones/diamond and colored gemstones studded jewelry/plain gold jewelry, (b) transacting in purchase/sale of rough or cut and polished diamonds/precious metal jewelry plain, minakari and/or studded with/without diamond and/or other stones, and (c) during the preceding three licensing years (April–March) having an average annual turnover of ₹ 30 million or above.

7.3 Advance Payment Against Export

If the trade transaction is under advance payment method then the exporter is obliged to send the shipment of goods within one year from the date of receipt of advance payment. From a buyer outside India, advance payment may be received with or without interest; the rate of interest, if any, payable on the advance payment, does not exceed London Inter-Bank Offered Rate (LIBOR) + 100 basis points. It may be noted that the documents covering the shipment are routed through the AD Category — I bank through whom the advance payment is received.

If exporter fails to ship the goods within one year from the date of shipment: Within one year from the date of receipt of advance payment, if the exporter fails to ship the goods either partly or fully, then there should not be any remittance towards refund of unutilized portion of advance payment or towards payment of interest. After the expiry of the said period of one year, any such remittance requires a prior approval of the RBI.

When advance can be extended beyond one year: There may be some goods which require more than one year to manufacture and ship. For such goods, AD Category-I banks may allow exporters to receive advance payment for more than one year. Also, to get export advance for more than one year, the "export agreement" for shipment of goods should mention that the period of shipment is beyond one year from the date of receipt of advance payment. Advance payment beyond one year is subject to the following conditions:

1. AD Category–I bank is satisfied with the KYC and due diligence exercise has been done for the overseas buyer;

2. Compliance with the anti-money laundering standards has been ensured;

3. The AD Category–I bank should ensure the end use of the export advance. If advance is received by the exporter then that should be employed to implement export and not for any other purpose, that is the transaction is a bona fide transaction;

4. Progress payment, if any, should be received directly from the overseas buyer strictly in terms of the contract;

5. If there is any rate of interest, payable on the advance payment, then it shall not exceed LIBOR + 100 basis points;

6. Advance payment is not allowed beyond one year if in the last three years exporter had to refund the advance and the refund amount exceeds 10% of the advance payment;

7. The documents covering the shipment should be routed through the same AD bank through which advance is received; and

8. In the event of failure, or if the shipment does not happen partly or fully, no remittance towards refund of unutilized portion of advance payment or towards payment of interest should be made without the prior approval of the RBI.

7.3.1 Advance with Maximum Tenure 10 Years

Exporters having a minimum of three years' satisfactory track record are allowed to receive long-term export advance up to a maximum tenor of 10 years. Exporters are likely to utilize this advance for completing long-term supply contracts of goods. However, this is subject to the following conditions:

1. The supply contract should be executed on the basis of firm irrevocable supply orders. Product pricing should be in consonance with prevailing international prices.

2.   To ensure that the exporters or the firms have the capacity, systems and processes in place to execute the orders over the duration of the said tenure.

3.   The entities that have not come under the adverse notice of the Enforcement Directorate or any such regulatory agency or have not been caution listed are eligible for long-term advance.

4.   Such advances should be adjusted through future exports.

5.   If exporter has any rate of interest to pay, then it should not exceed LIBOR + 200 basis points.

6.   All the documents related to the trade transaction should be routed through one AD bank only.

7.   Compliance with Anti Money Laundering (AML)/KYC guidelines to be ensured by the AD bank.

8.   Such export advances shall not be permitted to be used to liquidate Rupee loans classified as NPA.

9.   If long-term advance is provided, then double financing for working capital for execution of export orders should be avoided.

10. If advance is received with the amount of USD 100 million or more, then AD Category–I bank should immediately report to the Trade Division, Foreign Exchange Department, RBI, Central Office, Mumbai.

11. AD banks can issue a BG/SBLC for advance against export performance. However, the issuance of BG or SBLC should be done only after prudential evaluation of the credit.

   a.   BG/SBLC may be issued for a term not exceeding two years at a time, and further rollover of not more than two years at a time.

   b.   BG/SBLC should cover only the advance on reducing balance basis.

   c.   Overseas branch/subsidiary of a bank in India is not allowed to discount BG/SBLC issued from India in favor of an overseas buyer.

12. If AD Category–I banks have to refund advance payment credited to EEFC account, and if the entire balances held in the exporter's EEFC accounts maintained at different branches/banks are fully utilized, then the banks may allow the purchase of foreign exchange.

7.4 Consignment Exports

Under consignment export, the AD Category–I bank can forward shipping documents to its overseas branch/correspondent, only with the instruction that the overseas branch/correspondent can deliver them only against trust receipt/undertaking to deliver sale proceeds by a specified date within the period prescribed for realization of proceeds of the export. This procedure should be followed even if a bill is partly drawn in advance against the exports.

Direct dispatch of documents by the exporter:

1.   AD Category–I banks can dispatch the shipping documents directly to the consignees or their agents resident in the country of final destination of goods instead to their overseas

branches/correspondents. However, sending of documents directly to the consignees/their agents depend on:

   a.   Advance payment or an irrevocable LC has been received for the full value of the export shipment and the underlying sale contract/LC has a clear mentions that the documents should reach directly to the consignee or his or her agent resident in the country of final destination of goods.

   b.   The AD Category–I banks may also comply to the request of the exporter provided the exporter is a regular customer.

2.   "Status holder exporters" (as per the definition of FTP), and units in SEZs are permitted to dispatch the export documents directly to the consignees outside India.

3.   If the exporter is a regular customer of an AD Category–I bank for a period of at least six months and the export proceeds have been realized in full amount, then AD Category–I may regularize cases of dispatch of shipping documents by the exporter direct to the consignee or his or her agent resident in the country of the final destination of goods, up to USD 1 million or its equivalent, per export shipment.

7.5 Counter-trade Arrangement

Under counter trade, the value of goods imported into India gets adjusted against the value of goods exported from India. The payment between the Indian party and the overseas party happens through an escrow account opened in India in US Dollar.

1.   The prices of all imports and exports should be scaled at international prices in conformity with the FTP and Foreign Exchange Management Act, 1999 and the rules and regulations made thereunder.

2.   If there is an excess balance in the escrow account, no interest will be payable. However, the surplus fund may be held in a short-term deposit up to a total period of three months in a year and the banks may pay interest at the applicable rate.

3.   No fund-based/or nonfund-based facilities would be permitted against the balances in the escrow account.

7.6 Export of Goods by SEZs

If the processing/manufacturing charges are suitably loaded in the export price and are borne by the ultimate buyer, then the units in SEZs are permitted to undertake work abroad and export goods from that country itself. Also, the realization of the export proceeds should be in full value.

It may be noted that AD Category–I banks may permit units in DTAs to purchase foreign exchange for making payment for goods supplied to them by units in SEZs.

7.7 Export of Services by SEZs to DTA Units

For service export rendered by SEZ to DTA, an AD bank can sell foreign exchange to a unit in the DTA for making payment in foreign exchange to a unit in the SEZ. However, the SEZ unit which renders the services to the DTA unit must ensure that the letter of approval (LoA) issued to the SEZ unit by the development commissioner (DC) of the SEZ, carries the provisions relating to the services (applicable for goods unit as well) supplied by the SEZ unit to the DTA unit, and for payment in foreign exchange for the same should be mentioned.

7.8 Project Exports and Service Exports

Project exports relate to the export of engineering goods on deferred payment terms and implementation of turnkey projects and civil construction contracts abroad. Indian exporters who want to offer deferred payment terms to overseas buyers and the exporters who want to participate in global tenders for undertaking turnkey/civil construction contracts abroad are required to obtain the approval of the AD Category–I banks/EXIM Bank. This approval is required at the post-award stage before undertaking execution of such contracts. Regulations relating to "project exports" and "service exports" are laid down in the revised *Memorandum of Instructions on Project and Service Exports* (PEM-July 2014).

1. The respective AD bank/EXIM Bank should monitor the projects for which post-award approval has been granted by them.

2. In order to provide greater flexibility to project and service exporters in conducting their overseas transactions, facilities have been provided as under:

a. Inter-Project Transfer of Machinery

It provides the provision of inter-project transfer of machinery. The provision regarding recovery of market value (not less than book value) of the machinery, etc. from the transferee project has been withdrawn. Moreover, subject to the satisfaction of the sponsoring AD Category–I bank(s)/EXIM Bank, exporters are entitled to use the machinery/equipment for performing any other contract secured by them in any country.

b. Inter-Project Transfer of Funds

To boost the production by removing additional hazards, AD Category–I bank(s)/EXIM banks are allowed to permit exporters to open, maintain and operate one or more foreign currency account/s in a currency(ies) of their choice. All these accounts are subject to inter-project transferability of funds in any currency or country. AD Category–I bank(s)/EXIM Bank are authorized to monitor the inter-project transfer of funds.

c. Deployment of Temporary Cash Surpluses

Subject to monitoring by the AD Category–I bank(s)/EXIM Bank, project/service exporters may deploy the followings as deposits with branches/subsidiaries outside India of AD Category–I banks in India:

   i. Their temporary cash surpluses, generated outside India.

  ii. Investments in short-term paper abroad which includes treasury bills and other monetary instruments. However, investments in such documents needs to be with a maturity or remaining maturity of one year or less, and the rating of which should be at least A-1/AAA by Standard & Poor, or P-1/AAA by Moody's, or F1/AAA by Fitch IBCA and so on.

 iii. Repatriation of Funds in case of on-site software contracts.

The requirement of repatriation of 30% of contract value in respect of on-site contracts by software Exporter Company/firm has been dispensed with. However, repatriation of the profits of on-site contracts after completion of the contracts is mandatory.

7.9 Export of Currency

As per FEMA, permission of the RBI is required for any export of Indian currency except to the extent permitted under any general permission granted under the regulations as under:

1. Any person resident in India is allowed to take currency notes of Government of India and the RBI notes up to an amount not exceeding ₹25,000 (Rupees twenty five thousand only) outside India (other than to Nepal and Bhutan).

2. Any person resident outside India, except the citizen of Pakistan and Bangladesh and also not a traveler coming from and going to Pakistan and Bangladesh, and visiting India may take up to an amount not exceeding ₹25,000 (Rupees twenty five thousand only) currency notes of Government of India and the RBI notes outside India. This amount is applicable only while exiting only through an airport.

7.10 Switching from Barter Trade to Normal Trade at the Indo-Myanmar Border

It has been decided that the barter system of trade at the Indo-Myanmar border that had been prevailing for long has to face a switch to normal trade. Accordingly, with effect from December 1, 2015, this barter system is switched over to normal trade Accordingly, all trade transactions with Myanmar, including those at the Indo-Myanmar border with effect from December 1, 2015, are settled in any permitted currency in addition to the ACU mechanism.

7.11 Counter-trade Arrangements with Romania

Counter trade proposals from Indian exporters with Romania is accepted by the RBI subject to the following conditions:

1. Involving adjustment of value of exports from India against value of imports made into India in terms of a voluntarily entered arrangement between the concerned parties,

2. The Indian exporter should utilize the funds for import of goods from Romania into India within six months from the date of credit to escrow accounts allowed to be opened.

7.12 Handing Over Negotiable Copy of BL to Master of Vessel/Trade Representative

AD Category–I banks are allowed to deliver one negotiable copy of the BL to the master of the carrying vessel or trade representative for exports to certain landlocked countries. This condition is applied only if the shipment is covered by an irrevocable LC and the documents conform strictly to the terms of the LC which, inter alia, provides for such delivery.

7.13 Follow-up of Overdue Bills

If bills remain outstanding beyond the due date for payment from the date of export, then the problem with the realization of bills should be promptly taken up with the concerned exporter. The regional office of the bank has to be notified if the exporter fails to arrange for delivery of the proceeds within the stipulated period or seek extension of time beyond the stipulated period. Also, the RB requires the matter to be reported to the concerned of the RBI stating, where possible, the reason for the delay in realizing the proceeds.

7.14 Change of Buyer/Consignee

In the event of default by the original buyer, after goods have been shipped, they can be transferred to a buyer other than the original buyer. This transfer is subject to two conditions:

1. Provided the reduction in value, if any, involved does not exceed 25% of the invoice value, and

2. The realization of export proceeds is not delayed beyond the period of 12 months from the date of export.

Given that the above conditions are fulfilled, this transfer from one buyer to another buyer does not require prior approval of the RBI.

7.15 Shipments Lost in Transit

1. The AD Category–I banks must ensure that an insurance claim is made when shipments from India for which payment has not been received either by negotiation of bills under LCs or otherwise are lost in transit. The insurance claim should be made as soon as the loss is known.

2. The AD Category–I banks must arrange to collect the full amount of claim due on the lost shipment, in cases where the claim is payable abroad. The collection of the claim has to be through the medium of banks' overseas branch/correspondent.

3. A certificate for the amount of claim received should be furnished on the reverse of the duplicate copy.

4. AD Category–I banks should ensure that amounts of claims on shipments lost in transit which are partially settled directly by shipping companies/airlines under carrier's liability abroad are also repatriated to India by exporters.

7.16 Netting Off of Export Receivables Against Import Payments: Units in SEZs

Exporters may request the AD Category–I banks for "netting off" of export receivables against import payments for units located in SEZs subject to the following:

- The "netting off" of export receivables against import payments is in respect of the same Indian entity and the overseas buyer/supplier (bilateral netting), and the netting may be done as on the date of balance sheet of the unit in SEZ.

7.17 Financing Export Credit

For a long time now, the RBI and the government have been emphasizing on the requirement of exporting sector. It is one of the important schemes of the government to make the export credit reach the exporters at an affordable interest rate. For the development of export growth and to make the product internationally competitive, the government has come up with an interest equalization scheme, effective from April 2015. Prior to that, there was a scheme, namely, interest subvention scheme, operational from 2007 to 2010. The government encourages commercial banks to finance the credit requirements of exporters and to provide the packing credit to those sectors on which export growth depends. Export credit is, therefore, made available by commercial banks at a concessional rate of interest. Besides, the RBI has prescribed that the individual banks need to extend credit as conscious credit planning. In view of the high degree of importance attached to export finance in Indian economy, the RBI monitors the position of the outstanding export credit facilities provided by individual commercial banks on a regular basis. In the following sections, therefore, we discuss the salient provisions covering export finance. Our discussions shall, however, be mainly confined to the rupee export credit facilities provided by the banks and foreign currency lending to the exporters.

An exporter may require credit facility for completion of export contracts at two stages, namely, pre-shipment and post-shipment. The pre-shipment credit facility, as defined by the RBI, is provided for working capital requirements required till the shipment stage, namely, for purchase of raw materials, processing, manufacturing, packaging, transportation and warehousing of goods meant for exports. On the other hand, post-shipment credit facility, as the name suggests, is the facility extended by the commercial banks to the exporter after the goods are shipped. Post-shipment credit extended by banks takes care of the working capital requirements of the exporter. At the post-shipment stage, the credit is locked in the form of export receivables and the period is counted as the period from the shipment of goods to the realization of export proceeds. In respect of stand-alone export orders (may be backed by confirmed LCs), disbursement of the post-shipment liquidates the outstanding balance in the pre-shipment credit account of the exporter. Therefore, it can be said that pre-shipment credit is nothing but the self-liquidating advance. The outstanding balance in the post-shipment credit, in its turn, gets liquidated from the realization proceeds of the export bill. This may also be in the form of foreign bills purchasing/negotiating limits provided against LCs drawn on the financing bank. The commercial bank has to ensure the end use of the export credit. Export credit should not be extended for funding investments such as import of foreign technology, equipment, land development and so on, or any other item that cannot be regarded as a financing working capital requirement.

7.17.1 Pre-shipment Credit

As per the definition of the RBI, pre-shipment or packing credit can be defined as the following:

"Pre-shipment/packing credit means any loan or advance granted or any other credit provided by a bank to an exporter for financing the purchase, processing, manufacturing of packing of goods prior to shipment or estimated cost of working capital expenditure required for the proposed service on the basis of an LC opened in his or her favor or in favor of same other person, by an overseas buyer or a confirmed and irrevocable order for the export of goods/services from India or any other evidence of an order from export from India having been placed on the exporter or some other person, unless lodgment of export orders or LC with the bank has been waived".

Pre-shipment finance can be broadly classified into the following:

- Packing Credit in INR
- Advance against Duty Drawback Entitlements and
- Packing Credit in Foreign Currency (PCFC)

According to the guidelines prescribed by the RBI, within 45 days from the date of receipt of application seeking export credit limit, the sanction of fresh/ enhanced export credit limits should be made. Such application, should, however, be accompanied with the required details and information supported by financial/operating statements. In case the credit application is for renewal of limits or ad-hoc credit limits, the time taken by the banks should not exceed 30 days and 15 days respectively in that order.

Packing credit can be sanctioned either against irrevocable LC or against a confirmed order. Commercial banks feel more comfortable if the eligible exporters are able to provide irrevocable LCs established by the foreign buyers or importers in favor of the exporter through an internationally reputed bank. Copies of confirmed orders or contracts placed by the foreign buyers to the Indian exporters may also be accepted by the financing banks for the purpose. Appraisal of working capital requirements in the form of pacing credit is done in the usual manner using the holding level approach. However, the interest rate in packing credit in INR for a mid-corporate is much lower, ranging from 10%–16% than the otherwise available working capital loan 17%–22%.

In course of appraisal, the financing banks themselves decide the period for which a packing credit advance may be given after considering the various relevant factors including holding periods and so on. This is to ensure that the period is sufficient to enable the exporter to ship the goods. Exporting borrowers must ensure that the pre-shipment credit is adjusted by submission of export documents within 360 days from the date of advance, failing which the concessive credit facility from banks will not be available to them.

In course of disbursement, ordinarily, each packing credit sanctioned should be maintained as a separate account. This facilitates a proper monitoring of the period for which the packing credit has been availed and also the end use of funds. The following points are important in the context of disbursement of export credit facilities:

- Packing credit may be released in one lump sum or in stages as per the requirement for executing the orders/LC, depending upon operating cycle of the goods/services.

- Lending banks may also maintain different accounts in tune with their lending practices at various stages of processing and manufacturing, etc. This may depend on the type of goods to be exported and also the type of charge over the current assets, for example, hypothecation, pledge and so on. Lending banks have to ensure that the outstanding balance in all such accounts are adjusted by transfer from one account to the other and finally by proceeds of relative export documents on purchase/ discounts etc.

However, it may happen that the LCs or the orders are delayed on account of some reasons. However, the reasons to be checked by the bank granting the packing credit. Currently, to deal with such cases, the RBI permits commercial banks to grant advances without lodgment of LCs or confirmed order/contract at the initial stage. However, this facility is granted only if the financing banks are satisfied about the track record of the exporter and also if the bank is convinced about the genuineness of the reasons for delayed submission of LC/orders. In case of exporters of repute, banks may accept information by way of cable/telex as the relevant evidence of the LC, confirmed order or the contract which are expected in near future. Such communication however, should contain the following minimum information:

- Name of the Buyer

- Value of the Order

- Quantity and Particulars of the Goods to be Exported

- Date of Shipment

- Terms of Payment

The financing banks should follow up the submission of the final contract/LC when these are available.

The RBI has prescribed these liberalized steps in the running account facility recently introduced in the context of export credit. However, the concerned exporter is under obligation to submit monthly statements of outstanding export orders vis-à-vis EPC/PCFC availed.

Running account packing credit facility (RAPC) is maintained on FIFO (first in first out) principle. The outstanding packing credit can be cleared by submission of export documents even if packing credit is not disbursed against the said order. In other words, outstanding packing credit is cleared immediately on submission of documents irrespective of fact whether the export packing credit is availed against the shipment or not. Any packing credit disbursed can be cleared by any shipment provided the export is FTP and FEMA compliant.

Factors to be taken into account while assessing export credit requirements:

1. The factors such as capacity, viability, integrity and past performance of the exporter.

2. The exporter should have registered with the DGFT and obtained an IEC number, and possess membership of the relevant Federation of Indian Export Organization (FIEO)/Promotion council or any of its regional outfits.

3. The exporter should not figure in the specific approval list of ECGC. In case it does, specific approval of ECGC is required for covering any fresh credit exposure is taken in favor of the unit.

4. Similarly, if the name of the exporter figures in the caution list circulated by the RBI, the lending bank has to take their permission before a fresh credit exposure is taken in favor of the unit.

5. The quantum of incentives receivable is a very important aspect of a credit proposal and very often, the overall viability of the proposal depends on it. The quantum of export incentives should be properly factored in the assessment of EPC.

6. The capacity of the exporter to execute the orders as per the agreed time schedule needs to be properly assessed on the basis of installed capacity, availability of raw material and so on.

7. The general level of preparedness of the exporter for adhering to quality requirement may prove crucial, as nonpayment by the purchaser on account of deficiency in quality of the exported commodity are not insurable.

8. The county risk aspects have to be borne in mind as well. ECGC cover may not be offered to those country having very high country risk.

9. The credit officer should verify the necessary allotments in case the exporter deals in quota items.

10. If the EPC is extended under consortium arrangement, once the consortium has approved the assessment of the limits, it may perhaps be necessary to initiate action for completing the sanction process by individual bank forthwith, as time is a crucial factor especially in case of an export transaction. The exchange risk in realization of foreign exchange also needs to be looked into.

7.17.1.1 Quantum of Finance

As for quantum, the golden rule is "need-based." The credit officer would need to take care of the following aspects while assessing the quantum of finance against EPC:

1. At the time of sanction/renewal of credit facilities in the usual manner, the EPC limits are also assessed as part of the overall credit requirements (working capital assessment), with justifications for the limits arrived at. In the case of borrowers having both domestic and export business together, it is necessary to ensure that the export credit facility is commensurate with the past and projected volume of export business vis-à-vis the domestic turnover. The level of utilization of the export credit facility during the preceding year and the general conduct of the account should also be examined in this regard.

2. Sometimes, it may be necessary to allow inter-changeability between domestic and export credit limits, where the unit has both domestic and export operation. Similarly, inter-changeability between pre-and post-shipment export credit also may be allowed at the time of sanctions itself, if necessary.

3. EPC loans are usually restricted to the lower of 90% of FOB value of the contract, or the domestic cost of production. In the export of Hand – picked and selected (HPS) groundnut, de-oiled and de-fatted cakes, the disbursements may be allowed up to the value of raw material required. The excess amount disbursed should be liquidated by sale proceeds locally, within 30 days in case of oils and 15 in case of groundnuts.

4. Relaxations in respect of net working capital (NWC), current ratio could be permitted if the unit is otherwise healthy with acceptable levels of profitability and cash flows. Inadequacy or nonavailability of collateral cannot be a ground for rejecting a proposal for export finance.

5. The period of credit would depend on the manufacturing/trade/operating cycle. This should not however, normally exceed 180 days, which may be relaxed up to a maximum period of 360 days on merits. As part of the special financial package prescribed by the RBI, which is currently in vogue, pre-shipment credit could be extended up to 365 days for large value exports of products relating to pharmaceuticals, agrochemicals, transport equipment, iron and steel, electrical machinery, leather and textiles packing credit beyond 365 days may be considered if operating cycle so warrants only after obtaining prior permission from ECGC.

7.17.1.2 Pre-shipment Credit in Foreign Currency (PCFC)

The scheme of providing EPC facility in designated foreign currencies is popularly known as Pre-Shipment Credit in Foreign Currency (PCFC). This scheme enables the exporters to avail packing credit in foreign currencies at the interest rates prevailing in the international market through ADs (LIBOR). The scheme covers the input cost of the items exported, both the domestic procurement cost as well as the cost of imported inputs of exported gods. Exporters normally resort to this mode of finance when they feel that INR may not depreciate much in comparison to the currency in which the credit is denominated during the life of the credit. It is because, this would mean a higher amount of payment in rupee terms to be made by the borrower to the lending bank at the time of liquidation of the PCFC loan, which leads to a reduced profit.

7.17.1.3 Who Are Eligible?

All exporters who have firm export orders/irrevocable LCs with them are normally eligible for PCFC. This is, of course, subject to their satisfactory compliance with the other credit norms. PCFC is part of the total EPC limit provided to the exporter and, therefore, the conditions regarding the eligibility of exporters for running account EPC facility (exporters with good track record) is also equally applicable in this regard. PCFC facility (exporters with good track record) is also equally applicable in these regards. PCFC can be provided to a manufacturer/supplier against an LC or an export order received by a separate export order holder. PCFC can also be made available to the EOUs/units located in SEZs.

7.17.1.4 Mode of Availability of PCFC

PCFC is made available in the form of cash credit advance. Initially, PCFC is made available for a maximum period of 180 days as in the case of rupee export credit. PCFC can be availed in US dollar ($, pound sterling, EURO and Japanese Yen for the time being; if EPC has already been provide to an existing customer, the PCFC limit can be carved out of the existing EPC limits available to them. One should ensure that the total outstanding balance covering both the rupee and foreign currency facilities (converted at the prescribed notional rate of the lending bank) does not exceed the total EPC limit sanctioned.

Though the Rupee EPC (in part) may be provided against the same export order in order to meet the domestic and imported input cost elements separately, it is important to ensure to that the withdrawals already made against the Rupee EPC running account facility earlier is not converted into PCFC advances. Beside, before allowing PCFC facility to an exporter, a due diligence exercise to find out that the exporter has not availed PCFC/Export Bill Rediscounting Scheme (EBR) with any other bank in respect of the export order in question always makes sense.

Exporters desirous of availing PCFC are obligated to discount the export bills under EBR to enable them to repay the outstanding infringe currency.

7.17.1.5 Interest Rates Covering PCFC

The rate of interest to be charged on PCFC accounts is generally linked to the six months LIBOR/EUROLIBOR/EURIBOR rate a on the date of disbursement with a spread considered appropriate by the lending bank.

Besides, lending banks also recover transaction charges over and above the interest.

Since the interest rates on the loans are linked to LIBOR rates prevailing at the time of PCFC disbursals, it is necessary to raise the foreign currency funds through the foreign offices of the lending bank on the same day in respect of the disbursals made at the branches. The profitability of the lending bank inherent in the PCFC lending scheme, therefore, depends largely on the prompt and accurate reporting of the figures (including the maturity profile of the PCFC) for reconciliation.

In case of any extension of the credit, lending banks usually chare an additional interest over the spread initially charges by them above the six-month LIBOR ruling at the time of extension for the extended period. If no export takes place even within 365 days, PCFC is adjusted at the ruling TT selling rate for the currency concerned. Interest right from the date of disbursement until the date of payment should be recovered at 2% over the interest rate applicable for the cash credit of the exporter, and the interest earlier recovered at LIBOR related rates should be adjusted form that. Remittance of foreign exchange for repayment of principal with interest does not require the RBI's prior approval in such cases.

7.17.1.6 Repayment of PCFC

The export bill tendered in respect of export orders against which PCFC has been availed cannot be sent on collection basis. It is, therefore, necessary for the credit officer to ensure that the amount of foreign currency credit provided under the PCFC scheme is repaid out of the proceeds of the related export bill under EBR. However, the RBI has permitted the following relaxations in this regard:

1. It is possible that the exporter has already received advance remittances/separate inward remittances received against the orders in respect of orders against which PCFC has been provided by the lending bank. These remittances can be utilized to liquidate the PCFC. In this regard, care should be taken so that the foreign currency remittances received are not converted into Indian Rupees but the relative cover funds are be transferred to the respective main nostro accounts of the individual lending banks.

2. If the export is sent on collection basis and no PCFC/Packing Credit is provided against the export bills then the proceeds of such export bills can also be applied to liquidate the outstanding balance in the PCFC loan.

3. In the above cases, a declaration should be taken to the effect the he or she has not availed/will not avail PCFC credit facility from any bank against such orders/documents.

4. In case of liquidation of PCFC under the running account facility by advance remittances, effort should be made to restrict such adjustments to PCFC withdrawals which are not outstanding for more than 360 days from the date of withdrawal.

Some of the important issues concerning PCFC are as under:

1. The RBI takes a serious view if an exporter has not utilized the PCFC drawn for export purposes. Besides levying the prescribed penalties, the running account facilities provided to the defaulting export should, therefore, be withdrawn with immediate effect.

2. In a remittance outside the country, the issue of withholding tax may become very important. However, in a PCFC transaction, a lending bank usually avails the foreign line of credit from its own foreign offices. According to a school of thought, payment of interest to its own offices abroad against such line of credit may not therefore involve payment of withholding tax by the exporters.

3. ECGC cover is available in respect of PCFC advance as well. Lending bank branches would therefore do well to include the Rupee outstanding balances in PCFC advance under the Whole Turnover Packing Credit Guarantee (WTPCG) every month.

4. The exporter may book forward contracts also in respect of future PCFC withdrawals. They may also avail cross currency forward contracts in any of the permitted currencies against the invoiced currency in which PCFC is availed by him or her.

5. If a PCFC credit is provided for deemed exports, the exporter should liquidate the outstanding balance in the account by means of EBR within a maximum period of 30 days or up to the date of payment by project authorities, whichever is earlier. The PCFC credit would be governed by the other conditions relating to deemed exports, as in the case of a regular EPC.

7.17.2 Post-shipment Credit

The term post-shipment credit means any loan or advance granted or any other credit provided by lending bank to an exporter of goods from India from the date of extending credit after shipment of goods to the date of realization of export proceeds. Post-shipment credit facilities are generally provided in the form of:

1. Export bill purchased/discounted/negotiated,

2. Advances against bills for collection, and

3. Advances against duty drawback receivable from government.

As we have discussed earlier, outstanding balance in the post-shipment credit facility is liquidated by the proceeds of the export bills received from abroad. The following points are relevant in the context of ascertaining the period of advance in case of rupee post-shipment credit facility:

a. In case of usance bills, the period of advance is the NTP as specified by FEDAI.

b. In case of usance bills, post-shipment credit may be granted for a maximum duration of 180 days from date of shipment. This duration is inclusive of NTP and grace period, if any.

c. NTP means the average period normally involved from the date of negotiation/purchase/ discount till the receipt of bill proceeds in the nostro account of the bank concerned, as prescribed by FEDAI from time to time. NTP should not be treated as the time taken for the arrival of goods at overseas distinction.

7.17.2.1 Advance Against Undrawn Balances on Export Bills

Sometimes, the exporter draws bills on the overseas buyer to an extent of 90% to 98% of the FOB value of the contract in respect of export of certain commodities. The residuary amount is the undrawn balance, which the overseas buyer pays after satisfying himself or herself about quality/quantity of goods. Payment of undrawn balance is contingent in nature in the sense that it would be paid only if the overseas buyer is satisfied about the quality/quantity. However, the RBI allows banks to extend credit against undrawn balances at concessional rate of interest based on their commercial judgment and the track record of the buyer. Such advances are also eligible for concessional rate of interest for a maximum period of 90, days only to the extent of repayment done by actual remittances from abroad. This is subject to the condition that such remittances are received within 90 days after the export NTP in the case of demand bill and the due date in the case of usance bills. If the loan is repaid after 90 days, the rate of interest specified for the category "ECNOS" (Export Credit Not Otherwise Specified) at the post-shipment stage becomes applicable.

7.17.2.2 Advance Against Retention Money

Much like the advances against the undrawn portion of export bill, an exporter may also seek an advance against the retention money payable to him or her. This usually happens in the case of turnkey projects/ construction contracts, where the overseas employer makes progressive payments in respect of the services segment of the contract, and retains a small percentage of the progressive payments as retention money. This amount is payable after expiry of the stipulated period from the date of the completion of the contract. This requires certain certificate(s) from the specified authority. Retention money may also be sometimes stipulated against the supplies portion in the case of turnkey project. Likewise, it may arise in the case of sub-contracts. The payment of retention money is also contingent in nature, it becomes payable only on fulfillment of certain condition. The RBI has laid down the following guidelines which should be followed in case a lending bank considers granting advances against retention money:

1. Banks are not allowed to provide credit against retention money relation to services portion of the contract.

2. To the extent possible, exporters/lending banks should arrange for issuance of suitable guarantees instead of providing credit against retention money.

3. Even in respect of the supplies portion of the contract, granting of advances against retention money should be done on a selective basis. In cases where advance is granted against retention money in such situations, credit officers should take into account the size of the retention money accumulated, its impact on the liquid funds position of the exporter and the past performance

regarding the timely receipt of retention money. Besides, the payment of retention money may be secured by LC or BG where possible.

4. Advance against retention money will be eligible for concessional rate of interest only to the extent the advances are actually repaid by remittances received from abroad relating to the retention money and provided such payments are received within 180 days from the due date of payment of the retention money, according to the terms of the contract.

5. In cases where there retention money is payable within a period of one year from the date of shipment, according to the terms of the contract, interest at the prescribed concessive rates of interest (up to a maximum period of 90 days) becomes applicable. Beyond 90 days, the rate of interest prescribed for the category ECNOS at the post-shipment stage is applicable.

6. Where the retention money is payable after a period of one year from the date of shipment, according to the terms of the contract and the corresponding advance is extended for a period exceeding one year, it will be treated as post-shipment credit given on deferred payment terms exceeding on year, and the rate of interest for that category will apply.

7.17.2.3 Export on Consignment Basis

Export on consignment basis lends scope for a lot of misuse in the matter of repatriation of export proceeds. Therefore, export on consignment basis is treated at par with exports on outright sale basis on cash terms so far as the rate of interest to be charges by banks on post-shipment credit in concerned. The RBI has, therefore, clarified that lending banks will charge appropriate concessive rate of interest only up to the notional due date (depending upon the tenor of the bills), subject to a maximum of 270 days in the case of exports on consignment basis. This will be applicable even if the Foreign Exchange Department grants an extension in the period beyond 270 days for repatriation of export proceeds.

Precious and semi-precious stones, etc. exported mostly on consignment basis and the exporters are not in a position to liquidate pre-shipment credit account with remittances received from abroad within a period of 270 days from the date of advance. It would, therefore, be necessary to adjust packing credit advances in the case of consignment exports, as soon as the export takes place, by transfer of the outstanding balance to a special (post-shipment) account. The balance in this special account should in turn be adjusted as soon as the relative proceeds are received from abroad but not later than 180 days from the date of export or the period extended by the RBI, if any.

7.17.2.4 Post-shipment Advance Against Duty Drawback Entitlement

The government is encouraging exporters, and various incentives are provided to them for this purpose. Exporters enjoy certain duty drawback entitlements as an incentive. The RBI allows commercial banks to grant post-shipment advances to exporters against their duty drawback entitlements as provisionally certified by Customs authorizes pending final section and payment. The advance against duty drawback receivables can also be made available to exporters against export promotion copy of the shipping bill containing the EGM number issued by the customs department. The financing bank usually makes arrangement for noting lien with the designated bank. The designated bank then transfers funds to the financing banks as and when duty drawback is credited by Customs. Credit provided against duty drawback entitlements is also for concessional rate of interest and refinance from the RBI up to a maximum period of 90 days from the date of advance.

7.17.2.5 Post-shipment Export Credit in Foreign Currency

EBR is a post-shipment credit in foreign currency provided by lending banks to their exporter customers. This scheme allows banks to rediscount export bills aboard at rates linked to international interest rates at the post-shipment stage. In the EBR scheme, it is convenient to provide a facility against the bills portfolio (covering all eligible bills) than to have rediscounting facility abroad on a bill by bill basic. The RBI, however, allows banks to provide the facility even on a bill-to-bill basis in case of specific exporters, especially for large value transactions.

Besides, the exporters can also arrange for themselves a line of credit with an overseas bank or any other agency (including a factoring agency) for discounting their export bills direct on their own. They have to satisfy the following term and conditions in this regard:

1. Direct discounting of export bills by exporters with overseas bank and/or any other agency will be done only through the branch of a bank designated by him or her for this purpose.

2. Discounting of export bills will be routed through the designated bank that has provided the packing credit facility. In case these are routed through any other bank, the latter will first arrange to adjust the amount outstanding under packing credit with the concerned bank out of the proceeds of the rediscounted bills.

The salient features of the EBR scheme are discussed below:

Eligibility: The scheme covers mainly export bills with usance period up to 270 days from the date of shipment (inclusive of normal transit period and grace period, if any) demand bills can also be included if the overseas institution does not object to it, EBR facility may be offered in any convertible currency and banks have been allowed by the RBI to extend the EBR facility for exports to ACU countries.

Utilization of on-shore funds: Lending banks can utilize the foreign exchange resources available with tem in EEFC Resident Foreign Currency Accounts (RFC), Foreign Currency (Nonresident) Accounts (Banks) Scheme, to discount usance bills and retain them in their portfolio without resorting to rediscounting. In the case of demand bills, these need to be routed through the existing post-shipment credit facility or by way of foreign exchange loans to the exporters out of the foreign currency balances available with banks.

7.18 Interbank Market for Rediscounting

To facilitate the growth of local market of rediscounting export bill, the establishment and development of an active interbank market is desirable. It is possible that banks hold bills in their own portfolio without rediscounting. However, in case of need, the banks should also have access to the local market which will enable the country to save foreign exchange to the extents of the cost of rediscounting. Further, as different banks may be having bank's acceptance facility (BAF) for varying amounts, there may arise a situation when a bank that has balance available in its limit may offer rediscounting facility to another bank which may have exhausted its limit or could not arrange for such a facility. The RBI has, therefore, allowed banks to avail lines of credit from other banks in India if they are not in a position to raise loans from abroad on their own, or they do not have branches abroad. The ceiling on borrowing cost to the exporter is 0.75% above LIBOR/ERO LIBOR/EURIBOR excluding withholding tax. The borrowing and lending bank may, however, fix the spread as per their discretion.

Further, in view of the fact that it may be difficult to get the bills rediscounted "without recourse" facility from abroad under BAF, the RBI has permitted commercial bank to rediscount "with recourse."

Accounting Aspects: As per the provisions of EBR, the lending bank pays the rupee equivalent of the discounted value of the export bills to the exporter which is utilized to liquidate the outstanding export packing credit. As the discounting of bills/extension of foreign exchange loans (DP bill) is in actual foreign exchange, the appropriate spot rate is applied for the transactions. The rupee equivalent of discounted amounts/ foreign exchange loan is now held in the banks books distinct from the existing post-shipment credit account. In case of overdue bills, the RBI allows banks to charge 2% above the rate of rediscounting of foreign exchange loan from the due date to the date of crystallization. The applicable rate of interest is as per the RBI interest rate directive for post-shipment credit in rupees. This is applicable from the date of crystallization. In case the export-bill is not paid, the RBI allows the lending bank to remit the amount (equivalent to the value of the bill earlier discounted) to the oversea bank/agency which had discounted the bill without the prior approval of the RBI.

7.19 Gold Card Scheme for Exporters

In order to provide a boost to exports, it is necessary that export credit is made easily available on best terms to exporters with good track record. The gold card scheme has been drawn up for this purpose. The scheme envisages certain additional benefits based on the record of performance of the exporters. The cold card holder would enjoy a simpler and more efficient credit delivery mechanism in recognition of his or her good track record. The salient features of the scheme are the following:

1. All creditworthy exporters, including those in small and medium sectors with good track record and satisfying the laid down conditions are eligible for issue of gold card by individual banks.

2. Depending on their track record and credit worthiness, gold card holder exporters will be granted better terms of credit including rate of interest than those extended to other exporters by the banks.

3. Applications for credit are processed at norms simpler and under a process faster than for other exporters. Individual banks are required to clearly specify the benefits offered by them to cold card holders. The charges, schedule and fee structure in respect of services provided by banks to exporters under the scheme also would be at a relatively lower level than those provided to other exports.

4. The sanction and renewal of the limits under the scheme will be based on a simplified procedure to be decided by the banks. Taking into account the anticipated export turnover and track record of the exporter, the banks would determine need-based finance with a liberal approach, for this purpose. "In principle" limits will be sanctioned for a period of three years with a provision for automatic renewal (technical review) subject to fulfillment of the terms and condition of sanction.

5. A standby limit should additionally be made available to facilitate urgent credit needs for executing sudden orders to the extent of minimum 20% of the assessed limit. In the case of exporters of seasonal commodities, the peak and off-peak level may be appropriately specified. Similarly, in case of unanticipated export orders, norm for inventory may be relaxed taking into account the size and nature of the export order.

6. Requests from card holders should be processed quickly by banks within 25 days, 15 days and 7 days for fresh applications/renewal of limits and adhoc limits, respectively.

7. Banks would consider waiver of collaterals and exemption from ECGC guarantee schemes on the basis of card holder's creditworthiness and track record. The facility of further value addition to their cards through supplementary services such as ATMs, Internet baking and international debit/credit cards may be decided by the issuing banks.

Gold card holders would be given preference for grant of packing of credit in foreign currency (PCFC). Similarly, their request for issuance of foreign currency credit cards for meeting urgent payment obligations etc. would also be given priority by banks on the basis of their track record of timely realization of export bills. Lending banks would give priority to their PCFC requirement over the loan against Foreign Currency Nonresident Account (Bank) FCNR (B) funds etc. provided to nonexporter customer.

References and Resources

Interest equalization scheme. Retrieved on January 31, 2017, from https://www.rbi.org.in/Scripts/BS_CircularIndex Display.aspx?Id=10159

Master circular on export gods and services. Retrieved on January 31, 2017, from ehttps://rbidocs.rbi.org.in/rdocs/ notification/PDFs/APD6883071E462E56498C99FF8DDB9DD8A916.PDF

Master circular: Rupee/foreign currency export credit and customer service to exporters. Retrieved on January 31, 2017, from rbi.org.in

QUESTIONS

Answer the Following Questions

1. What is Exchange Earner Foreign Currency Account or EEFC Account and Diamond Dollar Account? Explain.

2. Explain the salient features of advance payment against export. What would be the tenure of the advance payment? Is there any exception?

3. Explain about the consignment export.

4. Write about the main features of counter trade agreement.

5. Describe the main characteristics of export of goods and services by SEZs.

6. Write the project exports and service exports.

7. Write a brief note about the export of currency.

8. Write a brief note about the counter-trade arrangements with Romania.

9. Write the procedure of netting off' of export receivables against import payments units in SEZs.

10. Write the process to change of buyer/consignee.

11. Explain the salient features of export finance.

12. What is pre-shipment and post-shipment credit?

13. Explain the advance against undrawn balances on export bills.

14. Describe the characteristics.

15. What is advance against retention money?

16. Explain the process of post-shipment advance against duty drawback entitlement.

17. Post-shipment export credit in foreign currency.

18. Write the gold card scheme for exporters.

19. Write about interest subvention scheme and interest equalization scheme.

Chapter

8

Trade Credit: Buyer's Credit and Suppliers Credit for Import Financing

8.1 Trade Credit

Trade credits (TC) refer to credits extended for imports, permissible under the extant FTP, directly by the overseas supplier, bank, and financial institution for maturity up to five years. Depending on the source of finance, such trade credits include suppliers' credit or buyers' credit. Suppliers' credit relates to credit for imports into India extended by the overseas supplier, while buyers' credit refers to loans for payment of imports into India arranged by the importer from a bank or financial institution outside India.

It may be noted that buyers' credit and suppliers' credit for three years and above come under the category of external commercial borrowings (ECB) which are governed by ECB guidelines issued vide A.P. (DIR Series) Circular No. 60 dated January 31, 2004 and modified from time to time.

8.1.1 Amount and Maturity

- Maximum Amount Per Transaction: Upto US$20 million per transaction for all items permissible for imports.

- Maximum Maturity in Case of Import of Noncapital Goods: Up to one year from the date of shipment or up to the operating cycle, whichever is lower.

- Maximum Maturity in Case of Import of Capital Goods: Up to five years from the date of shipment with contract period of six months.

- Roll-over/Extension: No roll-over/extension can be permitted by the AD Category–I bank beyond the permissible period.

8.1.2 All-in-cost Ceilings

The all-in-cost ceilings include the arranger fee, upfront fee, management fee, handling/processing charges, and out of pocket and legal expenses, if any. The existing all-in-cost ceilings are as under.

Maturity period: Up to one year—All-in-cost ceilings over six months LIBOR* is 350 basis points.

More than one year and up to three years—All-in-cost ceilings over six months LIBOR* is 350 basis points.

More than three years and up to five years—All-in-cost ceilings over six months LIBOR* is 350 basis points.

Note: * for the respective currency of credit or applicable benchmark.

8.1.3 Guarantees

- AD banks are permitted to issue an LCs/guarantees/letters of undertaking (LoUs)/letters of comfort (LoCs) in favor of an overseas supplier, bank, and financial institution, up to USD 20 million per transaction; however, the tenure is different for capital and noncapital goods.

  o **For noncapital goods:** For a period up to one year for import of all noncapital goods permissible under FTP (except gold, palladium, platinum, Rhodium, silver and so on).

  o **For capital goods:** Up to three years for import of capital goods, subject to prudential guidelines issued by the RBI from time to time. The period of such LCs/guarantees/LoUs/LoCs has to be coterminus with the period of credit, reckoned from the date of shipment.

Tenure beyond three years: The AD banks are not permitted to issue LCs/guarantees/LoUs/LoCs in favor of an overseas supplier, bank, and financial institution for the extended period beyond three years.

AD banks are required to furnish data on issuance of LCs/guarantees/LoUs/LoCs by all its branches, in a consolidated statement, at quarterly intervals.

8.2 Trade Credit for Infrastructure Sector

Companies in the infrastructure sector (where "infrastructure" is as defined under the extant guidelines on ECB) are allowed to avail trade credit up to a maximum period of five years for import of capital goods as classified by DGFT, subject to the following conditions:

1. The trade credit is allowed only if the contracted period is not less than 15 months and should not be in the nature of short-term roll-overs; and

2. In such case, when trade credit for the import of capital goods is extended, *beyond three years*, AD banks are not permitted to issue LCs/guarantees/LoUs/LoCs in favor of an overseas supplier, bank, and financial institution for the extended period.

8.3 Buyer's Credit

It is an import financing facility. This loan is extended to the importer towards the payment for import coming to India. According to the definition of the RBI, buyer's credit refers to loans for payment of imports into India arranged on behalf of the importer through an overseas bank.

For example, under buyer's credit, the offshore branch credits the NOSTRO of the bank in India, and the Indian bank uses the funds and makes the payment to the exporter's bank as an import bill payment on the due date. The importer reflects the buyers' credit as a loan on the balance sheet.

8.3.1 Benefits of Buyer's Credit

The benefits of buyer's credit for the importer are as follows:

*   If importer has to arrange the loan from the domestic market for his or her import payment, then it might be much costlier than the loan from the international market. So, we can say that the most important factor for which the importer goes for buyers' credit is interest cost saving.

*   Many a times, it is much beneficial for the exporter who might be in urgent need of working capital finance. Under buyer's credit facility, the exporter can get early payment or immediate payment on the due date, whereas the importer gets extended date for making an import payment as per the cash flows.

*   The importer can deal with the exporter on sight basis, negotiate a better discount, and use the buyer's credit route to avail financing.

*   Depending on the preference of the customer, the funding currency can be in any foreign currency, for example, USD, GBP, EURO, JPY, and so on.

- The importer can use this financing for any type of payment mechanism, namely open account, documentary collections, or LCs.

- The currency of imports can be different from the funding currency, which enables importers to take a favorable view of a particular currency.

8.3.2 Buyer's Credit Process Flow

In international trade, an Indian importer can import goods under documentary credit/LC, documentary collections (both DA and DP), direct documents/ on open account basis.

- To avail buyer's credit finance, an Indian importer may request the buyer's credit consultant/agent before the due date of the bill.

- The consultant approaches an overseas bank for indicative cost of the credit. A competitive cost is intimated to the importer.

- If pricing is acceptable to the importer, the overseas bank issues an offer letter in the name of the importer. Let us assume that the invoice is in USD. So, an Indian importer has to pay in USD. This is possible only by debiting the nostro account of the bank.

- The importer, say A, approaches his or her existing bank, say the Bank of Baroda, to get either the LoU, issued in favor of overseas bank, for example City Bank, New York, or the LoC, issued in favor of the importer's bank subsidiary, for instance, the Bank of Baroda, New York via swift.

- On receipt of the LoU/LoC, the overseas bank, as per instruction provided in the LoU/LoC, will either fund the Bank of Baroda, India's nostro account or pay the supplier's bank, say, HSBC, New York, directly.

- If SBI India's client takes buyers' credit from SBI's overseas branches, SBI India will give an LoC, whereas if the funding is arranged from say Bank of India, overseas branches, SBI India will give an LoU.

- A cross-currency contract is utilized to effect the import payment by utilizing the amount credited (if the borrowing currency is different from the currency of imports then).

- On the due date, the existing bank is to recover the principal and interest amount from the importer and remit the same to the overseas bank on the due date.

8.3.3 Can Buyer's Credit be Availed from any Bank, Including the LC Opening Bank?

- Buyer's credit can be taken from any bank, including LC opening bank overseas branches. But few banks are insisting on taking buyers' credit from their own overseas branches or they are creating differential pricing for LoU.

- In case of LoU, capital requirement under Basel III is more, compared to LoC which is issued in case of parent subsidiary relationship.

- Normally, importers have a comparative view for choosing between LoC or LoU. However, a comparison based on the interest cost provided by a foreign bank (Indian bank overseas branches or foreign bank) on deciding which offer to accept may not be always the right approach. Importers should look at the overall cost. Overall cost would be foreign bank interest cost and LoU charges of your bank. For instance, a customer having limits with Bank of Baroda and getting letter of comfort (LoC) or undertaking issued from them for buyer's credit.

8.4 Difference Between Letter of Comfort (LoC) and Letter of Undertaking (LoU)

Particular	Letter of Comfort	Letter of Undertaking
Definition	LoC is referred to a document which is provided by a partner in subsidiary relationship of the LoC Provider that is the importer's bank, assuring the financial soundness of the borrower to repay its debt(s).	A contract to perform the promise, or discharge the liability, of a third person in case of his default
Parties	Between Branches or Partner Subsidiary; SBI and SBI overseas branches	Inter-Bank; for example between SBI and HSBC, or SBI and City bank
Basel III	Low Provisioning	High Provisioning
Interest Charges to Customer	Low	High

8.4.1 LoC and LoU: A Comparison

Is it necessary that LoC is always having lower cost than the LoU: An example of the cost incurred by the importer: LoC/LoU charges of XYZ branches.

- Buyer's credit availed with XYZ branches at the interest cost 1% p.a.

- Buyer's credit availed with ABC overseas banks at the interest cost 1.5% p.a.

Say 90 days LIBOR is 0.25%.
For the importer's bank, say, XYZ Indian bank.

- XYZ Bank offer: L+1.50.
  Overall cost in case of XYZ Bank BC: 0.25+1.50+1.50=3.25%.

- ABC branch: L+1.75.
  Overall cost in case of ABC Overseas: 0.25+1.75+1=3.00%.

- As you see in the example, even after ABC overseas branch cost was higher, the overall transaction cost for the customer is still cheaper.

Issuance of buyer's credit limit as a sub limit to the LC.

- All banks have different buyer's credit limits. Precisely, buyer's credit is used by issuing LoU or LoC. LoU/LoC which forms a part of nonfund-based limit and is a type of financial guarantee.

- Sometimes banks classify them under sub-limits of LC or BG, and sometimes they are classified under nonfund-based limits in the name of buyer' credit.

Case Study

- A bank has opened an import LC for importing raw material which is due for payment on December 27, 2016. Now the importer has requested the bank to convert the LC as buyer's credit payable after 180 days as the rate for realization of LC is costly. Is the request of the importer correct?

- The RBI Master Circular on External Commercial Borrowing and Trade Credit says that the AD can approve trade for import of raw material up to 360 days from date of shipment. For the approval of any tenure as buyer's credit, it depends on the working capital cycle of the importer, which is ascertained by the bank at the time of sanctioning of limits. So, if the sanction limits say tenure of 180 days from the day of shipment, then it cannot be allowed beyond 180 days.

- If the branch is convinced about a particular case there may be an extension. A bank can go back to credit manager/approving authority for extension of tenure beyond 180 days with justification. Once approved, the same can be converted to buyer's credit for further approved tenure. Again, specific to this case, LC was due on December 29, 2016 and the question was asked on January 2, 2017, which means already there is delay of four days on the payment. Banks should go ahead and make the payment immediately.

8.5 Buyer's Credit in Cross Currency

International trade is carried out in USD, EUR, JPY, and other currencies. But when it comes to arranging buyer's credit against USD and EUR, it is much easier. Buyer's credit in these two currencies is available with better price range. Also, there are always more options of banks to choose from than in other currencies. But even with the above understanding, at times it is not possible to transact in these currencies and thus cross-currency buyers' credit is required.

8.6 Difference Between Buyer's Credit and LC

- *Definition:*

  o LC is one of the payment methods used in the international trade between the importer and the exporter in which the bank undertakes to pay the payment obligation on behalf of the importer if the documents are complied. It means that even if the importer defaults, his or her bank will have to pay on his or her behalf.

o   Whereas, buyer's credit is a funding mechanism used by the importer to fund his or her transaction. Buyer credit is available under LC payment method. Also, it is available with other payment methods, such as documentary collection and open method.

- *Parties involved during the transaction:*

    o   Under LC: Importer, Importer's Bank, Exporter, Exporters Bank

    o   Under Buyers Credit: Importer, Importer's Bank, Foreign Bank funding the transaction

- *Transaction flow*:

    o   Under LC, there is movement of goods between export and import and movement of documents and funds between importers bank and exporters' bank. Whereas in buyers' credit, there is only movement of fund.

- *Bank charges:*

    o   Under LC, the transaction bank charges LC commission and usance charges (mainly with PSU). In case of buyer's credit, bank charges LoC/LoU charges. In addition to these charges, the foreign bank charges its interest cost.

    o   LC is governed by UCP 600 issued by the ICC. Every LC has a mention of the same. In case of any dispute between importer's bank and exporter's bank, norms given in UCP 600 becomes the guiding factors to resolve the cases. However, there is no specific governing rule for LoU or LoC. Letter of comfort does not mention any specific rules.

8.7 In Which Case Buyer's Credit is Not Allowed

- In case of local trade.

- Advance payment for imports: Buyer's credit for any amount paid as advance either part or full is not allowed as per the RBI Circular on External Commercial Borrowing and Trade Credit.

- Any advance payment is always made before shipment of goods. And thus, not allowed.

- Not allowed for import of services.

8.8 Type of Transaction Where Buyer's Credit Can be Availed for Limited Amount

- If the *import bill is directly received* by importer from his or her overseas supplier, the buyers' credit amount is restricted up to $ 300,000.

Except for:

- If the import bill is received by wholly owned Indian subsidiary of foreign companies from their principal.

- If the import bill is received by status holder exporters as defined in the FTP, 100% export-oriented units, units in special economic zones, public sector undertakings and limited companies.

- Import bills received by all limited companies, namely, public limited companies, deemed public limited and private limited companies.

8.9 Availability of Buyer's Credit for Limited Tenure

- As per RBI guidelines, buyer's credit and suppliers credit is not likely to exceed 90 days from the date of shipment for the below goods:

    o   Rough, cut, and polished diamonds

    o   Gold

    o   Silver, platinum, palladium, rhodium

8.10 Supplier's Credit

Supplier's credit relates to credit for imports into India extended by the overseas suppliers or financial institutions outside India. Under supplier's credit, bills issued by the Indian bank branches on behalf of their importers are discounted by Indian bank overseas branches or foreign banks. This supplier's credit facilitates the payment to the suppliers at sight against usance bill under LC transaction.

8.10.1 Why Required?

- Suppliers requires sight payment, whereas importers wants credit on the transaction.

- At times, in capital goods, banks would insist on using the term loan instead of buyer's credit. This way you can avail cheap LIBOR rate funds and your supplier would also not mind as he or she is getting funds at sight.

8.10.2 Benefits/Advantages

- *For Importer:*

    o   Availability of cheaper funds for import of raw materials and capital goods

    o   Ease short-term fund pressure as able to get credit

    o   Ability to negotiate better price with suppliers

    o   Able to meet the suppliers' requirement of payment at sight.

- *For Supplier:*

    o   Realize at-sight payment

    o   Avoid the risk of importer's credit by making settlement with the bank.

8.10.3 Process Flow of Transaction

With transaction details, the importer approaches the arranger to get supplier's credit for the transaction.

- The arranger gets an offer from the overseas bank on the transaction.

- The importer confirms on pricing to the overseas bank and gets an LC issued from his or her bank, restricted to overseas bank counters with other required clauses.

- The supplier ships the goods and submits the documents at his or her bank counters.

- The supplier's bank sends the documents to the supplier's credit bank.

- The supplier's credit bank post checking documents for discrepancies and sends the document to the importer's bank for acceptance.

- The importer accepts the documents. The importer's bank provides acceptance to the supplier's credit bank LC guaranteeing payment on due date.

- The supplier's credit bank, based on acceptance, discounts the bill and makes payment to the supplier.

- On maturity, the importer makes the payment to his or her bank and the importer's bank makes payment to the supplier's credit bank.

8.10.4 Cost Involved (May Vary Bank to Bank)

- Foreign bank interest cost

- Foreign bank LC confirmation cost (case-to-case basis)

- LC advising and or amendment cost

- Negotiation cost (normally in range of 0.10%)

- Postage and swift charges

- Reimbursement charges

- Cost for the usance (credit) tenure. (Indian bank cost)

- RBI regulations, all in cost, amount, and maturity is same as buyer's credit

8.11 Difference between Buyer's Credit and Supplier's Credit

Criteria	Buyers Credit	Suppliers Credit
Mode of Payment	Can be used for payment mode such as LC, LC usance, DA, DP, & Direct Doc	Can be used only in case of LC transactions

LC Clauses	No additional clauses or Amendment is required in LC	At the time of opening LC or amending LC clauses given by Suppliers Credit bank needs to be mentioned; Such as, Negotiation Clause, Confirmation Clause, Reimbursement Clause
Arrangement	Can be arranged after documents have reached the bank or documents are received by Importer directly	Has to be arranged at the time of opening LC
Cost	Interest Cost+LoU/LoC	LC Advising Cost, LC Amendment Charges, Document Processing Charges, Courier Charges, Conformation Cost and Interest Cost

8.12 Case Studies

Case 1

Triotreat Foods Ltd is importing raw material amounting to US$ 10 million on 180 days DA basis for which the supplier has sought immediate payment. Is this permissible? If so, how can the transaction be undertaken?
What are the rules & documentation requirements? What are the risk implications? Risk mitigation?

As per FEMA regulations, imports can be made with maximum CREDIT OF 180 days credit from date of shipment. Hence, 180 days DA is not permissible.

A buyer's credit can be arranged by the bank at the request of the importer, subject to the ceiling of interest rate being within the ceiling of 350 bps over LIBOR for the currency.

The importer, however, is exposed to the exchange rate risk, which can be managed by fully or partially covering the loan and interest amount under the forward contract. The importer's application has to be cleared by the AD under the delegated authority.

The AD bank has to give a unique code number for each loan. Where the amount of credit is exceeding USD 20 MIO or the tenure of loan exceeds one year for noncapital goods, clearance is to be obtained from the RBI (Form TC).

Case 2

Triotreat Foods Ltd is required to import machinery, for which the supplier has sought advance payment of 10% and the balance is to be paid on deferred terms in three years. Is this permissible?
How will the transaction be handled?

Advance payment as sought can be remitted subject to the condition that actual evidence of import is submitted within 180 days.

For supplier's credit of three years, the same can be treated as trade credit and the AD has to consider and approve the seller's credit subject to interest rate ceiling and other conditions of trade credit. The interest payable to the nonresident lender (seller) will be subject to deduction of tax (Sec 195).

Case 3

Triotreat Foods Ltd is required to import raw Material, for which the Supplier has offered credit terms of 90 days. Triotreat Foods, however, desires a total credit period of 180 days. Is this permissible?

Presuming the seller is offering interest free credit period of 90 days, Buyers' credit can be arranged for the remaining 90 days.

Case 4

Slingbag Inc is required to import raw material, for which the supplier has offered credit terms of 270 days. Is this permissible?
How can the transaction be handled?
What are the rules and documentation requirements?
What are the risk implications? Risk mitigation?

For import of noncapital goods payment to the supplier has to be made before 180 days.

Case 5

Stitch-in-time Pvt. Ltd desires to import raw material on 180 days DA terms, but the supplier is not prepared to offer credit. What are the alternatives available to them to raise credit for the transaction? Is this permissible?
    What are the risk-implications? Risk mitigation?

The 180 days DA payment terms are not permissible. The maximum it can be is 180 days from shipment date.
    Supplier can be paid on sight basis and recovery from the importer can be deferred under buyer's credit.
    If buyer' credit is arranged through a foreign bank, the withholding tax is applicable.
    Forward cover for the maturity of loan can be booked in case of a strengthening currency.

Case 6

Smart-o-one Import Inc does not have any exports but does import substantially. Is it possible to minimize the company's borrowing cost? What are the alternatives available and how can they decide upon the most cost-effective method?
    What are the factors that they will need to take into account? What are the risk implications? Risk mitigation?

ECB cannot be availed for liquidating or repaying working capital finance. However, the trade finance route can be utilized to reduce the cost of borrowing. Buyer's credit can be arranged for large value imports. The risk factor would be long term exchange rate risk. Since the importer is not having any foreign exchange earning the exposure is high. The real interest rate applicable has to be valued with reference to the annualized premium rate for the currency.

Case 7

Excel-scent desires to raise foreign currency finance. Is this permissible? What are the alternatives available and what are the attendant rules and regulations?

Is it possible to minimize the company's foreign currency resource cost? What are the alternatives available?

What are the factors that they will need to take into account? What are the risk implications? Risk mitigation?

Excel-scent is eligible to raise a foreign currency loan if it is a limited company engaged in manufacturing sector.

The purpose of the finance should be either for doing capital expenditure or modernization/expansion of the existing project or refinancing existing trade credit for import of capital goods. The finance should be minimum average maturity of three years (maximum 5) and the total cost of finance should not be more than 350 bps over six months LIBOR for the currency of borrowing. The lender should be an international bank or the supplier of the capital goods being financed.

The risk is mainly the exchange fluctuation risk. If the currency of borrowing is prone to volatile fluctuations, the risk can be managed by forward cover or changing the currency of exposure by swap.

Case 8

Wonderful Inc, USA, is an equity holder in India, holding equity of 27%.

Wonderful India desires to avail ECB of US$ 10 million from Wonderful Inc, USA, under automatic route.

Is this permissible? If so, are there any other conditions?

Risk involved and risk mitigation?

Availment of ECB from equity holder is permissible subject to following conditions:

Interest rate: Maximum 500 bps over the six-month LIBOR rate for that currency;

The loan cannot be used for real estate activities or investing in share market or for on lending.

The other conditions (like application through AD for clearance and obtaining UI Code) are applicable as also the reporting through the AD about the withdrawals and repayments are also to be followed.

Risk is mainly the exchange rate risk. A long term hedging either option/forward cover can be considered.

Case 9

Sweet Dreams Hotels Ltd has plans to set up a tourist resort near Ratnagiri and desire to avail ECB of US$ 1 billion for acquiring land for this purpose.

Is this permissible and, if so, whether it would be under automatic route or approval route?

Risk involved and risk mitigation?

ECB cannot be used to acquire land. The amount is also exceeding the ceiling of USD 750 million. The case will be required to be routed through approval route. The application in Form 83 along with the enclosures will have to be forwarded through the AD.

"Peacock Airlines" desires to avail ECB of US$ 800 million from their strategic partner for working capital requirements.

    Is this permitted? If so, what are the conditions to be fulfilled?

This case is not covered under the automatic route. Since the amount is exceeding 700 million, the case will have to be routed through approval route.

References and Resources

RBI notification. Retrieved on January 31, 2017, from http://rbidocs.rbi.org.in/rdocs/notification/PDFs/CDS050511F. pdf

Master circular on external commercial borrowings and trade credit. Retrieved on January 31, 2017 from https://www. rbi.org.in/scripts/BS_ViewMasDirections.aspx?id=10204

Letters of credit. Blog, Retrieved on January 31, 2017, from www.letterofcredit.biz/Types_of_letters_of_credit.html

QUESTIONS

Answer the Following Questions

1. What is trade credit? What is the major difference with external commercial borrowings?

2. What is buyer's credit? Explain the cost structure of buyer's credit.

3. Is there any restriction for availing buyer's credit for capital goods and noncapital goods?

4. Write about the availability of buyer's credit for the infrastructure sector.

5. Explain the process flow of buyer's credit.

6. Explain the process flow when buyer's credit is availed under LoC and under LoU. Give example.

7. Compare the cost borne by the importer under LoC and LoU?

8. What are the differences between LoC and LoU?

9. What is supplier's credit? Can it be opened for all types of payment methods?

10. Explain the process flow under supplier's credit.

11. Write some differences between buyer's credit and supplier's credit.

Merchanting Trade

9.1 Merchanting Trade: Meaning

Merchanting trade, as the term refers to, is essentially intermediary trade. It involves three parties, namely, the buyer, the seller, and the intermediary, who is the facilitator of the trade. In the Indian context, merchanting trade refers to the purchase of goods from one country and sale of the same in another country, where the goods are directly shipped by the supplier to the ultimate buyer. Thus, as these goods do not reach Indian shores, there are no import or export clearance and customs formalities to be completed in India, and there shall be no document substantiating or evidencing import into India and export from India.

The intermediary earns foreign exchange to the extent of the difference between the cost of the import and the earnings from the export.

Example of a merchanting trade transaction: Party "A" in India has sighted "B." a supplier of silk ties in Singapore for the supply of ties. Party "A" also has a ready buyer "C" in Dubai who is willing to buy these ties. Here, party "A" is the intermediary' who undertakes the transaction for earning the difference in the import and export price, which provides the intermediary "A" an opportunity to earn profits.

Suppose the import cost of the ties is USD 3 per piece Cost, Insurance and Freight (CIF) Dubai and the export price per piece is USD 5 per piece CIF Dubai, the intermediary 'A' stands to earn USD 2 per piece CIF Dubai.

9.2 Parties to Merchanting Trade Transaction

1. Supplier: The person/firm overseas that supplies the product.

2. Buyer: The person/firm overseas that buys the product.

3. Intermediary: The facilitator of the trade transaction, who is located in India.

Figure 9.1   Merchanting Trade: Documents and Payment Flow

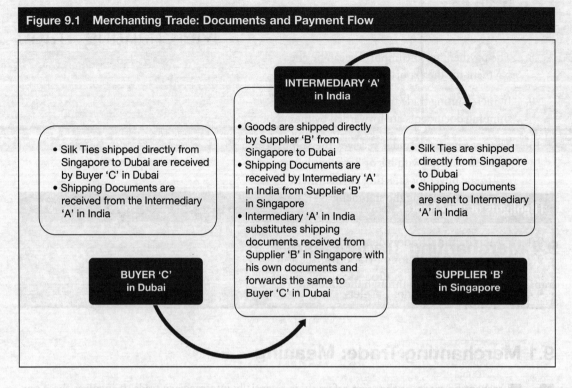

4. Supplier's Bank: The bank through whom the supplier forwards the shipping documents.

5. Intermediary Bank: The bank in India that handles the export and import leg of the transaction, on behalf of the intermediary.

6. Buyers Bank: The bank through whom the shipping documents are routed, for onward delivery to the buyer, as per contractual terms and as instructed by the intermediary's bank.

9.3 Merchanting Trade: Process

1. There are two legs to the merchanting trade transaction—the import leg and the export leg.

2. The intermediary trader, the supplier, and the buyer reside in different countries.

3. The import and the export leg are interlinked but the timing of the payment can be different.

4. The intermediary trader can receive export payment before effecting import payment or he or she can effect import payment first and then receive the export payment subsequently.

5. Import payment can be effected by availing a buyer's credit for the transaction and the export payment can be utilized to repay the buyer's credit.

6. An export order is placed by the buyer upon the intermediary trader who in turn places an import purchase order upon the supplier.

7. The entire transaction can be partly or entirely undertaken under firm order and LC or entirely under back-to-back LC.

8. The payment for the import leg can be effected to the supplier before or after shipment and the payment for the export leg can be received in advance or after shipment has been effected.

9. In merchanting trade transactions, shipment is effected by the supplier directly to the buyer but shipping documents are forwarded by the supplier to the intermediary trader.

10. The intermediary trader receives the shipping documents from the supplier and substitutes these documents with his or her own documents and forwards documents prepared by him or her to the buyer for effecting payment. The buyer can clear the shipment on receipt of shipping documents covering the shipment.

9.4 Merchanting Trade: Caselets

Transaction flow is explained through the following caselets depicting different situations. All the caselets are related to the following flowcharts.

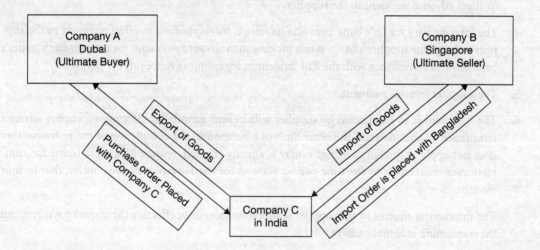

Case 1: Where Export Advance is Received First and Import Payment Too is Made in Advance

1. The export order is received by the intermediary trader and the export advance is also received by him or her from the overseas buyer through the intermediary trader's bank.

2. The import purchase order is placed by intermediary trader upon the overseas supplier.

3. As the supplier insists on immediate payment, the export advance received is utilized for effecting payment to supplier and, accordingly, the intermediary trader instructs his or her bank to effect payment to the supplier.

4. Intermediary trader's bank instructs its nostro correspondent bank to effect payment to the supplier through the supplier's bank.

5. The supplier receives payment.

6. The shipment is to be made by the supplier within four months of effecting of import advance remittance, and in any case within nine months from the date of receipt of export advance by the intermediary trader.

7. The shipment is effected by the supplier within the time prescribed in point (4) and the transaction is completed.

Case 2: Where Import Remittance is Effected in Advance Prior to Receipt of Export Advance

1. The export order is received by the intermediary trader but the export advance is not received by him or her from the overseas buyer.

2. The import purchase order is placed by the intermediary trader upon the overseas supplier.

3. As the supplier insists on immediate payment, the intermediary trader instructs his or her bank to effect advance payment to the supplier.

4. The intermediary trader's bank instructs its nostro correspondent to effect payment to the supplier through the supplier's bank. While making such advance payment, the intermediary trader's bank ensures compliance with the RBI guidelines regarding advance import payments.

5. The supplier receives payment.

6. The shipment is to be effected by supplier within four months of effecting of import advance remittance. In this instance, the outer limit of nine months for completion of entire transaction does not apply as foreign exchange outlay is already effected, reducing the time frame for completion of transaction to the time-period allowed for the Foreign exchange outlay, that is, four months.

7. The shipment is effected by the supplier within four months of effecting the import payment, and the transaction is completed.

Case 3: Where Import Payment is Made Against Sight Documents—Whether Under LC or Not and Export Payment is Received Thereafter

1. The export order is received by the intermediary trader but the export advance is not received by him or her from the overseas buyer.

2. The import purchase order is placed by the intermediary trader upon the overseas supplier.

3. As overseas supplier insists on sight payment, the intermediary trader instructs his or her bank to effect payment to the supplier against the sight documents as and when they are received by the intermediary's bank, whether under sight LC or otherwise.

4.   The supplier effects shipment and forwards sight documents through his or her bank to the intermediary trader's bank.

5.   If the documents are on collection basis, payment is effected to the debit of the suppliers account upon receipt of instructions from the supplier.

6.   If sight LC has already been established by the intermediary trader's bank in favor of the supplier, at the instance of the intermediary trader, the intermediary trader's bank shall, upon receipt of documents, effect import payment to the debit of the intermediary trader's account *provided that the presented documents are in conformity with LC terms.*

   If the documents received under the LC are discrepant documents, the same are to be dealt with in terms of UCP 600 and payment effected in conformity with such provisions.

7.   The intermediary trader substitutes the shipping documents received from the supplier, with documents prepared by him or her for the export leg of the transaction, and forwards these documents to the buyers bank through the intermediary trader's own bank for collecting export payment.

8.   Export payment should be received within four months of effecting of import payment, and the entire transaction should be completed within nine months from date of shipment.

9.   Sometimes the export payment is received even before the documents are submitted by the intermediary trader to his or her bank in India. In such an event, as the goods have been shipped and the export payment is received, the transaction is completed.

10. Alternatively, the buyer receives the export documents and releases export payment which is received by the intermediary trader's bank from the buyer's bank and the transaction is completed.

11. The intermediary trader's bank credits the export payment received to the intermediary trader's account.

12. The transaction is completed.

Case 4: Where Import Payment is Made Against DA Documents—Whether Under LC or Not and Export Payment is Received on Sight Basis

1.   The export order is received by the intermediary trader but the export advance is not received by him or her from the overseas buyer.

2.   The import purchase order is placed by the intermediary trader upon the overseas Supplier.

3.   As overseas Supplier is willing to extend a credit period of 'n' days (not exceeding 180 days) without insisting upon an LC, the Intermediary trader awaits the shipping documents from the supplier.

   If the supplier insists on an LC to cover the credit period, the intermediary trader instructs his or her bank to establish an LC in favor of the overseas supplier on 'n' days DA basis.

4.   The supplier effects shipment and forwards/presents the DA documents through his or her bank to the intermediary trader's bank.

5. Once the documents are received by the intermediary trader's bank, the documents are presented to the intermediary trader for his or her acceptance to pay on due date. The intermediary trader accepts the documents for payment on the due date and due date confirmation is given by the intermediary trader's bank to the supplier's/presenting bank, without any commitment on the part of the bank as regards payment on due date.

   In the event that the DA documents received are under LC and compliant with LC terms, the documents are accepted by the bank for payment to be made on the due date and the documents are released to the intermediary trader and his or her commitment is obtained for payment on the due date. The intermediary trader's bank conveys due-date confirmation to the supplier's/negotiating bank under the LC, with a commitment to pay on due date.

   If the documents received under the LC are discrepant documents, the same shall be dealt with in terms of UCP 600 and acceptance and payment on due date is effected in conformity with such provisions.

6. The intermediary trader substitutes the shipping documents received from the supplier, with documents prepared by him or her for the export leg of the transaction, and forwards these documents to the buyer's bank through the intermediary trader's own bank for collecting the export payment.

7. Export payment should be received within four months of effecting of the import payment, and the entire transaction should be completed within nine months from the date of shipment.

8. The buyer receives the export documents and releases the export payment, which is received by the intermediary trader's bank from the buyer's bank.

   In some cases, the buyer effects payment before the import documents fall due for payment. Such payment, whether received before or after the export documents reach the buyer, can be used to effect import payment—either before due date or on due date.

   If payment is made before due date of the import bill, it shall be in conformity with the provisions relating to pre-payment of import bills, more especially as regards deduction of interest amount for the unexpired period up to due date of the import bill.

   If there is a sufficient time-lag between the receipt of the export payment and the due date of payment of the documents representing the import leg of the transaction, such export proceeds can be retained by the intermediary trader in an interest-bearing account and earmarked for the import payment on the due date of the import bill.

10. The intermediary trader's bank credits the export payment received to the intermediary trader's account, if he or she has already effected the import payment or the export proceeds are used to settle the import payment, as stated at point (8) above.

11. The transaction is completed.

Case 5: Where Import Payment is Made on Due Date from Proceeds of Discounting of Export Documents or from Export Payment Made by the Buyer

1. The export order is received by the intermediary trader but the export advance is not received by him or her from the overseas buyer.

2. The import purchase order is placed by the intermediary trader upon the overseas supplier.

3. As the overseas supplier is willing to extend a credit period of 'n' days (not exceeding 180 days) without insisting upon an LC, the intermediary trader awaits the shipping documents from the supplier.

   If the supplier insists on an LC to cover the credit period, the intermediary trader instructs his or her bank to establish an LC in favor of the overseas supplier on "n" days DA basis.

4. The supplier effects shipment and forwards/presents the DA documents through his or her bank to the intermediary trader's bank.

5. Once the documents are received by the intermediary trader's bank, the documents are presented to the intermediary trader for his or her acceptance to pay on the due date. The intermediary trader accepts the documents for payment on the due date and due date confirmation is given by the intermediary trader's bank to the supplier's/presenting bank, without any commitment on the part of the bank as regards payment on due date, since the documents are on collection basis.

   In the event that the DA documents received are under LC and compliant with LC terms, the documents are accepted by the bank for payment to be made on the due date and the documents are released to the intermediary trader and his or her commitment is obtained for payment on due date. The intermediary trader's bank conveys due-date confirmation to the supplier's/negotiating bank under the LC, with a commitment to pay on due date.

   If the documents received under the LC are discrepant documents, the same are to be dealt with in terms of UCP 600 and acceptance and payment on due date is effected in conformity with such provisions.

6. The intermediary trader substitutes the shipping documents received from the supplier, with documents prepared by him or her for the export leg of the transaction and submits these export shipping documents to the intermediary trader's own bank for submitting to the buyer's bank for collecting payment thereof.

7. The intermediary trader's bank discounts the export bill and makes funds available to the intermediary trader who either uses this funds to effect the import payment, if fallen due or keeps these funds in an Interest-bearing account for utilization on due date for payment of the import bill.

8. Export payment is to be received within four months of effecting of the import payment, and the entire transaction is to be completed within nine months from date of shipment.

9. Buyer receives the export documents and releases the export payment which is received by the intermediary trader's bank from the buyer's bank.

   In certain cases, the buyer effects payment before the import documents fall due for payment. Such payment, whether received before or after the export documents reach the buyer, can be used to effect Import payment—either before due date or on due date.

10. If payment is made before due date of import bill, it shall be in conformity with the provisions relating to pre-payment of import bills, more especially as regards deduction of interest amount for the unexpired period up to due date of the import bill.

    If there is a sufficient time-lag between the receipt of export payment and the due date of payment of the documents representing the import leg of the transaction, such export proceeds can be retained by the intermediary trader in an interest-bearing account and earmarked for the import payment on the due date of the import bill.

The intermediary trader's bank credits the export payment received to the intermediary trader's account, if he has already effected the import payment or the export proceeds are used to settle the import payment, as stated at point "h" above.

11.   The transaction is completed.

Case 6: Where Import Payment is Effected Under Buyers Credit and the Buyers Credit is Liquidated by the Discounting of Export Documents or Receipt of Export Payment From the Buyer

1.   Export order is received by the intermediary trader but export advance is not received by him or her from the overseas buyer.

2.   Import purchase order is placed by the intermediary trader upon the overseas supplier.

3.   As overseas Supplier is not willing to extend a credit period, the intermediary trader awaits the shipping documents from the supplier.

      If the supplier insists on a sight LC, the intermediary trader instructs his or her bank to establish an LC in favor of the overseas supplier on sight basis.

4.   The supplier effects shipment and forwards/presents the documents through his or her bank to the intermediary trader's bank.

5.   In the meantime, the intermediary trader arranges for a buyer's credit of 'n' days in conformity with the RBI prescriptions on this score, which is approved by the intermediary trader's bank.

6.   Once the documents are received by the intermediary trader's bank, the documents are presented to the intermediary trader who gives a commitment to pay on the due date of the buyer's credit and takes delivery of the documents.

7.   An LC is issued by the intermediary trader's bank to the bank granting buyer's credit wherein the intermediary trader's bank commits to effect payment of the buyer's credit on its due date of payment.

8.   The intermediary trader's bank instructs the bank offering the buyer's credit to effect payment to the supplier's bank under the buyer's credit approved by that bank.

9.   The buyer's credit granting bank effects payment to the supplier through the supplier's bank and informs the due date of payment of the buyers credit to the intermediary trader's bank.

      As the intermediary trader has committed to make payment on the due date of the buyer's credit, due date confirmation is given by the intermediary trader's bank to the supplier's/presenting bank under the LC issued by it.

10.   In the event that the documents received are under LC and compliant with LC terms, the documents are accepted by the bank and process as per points (7) to (9) is followed.

If the documents received under the LC are discrepant documents, the same are to be dealt with in terms of UCP 600 and acceptance and payment on due date is effected in conformity with such provisions.

11. The intermediary trader substitutes the shipping documents received from the supplier with documents prepared by him or her for the export leg of the transaction and submits these export shipping documents to the intermediary trader's own bank for submitting to the buyer's bank for collecting payment thereof.

12. The intermediary trader's bank discounts the export bill and makes funds available to the intermediary trader who either uses this funds to effect repayment of the buyer's credit, if fallen due, or keeps these funds in an interest-bearing account for utilization on due date for repayment of the buyer's credit.

    Alternatively, the export documents are forwarded to the buyer through his or her bank, with instructions to release the DPs or acceptance by the buyer to pay on due date.

13. Export payment is to be received within four months of effecting of Import payment and the entire transaction is to be completed within nine months from date of shipment.

14. Buyer receives export documents and releases export payment which is received by the intermediary trader's bank from the buyer's bank.

    In certain cases, the buyer effects payment before the buyer's credit falls due for repayment. Such payment, whether received before or after the export documents reach the buyer, can be used to effect repayment of the buyer's credit—either before due date or on due date.

    If payment is made before due date of the buyer's credit, it shall be in conformity with the provisions relating to pre-payment of Import bills, more especially as regards deduction of interest amount for the unexpired period up to due date of the buyer's credit.

    If there is a sufficient time-lag between the receipt of export payment and the due date of repayment of the buyer's credit representing the import leg of the transaction, such export proceeds can be retained by the intermediary trader in an Interest-bearing account and earmarked for the repayment of the buyer's credit on its due date.

15. The intermediary trader's bank credits the export payment received to the intermediary trader's account, if he has already effected the repayment of the buyer's credit or the export proceeds are used to repay the buyer's credit, as stated at point "h" above.

16. The transaction is completed.

Reference and Resources

RBI master circular on merchanting trade, Retrieved from, https://www.rbi.org.in/scripts/BS_ViewMasCirculardetails. aspx?id=9041#C15

https://rbi.org.in/scripts/NotificationUser.aspx?Id=8812&Mode=0

Questions

Answer the Following Questions

1. Who are the parties to a merchanting trade transaction?

2. What are the RBI guidelines regarding the time-frame for completion of the merchanting trade transaction?

3. Is it necessary to receive payment for the export leg in advance?

4. If the export payment is received before the import payment falls due, what are the alternatives available for application of funds?

5. What is the role of the intermediary trader's bank in a merchanting trade transaction?

6. When can a merchanting trade transaction be said to have commenced, and when can it be said to have been completed?

7. Are there any trade control guidelines that need to be complied with while undertaking merchanting trade transactions?

8. How is a merchanting trade transaction different from a normal import and export transaction in terms of the RBI guidelines relating to exports and imports?

9. How can Buyer's credit be availed in undertaking a merchanting trade transaction?

10. Explain the flow of transactions in a merchanting trade transaction.

Appendix

Merchanting Trade: RBI Guidelines

1. The goods should not enter into India's DTA.

2. The goods should be in as-is condition and should not have been subjected to any transformation.

3. The goods should be such that they are permitted to be exported and imported in terms of the extant FTP as on the date of shipment.

4. All trade control and other rules and regulations and the RBI Guidelines relating to the import leg and export leg should be complied with, excepting the submission of bill of entry and export declaration form, since the goods shall not be entering the DTA.

5. Both the import and the export leg should be routed through the same AD bank.

6. All original shipping documents, namely, invoice, packing list, transport document (BL, airway bill and so on) and insurance documents should be verified by the bank handling the transaction. If original documents are not available, nonnegotiable copies duly-authenticated by the overseas bank handling the documents should be verified.

7. The AD should be satisfied about the genuine genuineness of the transaction.

8. The entire transaction should be completed within a period of nine months.

9. The period for which there is a foreign exchange outlay should not exceed four months.

10. Commencement of transaction:

    - Date of shipment, if shipment is made in advance

    - Date of receipt of export payment, if export advance is received

    - Date of import payment, if advance import payment is made

    whichever is first.

11. Completion of transaction:

    - Date of shipment, if effected after receipt of export advance/payment

    - Date of receipt of export proceeds, if shipment is made prior to receipt of export advance/payment

    whichever is last.

12. Suppliers' or buyer's credit can be provided for the transaction, to the extent not backed by an advance payment for the export leg.

13. Discounting of documents under export LC by the AD bank is allowed.

14. In the event of receipt of advance payment for exports, the advance should be earmarked for the Import payment but pending such payment, the amount of the Export advance can be invested in an interest-bearing deposit account.

15. Advance payment for the Import leg is permitted, based on the commercial judgement of the AD bank handling the transaction, in the event that Advance payment for the export leg is not received from the overseas buyer, before effecting such a remittance.

    In such situations, the RBI guidelines, rules, and provisions relating to Advance payment for imports should be complied with and receipt of a Bank Guarantee/LC from an international bank of repute should be ensured, where such advance remittance exceeds USD 200,000 (or its equivalent).

16. The AD bank handling the transaction can issue an LC favoring the overseas supplier against a confirmed Export order, taking into account the time frame for the foreign exchange outlay (four months) and for the completion of the transaction (nine months), as specified by the RBI.

17. The intermediary can utilize the balances held in EEFC for effecting payment of the import leg of the transaction.

18. One-to-one matching of the import and export leg of the transaction should be ensured by the AD bank that is handling the transaction.

19. Default in the import or export leg of the transaction by the Intermediary trader are to be reported by the AD bank handling the transaction to the Regional Office of RBI, in the prescribed form within 15 days from the close of each half-year, that is, June and December. The RBI would

be caution-listing such defaulting traders whose outstandings reach 5% of their annual export earnings.

20. KYC/AML guidelines should be scrupulously observed by the AD bank handling the transaction.

21. Confirmed export order should be received by the intermediary trader from the overseas buyer.

22. The AD bank handling the transaction should be satisfied about the Intermediary trader's capabilities to perform the obligations under the Export order and the transaction should result in a reasonable profit to him or her.

23. The intermediary trader should be a genuine trader of goods and should not be a mere financial intermediary and should have the capability.

Merchanting Trade with Nepal and Bhutan

In the case of merchanting trade with counterparties in Nepal and Bhutan, since these countries are landlocked, the facility of transit trade is available in transactions where goods are imported from third countries by buyers in Nepal and Bhutan under cover of Customs transit declarations in terms of the Government of India Treaty of Transit executed with these two countries. Thus goods consigned to importers in Nepal and Bhutan from third countries under merchanting trade transaction from India would be treated as traffic-in-transit, if otherwise compliant with the terms of the executed treaties of transit.

Foreign Exchange Markets, Merchant Deals and Interbank Cover Operation: Cash, Spot and Forward

10.1 Foreign Exchange Basics

Forex market is the largest financial market having more than USD 5 trillion traded every day (BIS Report 2016). Among all the segments (e.g., spot, forward, Forex swap and currency swap), the most liquid segment is Forex swap having 2.3 trillion transactions a day, followed by the spot segment with 1.6 trillion transactions a day (See Table 10.1).

Table 10.1 Net–net Basis Daily Averages in April, in Billions of US Dollars						
Instrument	2001	2004	2007	2010	2013	2016
Foreign exchange instruments	1,239	1,934	3,324	3,971	5,355	5,088
Spot transactions	386	631	1,005	1,488	2,046	1,654
Outright forwards	130	209	362	475	679	700
Foreign exchange swaps	656	954	1,714	1,759	2,239	2,383
Currency swaps	7	21	31	43	54	96
Options and other products	60	119	212	207	337	254

SOURCE: Triennial Central Bank Survey: Foreign Exchange Turnover, BIS Report 2016, retrieved from http://www.bis.org/publ/rpfx16fx.pdf

The Forex markets are essentially 24-hour markets and self-regulated. However, Indian market operates from 9 AM to 5 PM. The most traded currency is USD and the most traded currency pair is EUR/USD.

From Table 10.2, it is evident that more than 87% deals are done in USD. The euro holds its second position among all the traded currencies. The turnover of the Japanese yen is again in the third position with a little decrease in the amount traded. On the other hand, Mexican peso and Chinese renminbi entered the list of the top 10 most traded currencies since 2013.

10.1.1 Foreign Currencies Dealt by Banks

Banks deals in the following currencies and maintains exchange positions in USD, euro, GBP, yen, AUD, Swiss franc, Canadian dollar, Singapore dollar, Danish kroner, Swedish kroner, Hong Kong dollar, and so on.

Table 10.2 Currency Distribution of OTC Foreign Exchange Turnover (As There Are Two Currencies Involved, the Share Refers to the Percentage Out of 200)												
Currency	2001		2004		2007		2010		2013		2016	
	Share	Rank	Share	Rank	Share	Rank	Share	Rank	Share	Rank	Share	Rank
USD	89.9	1	88.0	1	85.6	1	84.9	1	87.0	1	87.6	1
EUR	37.9	2	37.4	2	37.0	2	39.1	2	33.4	2	31.3	2
JPY	23.5	3	20.8	3	17.2	3	19.0	3	23.1	3	21.6	3
GBP	13.0	4	16.5	4	14.9	4	12.9	4	11.8	4	12.8	4
AUD	4.3	7	6.0	6	6.6	6	7.6	5	8.6	5	6.9	5
CAD	4.5	6	4.2	7	4.3	7	5.3	7	4.6	7	5.1	6
CHF	6.0	5	6.0	5	6.8	5	6.3	6	5.2	6	4.8	7
CNY	0.0	35	0.1	29	0.5	20	0.9	17	2.2	9	4.0	8
SEK	2.5	8	2.2	8	2.7	9	2.2	9	1.8	11	2.2	9
MXN	0.8	14	1.1	12	1.3	12	1.3	14	2.5	8	2.2	10

SOURCE: Triennial Central Bank Survey: Foreign Exchange Turnover, BIS Report 2016, retrieved from http://www.bis.org/publ/rpfx16fx.pdf

Table 10.3 OTC Foreign Exchange Turnover by Currency Pair

Net-net basis[1] daily averages in April, in billions of US dollars and percentages

Currency pair	2001		2004		2007		2010		2013		2016	
	Amount	%	Amount	%	Amount	%	Amount	%	Amount	%	Amount	%
USD/EUR	372	30.0	541	28.0	892	26.8	1,098	27.7	1,292	24.1	1,173	23.0
USD/JPY	250	20.2	328	17.0	438	13.2	567	14.3	980	18.3	902	17.7
USD/GBP	129	10.4	259	13.4	384	11.6	360	9.1	473	8.8	470	9.2
USD/AUD	51	4.1	107	5.5	185	5.6	248	6.3	364	6.8	266	5.2
USD/CAD	54	4.3	77	4.0	126	3.8	182	4.6	200	3.7	218	4.3
USD/CNY	...	...	...	...	...	...	31	0.8	113	2.1	192	3.8
USD/CHF	59	4.8	83	4.3	151	4.5	166	4.2	184	3.4	180	3.5
USD/MXN	...	...	...	...	...	...	...	...	128	2.4	105	2.1

SOURCE: Triennial Central Bank Survey: Foreign Exchange Turnover, BIS Report 2016, retrieved from http://www.bis.org/publ/rpfx16fx.pdf

10.2 Forex Parlance

- **Interbank Dealing:** Transactions carried out between banks constitute interbank dealing. It is a wholesale market and the trading volume is very high.

- **Merchant Dealing:** The dealing is between a bank and a customer.

A deal in a foreign exchange market is unique in nature because of two-way quotes. For example, the USD/INR quote is 67.2500/5000. This is due to the fact that while giving the quote, the market maker does not know if the market taker is going to buy or sell.

- **Base Currency:** The currency which is priced. In USD/INR, USD is the base currency. In EUR/USD, the base currency is EUR.

- **Quoting Currency or Price Currency:** The currency which is the price. In USD/INR, the quoting currency is INR, and in EUR/USD, the quoting currency is USD.

- **Bid Rate:** The rate at which the market maker buys the base currency. If USD/INR is quoted as 66.70/72, then the bid rate is 66.70. It means that the market maker is willing to buy USD at the rate of 66.70 INR.

- **Offer Rate:** The rate at which the market maker sells the base currency. If USD/INR is quoted as 66.70/72, then the offer rate is 66.72. It means that the market maker is willing to sell USD at the rate of 66.72 INR.

- **Market Maker:** The bank which quotes the rate to the taker. Some of the major market makers presently are Deutsche Bank, J.P. Morgan, Citibank, Barclays, and UBS.

- **Marker Taker:** The bank which asks for the quote and approaches an interbank market for the quote.

Example of an Interbank Deal:

- Market taker calls a market maker and requests for a quote, say, USD/INR.

  o   MT: "Please quote me INR 1 million"

- Market maker gives a two-way quote.

  o   MM: "USD/INR 67.2500/5000"

- Market taker selects his or her choice.

  o   MT: "Mine"

- Deal is concluded by market maker confirming.

  o   "I sold $ 1 million at 67.5000"

Example: If the interbank quote for USD/INR is 68.71/72, then we can say that there are two parties to the trade: (a) price maker and (b) price taker. There are two actions or market sides in any transaction:

(a) buy and (b) sell. There are two currencies in Forex transaction: (a) base currency and (b) quoting currency. There are two sides to the two-way quote: (a) bid and (b) offer.

In other words, the price maker buys the base currency that is USD at the bid rate, that is, 68.71 and sells the base currency or USD at the offer rate 68.72.

In FX market, the action (i.e., buy, sell) may be specified in either base currency or quoting currency. But it is the base currency that is convenient to use in terms of quoting currency (QC). To conclude, we can say that if the market maker is buying the base currency, it will quote the bid rate to the customer and if market maker is selling the base currency it will quote the ask rate to the customer.

For example, on GBP/USD currency pair, buying GBP is the same as selling USD for any bank. When the action is stated in base currency, it is easy to follow because it is a price quotation.

Conventionally, Interbank quotes only the last two digits; popularly known as small figures.

For example, the EUR/USD quote 1.1112/1.1113 is abbreviated to 1.1112/13 or to simply 12/13.

USD/CHF quote 0.9091/0.9092 is abbreviated to 0.9091/92 or to 91/92.

The omitted part in the offer side is called the "big figure."

The rule to derive the full form of offer side is that the offer price will have as many decimal places as the bid price.

- **Purchase and Sale:** Any commercial bank transaction is classified as purchase and sale transaction. From the AD Category-I banks' point of view, conversion of foreign currency on behalf of an exporter into Indian rupees would involve a purchase and conversion of domestic currency into foreign currency on behalf of an importer would involve a sale transaction.

  Likewise, outward remittance would involve the sale of foreign currency, while inward remittance would involve the purchase of foreign currency.

  The maxim applied is buy low and sell high.

- **Long and Short Position:** Banks can maintain either overbought (long) or oversold (short) exchange positions in permitted currencies within prescribed limits. A long or short exchange position denotes the extent of the open (uncovered) quantity of the currency.

10.3 ISO Standard and the SWIFT Messages

The International Organization for Standardization (ISO) has given a three-letter code for every currency in their ISO 4217 standard.

The first two letters are the country code, defined by ISO in their standard ISO 3166, and the third letter is usually, but not always, the first letter of the currency name.

The ISO codes are adopted by the Society for Worldwide Interbank Financial Telecommunications (SWIFT), which is the communication and messaging network for banks the world over. Only these standard ISO/SWIFT codes, and not the special characters (e.g., $,), must be used in any standard Forex messaging.

The market practice for the notation of a currency pair is to write the BC code first, followed by the QC code, for example, EUR/USD. ISO 4217 is the international standard for currency code (See Table 10.4).

Table 10.4   Currency Code

Country	Currency	ISO Code
United Kingdom	Pound	GBP
European Union	Euro	EUR
United States	Dollar	USD
Japan	Yen	JPY
India	Rupee	INR
Switzerland	Franc	CHF
China	Renminbi	CNY

Table 10.5   An Overview of SWIFT MT Categories

Message Type	Description
MT0xx	System Messages
MT1xx	Customer Payments and Cheques
MT2xx	Financial Institution Transfers
MT3xx	Treasury Markets
MT4xx	Collection and Cash Letters
MT5xx	Securities Markets
MT6xx	Treasury Markets–Metals and Syndications
MT7xx	Documentary Credits and Guarantees
MT8xx	Travelers Cheques
MT9xx	Cash Management and Customer Status

SOURCE: (Retrieved from https://docs.oracle.com/cd/E19509-01/820-7113/6nid5dl2r/index.html)

10.4 Hierarchy of the Quote

For most of the currency pair, USD is quoted as base currency, except EUR, GBP, AUD, and NZD. It means, if AUD is quoted against NZD, USD, CHF or INR, AUD would be the base currency. If GBP is quoted against AUD, NZD, USD or INR, GBP would be the base currency.

The ongoing prices of currencies are known in the dealing room through two sources: (a) Information screens provided by vendors such as Reuters, Bloomberg and so on and (b) price-matching systems provided by a number of institutions (e.g., Deutsche bank, Barclays, Citibank, UBS, 360T).

10.5 Nostro and Vostro Account

Nostro Account: An account maintained in a foreign currency with a bank usually located in that country. For example, an Indian bank maintains a USD account with Citibank, New York, and maintains a euro account with Deutsche bank, Frankfurt. These accounts would be referred to as the Indian bank's USD nostro account and GBP nostro account, respectively. Nostro accounts are required to be maintained for the purposes of putting through inward and outward remittances in the respective currencies.

Vostro Account: An INR account maintained with a bank in India by a bank located abroad is referred to as a vostro account. For example, Citibank, New York, maintains a rupee account with Bank of Maharashtra, Mumbai. This account will be referred to as Citibank's vostro account. Vostro accounts are generally to be used for rupee payments to be made in India. Funding of the vostro account is done by the foreign bank, by selling foreign currency and buying rupee. The vostro account cannot be used for USD/INR trading by the foreign banks.

10.6 Value Dates or Settlement Dates

In a Forex transaction, two dates are involved—the date of the deal and the date of settlement of the deal. The date of settlement is also known as the value date of the transaction. For any inward remittances or for export transaction, the nostro fund would be credited, and for any outward transaction or import transaction, the nostro fund gets debited on the respective value dates (see Table 10.6).

Table 10.6 Example of Value Dates

Settlement	Settlement/Value Date	Definition
Cash	December 12	Deal Date, T=0
Value "Tomorrow Next"	December 13	One "Mutual Business Date After Deal date" T+1
Spot	December 14	Two "Mutual Business Date After Deal Date" T+2
Forward	December 15 or Later	Three Business Days or More After Deal date; Always Longer Than Spot

The classification of the value dates are as follows:

- **Cash value date:** Settlement is at T=0. The deal date and settlement date are both the same.

- **Tom value date:** Settlement is at T+1. It means the date of settlement falls due on the next working day for the non-USD center (between USD/INR non-USD center is INR center). On the settlement date, both the USD and non-USD centers should remain open.

- **Spot date:** Settlement is at T+2. "Value spot" means the date of settlement falls due on the second working day for the non-USD center (between USD/INR non-USD center is INR center) after the date of deal. On the settlement date, both the USD and non-USD center should remain open.

Spot is the most common value date used in the Forex transaction.

Algorithm of Spot Value Date

Case–I:
USD is one of the currencies in the currency pair.

- Spot value date is the date that must be a second business day at non-dollar center and a New York business day.
- It need not be a second business day at New York.
- If New York is closed on what is a second business day at the other center, then we move to the next business day on which both non-dollar center and New York are simultaneously open.

Case–II:
USD is not one of the currencies in the currency pair (i.e., cross rate).

- Spot value date is the date that must be second business day at each settlement center and a New York business day.
- Though not involved in settlement, New York must be opened because the cross rates are ultimately derived by crossing two USD-based rates.
- Therefore, New York will be indirectly involved in settlement. If any of the settlement centers or New York is closed on such date, we move to the next business day on which all the three are open.

SOURCE: TDG Practitioner Guide to Forex Market by The Derivatives Group.

- **Forward value date:** Any settlement date beyond spot would be categorized as "forward." The rate of forward cover is arrived at after taking into consideration the current spot rate and the current forward points (FPs) for the date of delivery.

10.6.1 Rules for Forward Value Dates

Case I: Suppose a forward contract is booked on July 15 for two months. So, to decide on the maturity of the forward contract, we first have to decide about the spot date. In this case, the spot is July 17 (assuming that this is the second working day of the non-USD center and the working day of the USD center). So, the maturity of two month forward would be September 17.

Case II: Suppose a forward contract is booked on June 28. So, the spot is June 30 (assuming that this is the second business day of the non-USD center and working day for the USD center). Now June 30 is the last working day of the month. So the two month forward contract would also fall on the last working of the two months, that is, August 31.

As per FEDAI rule, the date of delivery under a forward contract is considered as follows:

1. If bills or documents are purchased/discounted/negotiated: date of purchase/discount/negotiation and payment of rupee to customer.

2. Bills or documents under collection: date of payment of rupees to the customer on realization.

3. In case of retirement/crystallization of import bill/documents: date of retirement or crystallization of liability, whichever is earlier. If an import bill is received under an LC and if the customer

does not pay within 10 days, his or her liability will be crystalized, that is, converted into Indian rupees, on the 10th day of the receipt of documentary by the bank.

The interbank bid rate or ask rate is quoted to the customer. Along with it, the cash/spot (C/S) or the tom/ spot (T/S) are the two pre-spot dates for settlement earlier to the spot dates. The forward market in India is liquid up to one year; however, there is no restriction in booking a forward contract beyond one year. In the Indian Forex market, FPs are always quoted in terms of paise.

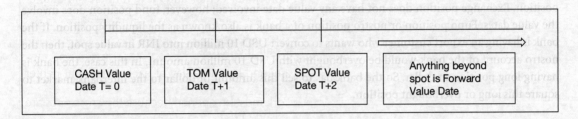

Forward booing can be categorized into two parts: (a) month-end rate and (b) rate for broken dates.

Month-end rate: Month-end rates are applicable for option forward, and FEDAI clearly prescribes the rules for this. Forward options are a type of forward; if booked, then they can be executed at any day of the month. However, FEDAI rules for TT and bill buying rate prescribe that if the market is in premium, then the premium rate for the last month cannot be passed on to the export customer. However, a premium would be charged to the import customer. For example, if USD/INR spot rate is 67.72/73 and the one-month forward rate is 4/5, then the export customer who wants to book one-month forward would be quoted the rate for USD as 67.72 INR-margin. He or she would not be given the benefit of premium. So, the customer would receive less INR against USD. This is for the benefit of the bank. Similarly, if the customer is an import customer, then he or she would be charged the premium price for USD. He or she would be charged $67.73 + 0.05 + margin = 67.78 + margin$.

Broken date: The FP are given for the month-end dates in India. However, forward contracts could be sold for any dates that fall within any of the months. Such contracts are called broken dates contracts. In case of the exporter, the bank has to give the bid rate, while for the importer, the bank has to give the ask rate as the bank on behalf of the market buys low and sells high.

We would discuss each of these cases in detail in the later sections.

10.6.2 Herstatt Risk or Settlement Risk

The 1974 failure of Bank Haus Herstatt concerns the complexity of assuring the settlement of both ends of a cross-border currency deal covering different time zones. Herstatt risk is the chance that a bank will deliver currency on one side of a foreign exchange deal and find that its counterparty cannot reciprocate. This can happen because banks operate in different time zones. For example, a bank selling yen and buying sterling pays yen to another bank in Japan during the Japanese business day and then waits until London opens to get sterling in return.

10.7 Merchant Deals and Cover Operation

Forex front office treasury handles all transactions in the merchant and interbank Forex markets. Deals originate from either merchant desks or proprietary trading desks. We concentrate mostly on the deals related to merchant transaction as the deals related to proprietary trading is beyond the purview of this book. Merchant deals allow the exporter or importer to hedge their foreign exchange risks with the bank. Consequently, banks get exposed to the foreign exchange risk. This is reflected in exchange and fund position. Exchange position does not have any value date involved; however, fund position does involve the value dates. Fund position or nostro position of a bank is also known as the liquidity position. If the bank is having an export customer who wants to convert USD 10 million into INR in value spot, then the nostro account of the bank would be overbought with USD 10 million amount. In this case, the bank is having long position in dollar. So the bank has to sell this amount of dollar to the interbank market to square this long or overbought position.

10.7.1 Spot Merchant Deals in USD/INR and Interbank Cover Operation

It is now clear that a spot deal may be initiated if a customer (for example, exporter/importer) wants a settlement on value spot. A spot deal helps to exit an existing position either by booking profit or by booking loss (read stop loss). For example, if an importer has to convert his or her payables in dollar value spot, then the bank nostro account would get debited on the settlement date, that is, on spot date. So, on the spot date bank is having oversold position in USD. To cover this position bank must buy dollar from interbank on value spot. So the nostro account in dollar on the spot date, that is, after two days of the deal date, gets squared off.

1. Import customer having USD 1 million to convert into INR.

Interbank spot rate USD/INR 67.75/76; deal date is December 14, 2016.

	Credit	Debit
Spot (16.12.2016)		Oversold Position

So, by booking a spot deal on December 14, 2016 (deal date), the import merchant transfers the risk of foreign exchange fluctuations to the bank book. The bank's nostro position would be debited with USD 1 million on December 16, 2016.

Cover Operation in Interbank:

	Credit	Debit
Spot (December 16, 2016)	+	Oversold Position

Subsequently, the bank has to cover its oversold position by buying the same in the interbank, unless there is an export customer having an equivalent transaction booked on the same day. If the bank goes to the interbank to buy USD 1 million, the interbank sells dollar at INR 67.76. So, the bank offers the rate of INR 67.78 to the import customer, keeping a 2 paise exchange margin.

2. Suppose interbank spot rate for USD/INR is 66.70/72.

An importer wants a conversion of USD value spot. The margin is 2 paise. The deal date is November 9, 2016. The value date or the settlement date would be:

	Credit	Debit
Spot (November 11, 2016)		-

The merchant desk quotes INR 66.74 per USD to the customer. With this deal, the bank's nostro position becomes oversold at value spot.

Cover Operation in Interbank:

	Credit	Debit
Spot (November 11, 2016)	Buy	-

The bank covers this deal by a buy transaction in the interbank at INR 66.72 per USD. The profit is 2 paise per dollar.

10.7.2 Spot Deals in Cross Rate and Interbank Cover Operation

In this example, we would learn about exchange position too. An exchange position is created with every purchase and sale transaction of the bank; however, unlike nostro position, it does not have any maturity date. From the next deal onwards, we would learn both the exchange position and fund position for each value dates.

1. Spot: EUR / USD: 1.1112 / 14
            USD / INR: 68.2500 / 2550

Calculate the merchant rate of EUR/USD for an export client with 5 paise margin and explain the cover operation.

Merchant Rate:
Bank purchases EUR from the export client at 1.1112.
   EUR/INR rate is $1.1112 \times 68.2500 = 75.8394$ INR per EUR.
   With the margin, the rate is 75.8194 INR per EUR.

Cover Operation:
Initial position is created as bank has booked a deal to settle the receivables of the export customer on value spot.

EUR						USD					
Exchange Position			Fund Position			Exchange Position			Fund Position		
	P	S		C	D		P	S		C	D
Customer	+		Spot	+		Interbank			Spot		
Interbank						Interbank					

i. Now, the foreign exchange risk in euro is transferred from the export customer to the bank book. To cover this position, the bank needs to first sell euro and buy dollar in the interbank. The corresponding transaction is sell euro and buy dollar value spot at 1.1112.

EUR						USD					
Exchange Position			**Fund Position**				**Exchange Position**			**Fund Position**	
	P	**S**		**C**	**D**			**P**	**S**		**C**	**D**
Customer	+		Spot	+	Sell	Interbank	Buy		Spot	Buy	
Interbank		Sell				Interbank					

So, the exchange position along with the fund position in euro is squared off. We can say that euro is having no maturity gap as the customer transaction requires the settlement to be on value spot. By doing a cover operation, the bank can always square off its position at value spot. For this, the bank has to do the opposite transaction to the customers deal. On the other hand, in dollar, both the exchange position and the fund position are open to cover. So, the bank sells dollar in the market and buys INR. The transaction in interbank is sell dollar buy INR value spot at 68.2500. With this transaction, the exchange and the fund positions are reported as:

EUR						USD					
Exchange Position			**Fund Position**				**Exchange Position**			**Fund Position**	
	P	**S**		**C**	**D**			**P**	**S**		**C**	**D**
Customer	+		Spot	+	Sell	Interbank	Buy	Sell	Spot	Buy	Sell
Interbank		Sell	Frw			Interbank					

Now the bank is having its dollar exchange position and the fund position covered or in squared off position.

So the cover operation rate for the bank for EUR/INR is $68.2500 \times 1.1112 = 75.8394$ INR per EUR. Deduct the margin. So, the customer rate for EUR/INR is $75.8394 - 0.02 = 75.8194$ INR per EUR.

2. Spot: EUR/USD: 1.1112/14
          USD/INR: 68.2500/2550

Merchant Rate for EUR/INR and cover operation for an import customer value spot:

Merchant Rate:

Bank sells EUR to the import customer

   EUR/INR rate is $1.1114 \times 68.2550 = 75.8586$ INR per EUR.

   With the margin of 2 paise the customer rate is 75.8786 INR per EUR.

EUR						USD					
Exchange Position			**Fund Position**				**Exchange Position**			**Fund Position**	
	P	**S**		**C**	**D**			**P**	**S**		**C**	**D**
Customer		-	Spot		-	Interbank			Spot		
Interbank						Interbank					

As the bank has to sell euro at spot to the customer, the bank must buy euro from interbank to cover its spot position. So, the first transaction is to buy euro and sell dollar value spot at 1.1114.

EUR					USD					
Exchange Position			**Fund Position**			**Exchange Position**			**Fund Position**	
	P	S		C	D		P	S		C	D
Customer		-	Spot	Buy	-	Interbank		Sell	Spot		Sell
Interbank	buy					Interbank					

By the aforementioned transaction, exchange and fund position get squared off in euro. However, the bank is over sold in dollar exchange and fund position.

EUR					USD					
Exchange Position			**Fund Position**			**Exchange Position**			**Fund Position**	
	P	S		C	D		P	S		C	D
Customer		-	Spot	+	-	Interbank	Buy	Sell	Spot	Buy	Sell
Interbank	+					Interbank					

To cover this position, the bank buys USD value spot against INR. The transaction is buy USD sell INR value spot at 68.2550.

The cover rate for EUR/INR is $1.1114 \times 68.2550 = 75.8586$ INR per EUR.

The margin is to be added. The rate to the customer is $75.8586 + 0.02 = 75.8786$ INR per EUR.

10.8 Forward Points or Swap Points

A forward contract is booked if there is any receivables or payables beyond spot transaction. A forward contract may be booked for one month, or two months and so on. If an exporter books a purchase contract with the bank for two months, then the fund or the nostro position of a bank becomes overbought on the settlement date, that is, after two months. However, banks are not allowed to book a cover for any purchase and sell transaction directly in the forward segment or in the cash segment. For such merchant deals, the bank has to involve spot segment and Forex swap to do a cover operation. Cash segment or forward segment are different from the spot by forward points. It should be noted that often Forward Points or FPs are also called 'swap points' as they are taken from interbank swap market. It reflects the interest rate differentials between the currencies for the forward period. Depending upon interest rate differential between the two currencies, FP can be positive or negative.

In India, the FPs are actually traded rates in the interbank swap market, which means they may not be strictly derived from interest rate differentials. Sometimes the market traded forward rates would be different from what the interest rate differentials warrant because of liquidity situation in the domestic money market.

- If FPs are positive, then they are added to the spot rate to arrive at the forward rate. In such case, forward rates will be higher than spot rate and we can say that the foreign currency is in "premium." If FP, on the other hand, is negative, then forward rate is arrived by subtracting forward points from spot rate, which is a case of foreign currency being in "discount".

- For example, if spot USD/INR 67.23/24 and S/1M is 9/10, then the forward rate is 67.32/67.34.

- Cash or tom value dates are also known as short dated forward. For cash or tom value dates, the application of exchange arithmetic is a little different. If foreign currency is in premium in C/S, then to arrive to cash rate, we have to deduct the FPs from the spot rate in the cross manner. As cash market represents a market segment in the previous time compared to spot in the timeline, if C/S represents premium condition, then it means that the foreign currency is in premium in the spot segment.

- For example, if spot USD/INR 67.23/24 and C/S is 3/4, then the cash rate is 67.19/67.21.

How the forward points are derived?
  Bid side swap points

$$= spot\ rate \times \frac{1+\dfrac{borrowing\ rate\ for\ offered\ currency \times swap\ days}{360\ or\ 365}}{1+\dfrac{lending\ rate\ in\ base\ currency \times swap\ days}{360\ or\ 365}} - spot\ rate.$$

Offer side swap points

$$= spot\ rate \times \frac{1+\dfrac{lending\ rate\ for\ offered\ currency \times swap\ days}{360\ or\ 365}}{1+\dfrac{borrowing\ rate\ in\ base\ currency \times swap\ days}{360\ or\ 365}} - spot\ rate.$$

Most currencies use a 360-day year, except the sterling pound and a few other currencies
  For example,
  USD/YEN spot rate=115.30/115.35
  One-month USD interest rates=5.93% 6.03%
  One-month Yen interest rates=0.09% 0.21%
  Bid side swap points

$$= 115.30 \times \frac{1+\left(0.0009 \times \dfrac{30}{360}\right)}{1+\left(0.0603 \times \dfrac{30}{360}\right)} - 115.30$$

  −0.57

Offer side swap points

$$= 115.35 \times \frac{1+\left(0.0021 \times \dfrac{30}{360}\right)}{1+\left(0.0593 \times \dfrac{30}{360}\right)} - 115.35$$

  −0.55

So USD/YEN one month forward differentials are −0.57 / −0.49

SOURCE: TDG Practitioner Guide to Forex Market by The Derivatives Group.

Here we represent the general rue for the calculation of forward rate and the cash or tom rate.

- **Case 1: When foreign currency is in premium:**

	Regular Forward			Short Dated Forwards or Value Cash	
	Bid	**Ask**		**Bid**	**Ask**
Spot rate	A (= 67.56)	B (= 67.57)	Spot rate	A (= 67.56)	B (= 67.57)
Swap points (S/1M)	C (= 0.05)	D (= 0.06)	Swap points (C/S)	E (= 0.03)	F (= 0.04)
Forward rate	A+C (=67.56+0.05) = 67.61	B+D (=67.57+0.06) = 67.63	Cash rate	A−F (=67.56−0.04) = 67.52	B−E (67.57−0.03) = 67.54

- **Case 2: When foreign currency is in discount:**

	Regular Forward			Short Dated Forwards	
	Bid	**Ask**		**Bid**	**Ask**
Spot rate	A (= 67.56)	B (= 67.57)	Spot rate	A (= 67.56)	B (= 67.57)
Swap points (S/1M)	C (= 0.11)	D (= 0.10)	Swap points (C/S)	E (= 0.07)	F (= 0.06)
Forward rate	A−C (=67.56−0.11) = 67.45	B−D (=67.57−0.10) = 67.47	Cash rate	A+F (=67.56+0.06) = 67.62	B+E (= 67.57+0.07) = 67.64

In case of USD/INR, USD is generally in premium as the interest in the USA is lower than the interest rate prevailing in India; forward is generally higher than spot rate.

Let an exporter sell EUR for April 31, 2017, roughly six months from November 30, 2016. He sells EUR 1 million on November 30, 2016 to an Indian bank for rupees and, hence, looking for EUR/INR six month forward price. Let the applicable FPs in the market be as follows:

Bid/Ask Rates	USD/INR	EUR/USD
Spot as on 30 November	67.84 / 67.86	1.0696 / 1.0698
FP for 31st April	121 / 123	93 / 94

For the quoting bank, the problem can be solved in three stages. First, arrive at the USD/INR forward rate in the interbank. Second, arrive at the forward EUR/USD buying rate in the interbank of EUR/USD. Third, based on the two, arrive at the EUR/INR buying rate as follows:

1	Interbank six month forward buying rate for USD / INR	Spot	67.84
		FP	(+) 1.21
		F (₹)	69.05
2	Interbank six month forward buying rate for EUR / USD	Spot	1.0696
		FP	(+) 0.0093
		F ($)	1.0789
3	EUR / INR forward purchasing price from exporter		69.05 × 1.0789
		₹	74.498045

Rule for Cross Currency

- If USD is at the same side in both the pairs - Divide

If USD remains at the same side for both the currency pairs then we divide. For example, if we need to calculate CHF / INR rate which is derived from USD / CHF and USD / INR, we divide. The same is true if we need to calculate EUR / GBP rate from EUR / USD and EUR / GBP rates.

- If USD is at the two opposite sides in both the pairs - Multiply

If USD is there at the opposite sides in both the pairs then we multiply. For example, if we need to calculate EUR / INR rate which is derived from EUR / USD and USD / INR, we multiply.

10.9 Forex Swap

Forex swap is purely an "interbank" product. Banks use swap market to plug the funds position gaps that arise out of their activities. Forex swap refers to simultaneous buy/sell or sell/buy a currency, say, EUR 1 million at two different value dates, say, spot and one-month forward with the differential rate. It has the following three characteristics: (a) the first transaction is likely to happen in the spot leg, (b) a reversing forward leg for the same amount as that of spot leg, and (c) counterparty for both the legs is the same.

Generally, corporates do not have much need for Forex swap products. There are two types of Forex swap

a. Buy/Sell swap and

b. Sell/Buy swap

For instance, in a buy/sell swap, the near leg is a BUY and the farther leg is a SELL. In general, near leg is spot. However, in swaps involving of pre-spot dates, near leg will be either cash date or tom date and farther leg would be spot (in international markets, there is also something called "next," meaning next to spot).

In market parlance, generally, a swap is always mentioned along with the two legs involved. For instance, "buy/sell, spot over three months," means that the first leg is spot and the second is three month forward. For pre-spot dated, it is either cash over spot (C/S, near leg cash and farther leg spot) or tom over spot (T/S).

The main instrument of cover operation in any segments of the Forex market except the spot is Forex swap or simply called as foreign exchange swap (FX swap).

10.10 The Fundamental Rules of Forex Swap

Case I: Currency is in premium. Suppose USD/INR spot is 66.51/52 and S/1M is 10/11.

So, in the forward market, USD becomes costlier. If the bank buys USD spot and sells USD in the forward market then it gains. This gain in interbank parlance is known as receive. The bank as a price taker receives low, that is, between 10/11, it receives 10 paise. On the other hand, if bank sells USD spot and buys USD in the premium market, then the bank or the price taker has to pay to the market or interbank. So, bank pays high: 11 paise.

- Receive—Buy spot sell forward

- Pay—Sell spot and buy forward

Case II: Currency is in discount. Suppose, USD/INR spot is 66.51/52 and S/1M is 11/10.

So, in the forward market, USD becomes cheaper. If the bank buys USD spot and sells USD in the forward market, then it pays. The bank pays high, that is, between 10/11, it pays 11. On the other hand, if bank sells USD spot and buys USD in the discount market, then the bank or the price taker receives and receives low: 10 paise.

- Receive—Sell spot and buy forward

- Pay—Buy spot and sell forward

Price takers receive low and pay high. It means that the price maker receives high and pays low. This whole transaction can be represented by the following matrix:

Pay or receive points depends on the transaction of the Bank		Swap Transaction	
		Receive	Pay
Forward market	Premium	B / S	S / B
	Discount	S / B	B / S

Irrespective of the market conditions, that is, forward market being in premium or in discount, the bank will either receive or pay depending on the traction, whether the bank is doing a buy/sell or sell/buy swap in the interbank. Table 10.7 shows the cash flow between price taker and the price maker for Forex swap transaction.

Table 10.7 Cash Flows in Forex Swap					
		Bank A		Bank B	
		Buy/Sell Swap		Sell/Buy Swap	
Date	Rate	USD	INR	USD	INR
Spot	55.50	+ 1,000,000	– 5,55,00,000	– 1,000,000	+ 5,55,00,000
Three Months	55.50+0.15	– 1,000,000	+ 5,56,50,000	+ 1,000,000	– 55,6,50,000
Net Flow		Nil	+ 1,50,000	Nil	– 1,50,000

10.10.1 Two Month Forward Deal in USD/INR

1. USD/INR: 64.2200 / 0.2300
    One month forward   0.0125 / 0.0225
    Two month forward   0.0250 / 0.0350

Renuka Ltd has secured an order for Indian saris worth USD 1 million. It needs two- month forward cover with a margin of 2 paise.

Renuka Ltd will receive USD 1 million after two months. The bank's nostro account would be overbought after two months.

Initial Position

Exchange Position (USD)			Fund Position (USD)		
	P	S		Credit	Debit
Customer	+1		Spot		
Interbank			2M FRD	+1 (expected after two months)	

The bank has to do the opposite transaction to cover its exchange position. So, the bank sells the dollar in interbank. We have already mentioned that this outright sell is possible only on the spot value date. So, the bank's fund position would be debited on the spot date.

i. The transaction is sell USD buy INR at value spot at 64.2200.

Exchange Position in USD			Fund Position in USD		
Customer	+1		Spot	Maturity GAP	−1
Interbank		−1	2M FRD	+1	Maturity GAP

With this, the bank's exchange position gets squared off. However, fund position is not squared off because of the mismatch in the dates of outflow and inflow of the fund. This mismatch is known as maturity gap. To cover this position, the bank needs to get into a swap deal.

ii. Buy USD spot sell USD forward. Buy/sell swap in USD.

As USD is in premium in forward market compared to spot market, by doing a buy/sell swap, the bank receives the points. As a market taker, bank receives lower points 0.0250 (between 0.0250 and 0.0350; FPs after two months).

Exchange Position			Fund Position		
	Purchase	Sale		Credit	Debit
Customer	+1		Spot	Buy	−1
Interbank		−1	2M FRD	+1	Sell
Interbank	+	−			

iii. So, the cover rate is $64.22005 + 0.0250 = 64.2450$.

iv. With an exchange margin of 2 paise the customer rate $= 64.2450 - 0.02 = 64.2250$.

2. USD / INR: 66.3200 / 0.3300
   One month forward   0.1500 / 0.1600
   Two month forward   0.3000 / 0.3100

TVS motors, Kolkata, wants a two month forward contract for USD 1 million import of Kuala engines for their mini two-seater car. The margin is 2 paise.

Initial Position: Importer has to pay his or her counterparty USD 1 million. The bank sells one million dollars to the importer after two months. So, after two months, the bank's nostro account gets debited with 1 million dollar. As the bank gives the rate to the customer on the deal date, the bank would like to give the rate what it gets from the interbank while covering its position.

Exchange Position			Fund Position		
Customer		−1	Spot		
Interbank			2M FRD		−1

The bank does an opposite transaction to be settled at value spot, that is, the bank buys USD 1 million value spot. As we have already mentioned that this outright buy is possible only on the spot value date, the bank's fund position would be credited on the spot date.

Exchange Position			Fund Position		
	P	S		Cr	De
Customer		−1	Spot	+1	↗ Maturity GAP
Interbank	+1		2M FRD	Maturity GAP ↗	−1

    i.   Buy USD sell INR spot at 66.3300.

With this transaction, the bank gets its exchange position covered. However, it remains open in its fund position because there remains a maturity gap. To cover this position, the bank does a swap transaction. It does a sell/buy swap.

    ii.   Sell USD/Buy INR Spot; buy USD/Sell INR forward. Sell/buy swap in USD.

    iii.   USD is in premium. As bank does a sell/buy swap, bank pays. It pays high, that is, 0.3100.

Exchange Position in USD			Fund Position in USD		
Customer		−1	Spot	+1	↗ Sell
Interbank	+1		2M FRD	Buy ↗	−1
Interbank	+1	−1			

    iv.   Cover rate = 66.3300 + 0.3100 = 66.6400.

    v.   With margin = 66.6400 + 0.0200.

3. The exporter needs two month forward cover for USD 10 million. Margin for the bank will be 2 paise. The USD/INR rates are:

USD / INR Spot	64.2275	64.2375
One month forward	0.0125	0.0225
Two month forward	0.0250	0.0350

In the forward market, USD is in premium. After two months, the exporter will sell USD 10 million to the bank as per the forward contract. The bank, in order to cover its position, will carry out a FX swap in the interbank.

The exchange position and the fund positions are as follows:

Exchange Position				Fund Position		
	Purchase	Sell			Credit	Debit
Customer	+		Spot			
Interbank			2 M		+	

The bank will buy the USD 10 million from the customer in value forward as the bank's nostro fund receives USD after two months and has to sell it in the interbank. However, the bank cannot book his or her position in the forward market directly. The bank does a buy/sell swap to cover its position

The cover operation of the bank in interbank will be:

i.   Sell USD value spot at 64.2275.

Exchange Position				Fund Position		
	Purchase	Sell			Credit	Debit
Customer	+		Spot		Maturity Gap	–
Interbank		–	2 M		+	Maturity Gap

ii. Now the exchange position is in square. But the maturity gap persists.

a.   Buy USD/sell INR value spot.

b.   Sell USD/buy INR value forward (Buy–Sell swap in USD), market is in premium, so receive low: 0.0250.

Exchange Position				Fund Position		
	Purchase	Sell			Credit	Debit
Customer	+		Spot		Buy	–
Interbank		–	2 M		+	Sell

iii. Cover rate to sell in the interbank will be $=64.2275+0.0250=64.2525$.

iv. Forward rate quoted to the exporter will be $=64.2525-0.02=64.2325$.

4. The exporter needs two month forward cover for USD 10 million. The margin for the bank will be 2 paise. The USD/INR rates are:

USD / INR Spot	64.2275	64.2375
One month forward	0.0225	0.0125
Two month forward	0.0350	0.0250

The exporter is going to receive USD after two months. So, the nostro position of the bank would be credited with USD after two months. As bank has to give the rate to the customer, the bank must know the cover rate in interbank. For this, the bank has to make the spot segment involved in the transaction as the bank cannot book a forward cover directly without involving the spot segment.

Initial Position:

Exchange Position				Fund Position	
	Purchase	Sell		Credit	Debit
Customer	+		Spot		
Interbank			2 M	+	

i. Sell USD value spot at 64.2275.

Exchange Position				Fund Position	
	Purchase	Sell		Credit	Debit
Customer	+		Spot	Maturity Gap	–
Interbank		–	2 M	+	Maturity Gap

ii. Exchange position is in square but nostro position is having a maturity gap. To cover this maturity gap, the bank does a buy/sell swap in USD

   a. Buy USD/sell INR value spot.

   b. Sell USD/buy INR value forward.

In the forward market, USD is in discount. So pay and pay high: 0.0350.

Exchange Position				Fund Position	
	Purchase	Sell		Credit	Debit
Customer	+		Spot	Buy	–
Interbank		–	2 M	+	Sell

iii. Cover rate to sell in the interbank will be = 64.2275 – 0.0350 = 64.1925.

iv. With the margin, the forward rate quoted to the exporter will be = 64.1925 – 0.02 = 64.1725.

5. The importer needs two month forward cover for USD 10 million. The margin for the bank will be 2 paise. The USD/INR rates are:

USD / INR Spot	64.2275	64.2375
One month forward	0.0125	0.0225
Two month forward	0.0250	0.0350

After two months, the importer has to make payment to his or her foreign counterparty, for which he or she needs USD. The bank will sell USD 10 million to the importer as per the forward contract. The initial position of the bank during the forward booking is as follows:

Exchange Position in USD			Fund Position in USD		
	Purchase	**Sell**		**Credit**	**Debit**
Customer		–	Spot		
Interbank			Forward		–

The nostro account of the bank in USD would get debited in two months' time. So, the bank needs to buy USD to be credited to his or her nostro account after two months. But he or she has to book it today to avoid the risk of exchange rate fluctuation. However, the bank cannot book this forward cover directly in two months' time. The bank, in order to cover its position, will involve the spot leg and use FX swap in the interbank.

    i.   Buy dollar spot at 64.2375. With this transaction, the exchange position is fully covered. However, there exists a maturity gap in the fund position as the USD outflow would be in two months' time, whereas the USD inflow is in spot.

Exchange Position in USD			Fund Position in USD		
	Purchase	**Sell**		**Credit**	**Debit**
Customer		-	Spot	+	Maturity Gap
Interbank	+		Forward	Maturity Gap	-

    ii.   To cover this maturity gap, the bank does a sell/buy swap.

        a.   Sell USD/buy INR value spot.

        b.   Buy USD/sell INR value forward.

    iii.   USD is in premium in the forward market. So, the bank pays, and as a market taker, the bank pays high: 0.0350.

    iv.   The cover rate to buy from the interbank = 64.2375 + 0.0350 = 64.2725.

    v.   After adjusting the margin, the forward rate quoted to the exporter = 64.2725 + 0.02 = 64.2925 INR per dollar.

6.   The importer needs two month forward cover for USD 10 million. The margin for the bank will be 2 paise. The USD/INR rates are:

USD / INR Spot	64.2275	64.2375
One month forward	0.0225	0.0125
Two month forward	0.0350	0.0250

After two months, the importer has to make payment to his or her foreign counterparty, for which he or she needs USD. The bank will sell USD 10 million to the importer as per the forward contract. The initial position of the bank during the forward booking is as follows:

Exchange Position in USD			Fund Position in USD		
	Purchase	Sell		Credit	Debit
Customer		-	Spot		
Interbank			Forward		-

The nostro account of the bank in USD would get debited in two months' time. So the bank needs to buy USD to be credited to his or her nostro account after two months. But he or she has to book it today to avoid the risk of exchange rate fluctuation. However, the bank cannot book this forward cover directly in two months' time. The bank, in order to cover its position, will involve the spot leg and use FX swap in the interbank.

i. Buy USD spot at 64.2375. With this transaction, the exchange position is fully covered. However, there exists a maturity gap in the fund position as the USD outflow would be in two months' time, whereas USD inflow is in spot.

Exchange Position in USD			Fund Position in USD		
	Purchase	Sell		Credit	Debit
Customer		-	Spot	+	Maturity Gap
Interbank	+		Forward	Maturity Gap	-

ii. To cover this maturity gap, the bank does a sell/buy swap.

   a. Sell USD/buy INR value spot

   b. Buy USD/sell INR value forward

iii. USD is in discount in the forward market. So, the bank receives, and as a market taker, the bank receives low; 0.0250.

iv. The cover rate to buy from the interbank = 64.2375 − 0.0250 = 64.2125.

v. After adjusting the margin, the forward rate quoted to the exporter = 64.2125 + 0.02 = 64.2325 INR per dollar.

10.10.2 Two Month Forward Deal in Cross Rate

7. Spot: EUR/USD: 1.1112/14;   S/1M 20/21
            USD/INR: 68.2000/2100;   S/1M 23/24

Calculate the rate and write the cover operation for an export client and an import client with a 5 paise margin.

Export Client:
   EUR/USD the rate is 1.1112 + 0.0020 = 1.1132
   USD/INR the rate is 68.2000 + 0.23 = 68.43
   EUR/INR = 1.1132 × 68.43 = 76.1763
   Deduct the margin. The rate for the export customer is 76.1563.

Export Client—Initial position in the bank book:

The exporter is having EUR. He wants to get it converted into INR. It is not possible to convert this EUR directly into INR. To convert this, the bank needs to make use of the USD channel. So, in simple language, the bank first has to convert EUR into USD and then convert USD to INR.

After having the customer deal booked, the exchange and fund position would look like the following:

EUR						USD					
Exchange Position			Fund Position			Exchange Position			Fund Position		
	P	S		C	D		P	S		C	D
Customer	+		Spot			Interbank			Spot		
Interbank			Fwd	+		Interbank			Spot		
Interbank						Interbank			Fwd		

The bank does sell euro in the interbank market at value spot to cover its position. The transaction is as follows:

    i.   Sell EUR and buy USD value spot at 1.1112.

EUR						USD					
Exchange Position			Fund Position			Exchange Position			Fund Position		
	P	S		C	D		P	S		C	D
Customer	+		Spot		-	Interbank	+		Spot	+	
Interbank		-	Fwd	+		Interbank			Spot		
Interbank						Interbank			Fwd		

Now, the exchange position in euro is squared off. However, the maturity gap remains, with fund position in euro. Also, the exchange position and fund position in USD are not squared off. To square off the position in USD, bank has to sell USD in interbank against INR. The transaction is as follows:

    ii.   Sell USD buy INR value spot at 68.2000.

EUR						USD					
Exchange Position			Fund Position			Exchange Position			Fund Position		
	P	S		C	D		P	S		C	D
Customer	+		Spot	Maturity gap	-	Interbank	+	-	Spot	+	-
Interbank		-	Fwd	+	Maturity Gap	Interbank			Spot		
Interbank						Interbank			Fwd		

Now, the bank has no position open in USD. However, the fund position in euro is still open. As there exists a maturity gap, the bank does a buy/sell swap in euro. The transaction is as follows:

iii. Buy EUR and sell USD value spot and ⎫
     Sell EUR and buy USD value forward ⎰

    a. Buy/sell in euro. Euro is on premium in the forward marker. So, the bank receives, and the bank receives low; 20 pips.

    b. The rate in EUR/USD is: $1.1112 + 0.0020 = 1.1132$.

With this transaction, exchange and fund positions in euro are squared off. However, the buy/sell swap in euro has a corresponding sell/buy swap in USD. So, we now have fund position in USD open at a different maturity date.

	EUR				USD				
Exchange Position		**Fund Position**			**Exchange Position**		**Fund Position**		
	P	S		C	D		P	S	C	D
Customer	+		Spot	Buy	-	Interbank	+		Spot	+	-1
Interbank		-	Fwd	+	Sell	Interbank		-	Spot	Maturity Gap	Sell
Interbank	+	-				Interbank	+	-	Fwd	Buy	Maturity Gap

The Bank now does a buy/sell swap in USD to cover the position. The transaction is as follows:

iv. Buy USD/Sell INR value spot ⎫
    Sell USD/Buy INR value forward ⎰

    a. Receive low: 23 paise.

    b. $68.2000 + 0.23 = 68.43$.

	EUR					USD				
Exchange Position			**Fund Position**			**Exchange Position**			**Fund Position**	
	P	S		C	D		P	S	C	D
Customer	+		Spot	Buy	-	Interbank	+		Spot	+	-1
Interbank		-	Fwd	+	Sell	Interbank		-	Spot	Buy	Sell
Interbank	+	-				Interbank	+	-	Fwd	Buy	Sell
						Interbank	+	-			

v. EUR/INR $68.43 \times 1.1132 = 76.1763$.

vi. Deduct the margin as the bank buys euro.
    The final rate is 76.1563. This rate is quoted to the customer.

8. ***Import client***

Spot: EUR/USD: 1.1112 / 14;   S/1M 20/21
USD/INR: 68.2000 / 2100;   S/1M 23/24
EUR/USD the rate is $1.1114 + 0.0021 = 1.1135$
USD/INR the rate is $68.2100 + 0.24 = 68.45$

EUR/INR $= 1.1135 \times 68.45 = 76.2191$.

Add the margin. The rate for the import customer 76.2391.

Import Client—Initial position in the bank book:

The importer is required to have EUR for making payment towards his or her import bill. He or she wants to get it converted from INR. However, it is not possible to convert INR into EUR directly. To convert this, the bank needs to make use of the USD channel. So, in simple language, the bank first has to convert INR into USD and then convert USD to EUR.

After having the customer deal booked, the exchange and fund position would look like the following:

	EUR					USD				
	Exchange Position		Fund Position			Exchange Position		Fund Position		
	P	S		C	D		P	S		C	D
Customer		-	Spot			Interbank			Spot		
Interbank			Fwd		-	Interbank			Spot		
Interbank						Interbank			Fwd		

The bank buys euro in the interbank market at value spot to cover its position. The transaction is as follows:

    i.   Buy EUR and sell USD value spot at 1.1114.

	EUR					USD				
	Exchange Position		Fund Position			Exchange Position		Fund Position		
	P	S		C	D		P	S		C	D
Customer		-	Spot	+	Maturity gap	Interbank		-	Spot		-
Interbank	+		Fwd	Maturity Gap	-	Interbank			Spot		
Interbank						Interbank			Fwd		

Now, the exchange position in euro is squared off. However, the maturity gap remains with fund position in euro. Also, exchange position and fund position in USD are not squared off. To square off the position in USD, the bank has to buy USD in interbank against INR. The transaction is as follows:

    ii.   Buy USD Sell INR value spot at 68.2100.

	EUR					USD				
	Exchange Position		Fund Position			Exchange Position		Fund Position		
	P	S		C	D		P	S		C	D
Customer		-	Spot	+	Maturity gap	Interbank	+	-	Spot	+	-
Interbank	+		Fwd	Maturity Gap	-	Interbank			Spot		
Interbank						Interbank			Fwd		

Now, the bank has no position open in USD. However, the fund position in EUR is still open. As there exists a maturity gap, the bank does a sell/buy swap in EUR. The transaction is as follows:

iii. Sell EUR and buy USD value spot and }
Buy EUR and sell USD value forward }

    a. Sell/buy in euro. Euro is on premium in the forward marker. So, the bank pays, and the bank pays high: 21.

    b. The rate in EUR/USD is: 1.1114 + 0.0021 = 1.1135.

EUR					USD					
Exchange Position			**Fund Position**		**Exchange Position**			**Fund Position**		
	P	S		C	D		P	S		C	D
Customer		-	Spot	+	Sell	Interbank	+	-	Spot	+	-
Interbank	+		Fwd	Buy	-	Interbank	+	-	Spot	Buy	Maturity Gap
Interbank	+	-				Interbank			Fwd	Maturity Gap	Sell

With this transaction, the exchange and fund position in euro are squared off. However, the sell/buy swap in EUR has a corresponding buy/sell swap in USD. So, we now have a fund position in USD open at a different maturity date.

The bank now does a sell/buy swap in USD to cover the position. The transaction is as follows:

iv. Sell USD/buy INR value spot }
Buy USD/Sell INR value forward }

    a. Pay high: 24.

    b. 68.2100 + 0.24 = 68.45.

EUR						USD					
Exchange Position			**Fund Position**			**Exchange Position**			**Fund Position**		
	P	S		C	D		P	S		C	D
Customer		-	Spot	+	Sell	Interbank	+	-	Spot	+	-
Interbank	+		Fwd	Buy	-	Interbank	+	-	Spot	Buy	Sell
Interbank	+	-				Interbank			Fwd	Buy	Sell

v. EUR/INR 68.45 × 1.1135 = 76.2191.

vi. Add the margin as the bank sells euro.
The final rate is 76.2393. This rate is quoted to the customer.

9.   The exporter needs 1 month forward cover for export to Switzerland. Margin for the bank will be 4 paise. Quote for CHF / INR is required to be given to the exporter by the bank. The USD/CHF and USD / INR rates are:

USD / CHF Spot	0.9543	0.9545		USD / INR Spot	62.0100	62.0200
S / F	0.0034	0.0033		S / F	0.0176	0.0178

For this, the exporter will sell the CHF and, hence, the bank will buy the CHF from the customer.

Exchange arithmetic
USD/CHF: 0.9545 – 0.0033 = 0.9512
USD/INR 62.0100 + 0.0176 = 62.0276
CHF/INR = 62. 0378 / 0.9512 = 65.2098
Customer rate = 65.1698 INR per CHF

The bank buys CHF one month forward from the customer and covers its position in the spot and forward market using FX swap. Here, the mechanism of cover position is illustrated in order to arrive at the final CHF/INR rate. For CHF, the initial exchange position and the funds position will be as follows:

CHF						USD					
Exchange Position			Fund Position			Exchange Position			Fund Position		
	P	S		C	D		P	S		C	D
Customer	+		Spot			Interbank			Spot		
Interbank			Fwd	+		Interbank			Spot		
Interbank						Interbank			Fwd		

The cover operation in the interbank for CHF will be as follows:

i.   Sell CHF and buy USD value spot at 0.9545. With this exchange, position in CHF is covered or squared off. However, the bank is open in CHF fund position and for USD both in exchange and fund position.

CHF						USD					
Exchange Position			Fund Position			Exchange Position			Fund Position		
	P	S		C	D		P	S		C	D
Customer	+		Spot		-	Interbank	+		Spot	+	
Interbank		-	Fwd	+		Interbank			Spot		
Interbank						Interbank			Fwd		

ii.   The bank sells USD buys INR value spot at 68.0100. By this operation, the bank covers its open position in USD both for exchange and fund position. But the bank is still having the position opened in CHF nostro.

CHF					USD					
Exchange Position			Fund Position			Exchange Position			Fund Position		
	P	S		C	D		P	S		C	D
Customer	+		Spot	↖	-	Interbank	+	-	Spot	+	-
Interbank		-	Fwd	+		Interbank			Spot		
Interbank						Interbank			Fwd		

iii. So, the bank does a swap operation

    a. Sell USD and buy CHF spot.

    b. Buy USD and sell CHF forward.

Since it is a sell/buy swap in USD and USD is in discount in forward segment, the bank receives, and receives low; 0.0033.

    Hence USD/CHF forward rate will be = 0.9545 − 0.0033 = 0.9512.

CHF					USD					
Exchange Position			Fund Position			Exchange Position			Fund Position		
	P	S		C	D		P	S		C	D
Customer	+		Spot	Buy↘	-	Interbank	+	-	Spot	+	-
Interbank		-	Fwd	+	Sell	Interbank	+	-	Spot		Sell
Interbank	+	-				Interbank			Fwd	Buy↙	

iv. Now, in euro as both the exchange and fund position are squared off bank does a buy/sell swap in USD:

    a. Buy USD and sell INR spot.

    b. Sell USD and buy INR forward.

Since it is a buy/sell swap in USD and USD is in premium in forward, the bank receives, and receives low: 0.0176.

    Hence, USD/INR forward rate will be = 62.0100 + 0.0176 = 62.0276.

CHF					USD					
Exchange Position			Fund Position			Exchange Position			Fund Position		
	P	S		C	D		P	S		C	D
Customer	+		Spot	Buy↘	-	Interbank	+	-	Spot	+	-
Interbank		-	Fwd	+	Sell	Interbank	+	-	Spot	Buy	-
Interbank						Interbank			Fwd	+	Sell

v. Hence cover rate of CHF/INR to sell CHF in interbank in forward market will be

$$= 62.0276 / 0.9512$$
$$= 65.2098.$$

vi. CHF/INR forward rate quoted to the exporter = 65.2098 − 0.04 = 65.1698.

10.10.3 Cash Settlement in USD/INR

1. USD/INR: Spot 64.8950/9050,
    C/S 0.0275/0.0300, margin 2 p.

The customer wants a cash rate for USD 1 million export.

As it is cash settlement, the bank needs to do a spot transaction as well as a swap deal to fill the maturity gap. Also, from the C/S quote, it is clear that the cash rate is less than the spot rate.

Exchange Arithmetic

The customer is having USD and wants to convert it into INR value cash.

Cash rate for an exporter in INR (64.8950 − 0.0300) = INR 64.8650

Customer Rate = INR 64.8450.

Initial Position:

Exchange Position in USD			Fund Position in USD		
	Purchase	**Sale**		**Credit**	**Debit**
Customer	+1		Cash	+1	
Interbank			Spot		

i. As it is not possible to sell USD directly at cash, the bank sells USD at value spot at the rate 64.8950.

Exchange Position in USD		Fund Position in USD		
Customer	+1	Cash	+1	Maturity Gap
Interbank	−1	Spot	Maturity Gap	−1

ii. Now as inflow of fund is at value cash and outflow of fund is at value spot, it creates a maturity gap. To cover this position bank has to do a swap operation.

iii. Sell USD/Buy INR cash and
    Buy USD/Sell INR spot (sell/buy swap in USD).
    Spot USD is in premium. So, to find the cash rate, we need to deduct swap points from the spot rate.

Exchange Position in USD			Fund Position in USD		
	Purchase	**Sale**		**Credit**	**Debit**
Customer	+1		Cash	+1	Sell
Interbank		−1	Spot	Buy	−1

iv.   The bank sells USD at discount rate and buys USD at premium rate.
      The bank pays, pays high: 0.0300.

v.   The cover rate is 64.8950 − 0.0300 = 64.8650.

vi.   The customer rate deduct margin = 64.8450.

2.   USD/INR is 62.50/52 and C/S is 4/3.

Explain the cover operation for USD importer who wants a conversion on value cash.

Exchange Arithmetic:
   Importer Rate: 62.52 + 0.04 = 62.55
   Add Margin: 62.55 + 0.02 = 62.57

Interbank Cover Operation:
   Initial Position:

Exchange Position in USD			Fund Position in USD		
	Purchase	**Sale**		**Credit**	**Debit**
Customer		−1	Cash		−1
Interbank			Spot		

As the customer wants a conversion on value spot and the bank is not allowed to buy USD directly from value cash, the bank involves spot segment and does a swap operation.

i.   The bank buys USD value spot in interbank at 62.52. With this transaction, the exchange
      position and fund position in USD becomes as follows:

Exchange Position in USD			Fund Position in USD		
	Purchase	**Sale**		**Credit**	**Debit**
Customer		−1	Cash	Maturity Gap	−1
Interbank	+1		Spot	+1	Maturity Gap

ii.   To cover the position, bank has to do a swap.

   a.   Buy USD/Sell INR cash

   b.   Sell USD/Buy INR spot,
        USD is in discount in the spot market, pay high: 0.04.

Exchange Position in USD			Fund Position in USD		
	Purchase	**Sale**		**Credit**	**Debit**
Customer		−1	Cash	Buy	−1
Interbank	+1		Spot	+1	Sell

iii. The cover rate = 62.52 + 0.04 = 62.56.

iv.   The exchange margin is 62.58.

v.   The customer rate 62.58.

A few more examples are given:

3.   The exporter wants a conversion on value cash for USD 10 million. The margin for the bank will be 2 paise. The USD/INR rates are as follows:

USD / INR Spot	64.8950	64.9050
Cash / Spot	0.0300	0.0375

Exchange Arithmetic:

Customer is having USD and wants a conversion on value Cash

Cover Rate: USD/INR = 64.8950 − 0.0375 = 64.8575 INR per USD.

Exporter Rate: 64.8375 INR per USD.

In this transaction, the nostro account of the bank is expecting a credit of USD 10 million. So, the bank has to give a rate to the customer for the conversion of USD into INR value cash. The rate the bank offer has to be booked in the interbank. The bank cannot book a cash rate directly without making a spot transaction.

The initial position of bank is as follows:

Exchange Position in USD				Fund Position in USD		
	Purchase	Sale			Credit	Debit
Customer	+			Cash	+	
Interbank				Spot		

a.   Sell USD value spot at 64.8950. So, the exchange position is covered but fund position is not because of the maturity gap in the inflow and outflow of fund.

Exchange Position in USD				Fund Position in USD		
	Purchase	Sale			Credit	Debit
Customer	+			Cash	+	Maturity Gap
Interbank		-		Spot	Maturity Gap	-

b.   Sell USD/Buy INR value cash and buy USD/Sell INR value spot.

So, it is a sell/buy swap. USD is in in premium in the spot market compared to cash. Pay and pay high: 0.0375.

Exchange Position in USD				Fund Position in USD		
	Purchase	Sale			Credit	Debit
Customer	+			Cash	+	Sell
Interbank		-		Spot	Buy	-

c.   With the sell/buy swap, not only is the exchange position in USD in square but the fund position also in square.

d. So, the cover rate to sell USD in the interbank$=64.8950-0.0375=64.8575$.

e. With the margin cash rate quoted to the exporter will be$=64.8575-0.02=64.8375$.

4. The exporter wants a conversion on value cash for USD 10 million. Margin for the bank will be 2 paise. The USD/INR rates are as follows:

USD / INR Spot	64.8950	64.9050
Cash / Spot	0.0375	0.0300

Exchange Arithmetic:

Customer is having USD and wants have it converted to INR on today

Cover Rate: $64.8950+0.0300=64.9250$ INR per USD

Exporter Rate: 64.9050 INR per USD

In this transaction, nostro account of the bank is expecting a credit of USD 10 million. So, the bank has to give a rate to the customer for the conversion of USD into INR value cash. The rate the bank offer has to be booked in the interbank. The bank cannot book a cash rate directly without making a spot transaction.

The initial position of bank is as follows:

Exchange Position in USD			Fund Position in USD		
	Purchase	**Sale**		**Credit**	**Debit**
Customer	+		Cash	+	
Interbank			Spot		

a. Sell USD value spot at 64.8950. So, the exchange position is covered but fund position is not because of the maturity gap in the inflow and outflow of fund.

Exchange Position in USD			Fund Position in USD		
	Purchase	**Sale**		**Credit**	**Debit**
Customer	+		Cash	+	Maturity Gap
Interbank		-	Spot	Maturity Gap	-

b. Sell USD/Buy INR value cash and buy USD/sell INR value spot.

So, it is a sell/buy swap. USD is in in discount in the spot market compared to cash. So, the bank received, and receives low as price taker: 0.0300.

Exchange Position in USD			Fund Position in USD		
	Purchase	**Sale**		**Credit**	**Debit**
Customer	+		Cash	+	Sell
Interbank		-	Spot	Buy	-

c. With the sell/buy swap not only exchange position in USD is in square but the fund position is also in square.

d. So, the cover rate to sell USD in the interbank=64.8950+0.0300=64.9250.

e. With the margin cash rate quoted to the exporter will be=64.9250−0.02=64.9050.

5. The importer wants a conversion on value cash for USD 10 million. The margin for the bank is 2 paise. The USD/INR rates are:

USD / INR Spot	64.8950	64.9050
Cash / Spot	0.0300	0.0375

Exchange Arithmetic:

The importer requires USD to pay to his or her foreign party on today's date. So, the bank has to buy dollar from the market.

Cover rate for Bank: 64.9050 − 0.0300=64.8750 INR per USD.

Importer Rate=64.8950 INR per USD.

The importer has to make payment to his or her foreign counterparty on the deal date or on today's date. For which he or she needs USD immediately. The bank will sell USD 10 million to the importer on today (T=0). The initial position of the bank during the booking of USD conversion is as follows:

Exchange Position in USD			Fund Position in USD		
	Purchase	Sell		Credit	Debit
Customer		-	Cash		
Interbank			Spot		

The nostro account of the bank in USD would get debited today on account of the payment of the customer. So bank needs to buy USD to be credited to his or her account immediately on the same date as the deal date. However, the bank cannot book this directly in cash market segment. The bank, in order to cover its position, will involve the spot leg and the use FX swap in the interbank.

i. Buy USD spot at 64.9050. With this transaction, the exchange position is fully covered. However, there exists a maturity gap in the fund position as USD outflow would be on today, whereas USD inflow is in spot leg; that is on T+2 day.

Exchange Position in USD			Fund Position in USD		
	Purchase	Sell		Credit	Debit
Customer		-	Cash	Maturity Gap	-
Interbank	+		Spot	+	Maturity Gap

ii. To cover this maturity gap bank does a buy/sell swap.

a. Buy USD/Sell INR value cash.

b. Sell USD/Buy INR value spot.

iii. USD is in premium in the spot market compared to cash market. So, the bank receives, and as a market taker, the bank receives low; 0.0300.

iv.   The cover rate to buy from the interbank=64.9050−0.0300=64.8750.

v.   After adjusting the margin, the forward rate quoted to the exporter=64.8750+0.02=64.8950 INR per USD.

6.   Importer wants a conversion on value cash for USD 10 million. The margin for the bank will be 2 paise. The USD/INR rates are:

USD / INR Spot	64.8950	64.9050
Cash / Spot	0.0375	0.0300

Exchange Arithmetic:

The importer requires USD to pay to his or her foreign party on today's date. So, the bank has to buy dollar from the market.

Cover rate for Bank: 64.9050+0.0375=64.9425 INR per USD.

Importer Rate=64.9625 INR per USD.

The importer has to make payment to his or her foreign counterparty on the deal date or on today's date for which he or she needs USD immediately. The bank will sell USD 10 million to the importer on today (T=0). The initial position of the bank during the booking of USD conversion is as follows:

Exchange Position in USD			Fund Position in USD		
	Purchase	Sell		Credit	Debit
Customer		-	Cash		-
Interbank			Spot		

The nostro account of the bank in USD would get debited today on account of the payment of the customer. So the bank needs to buy USD to be credited to his or her nostro account immediately on the same date as the deal date. However, the bank cannot book this directly in cash market segment. The bank, in order to cover its position, will involve the spot leg and the use FX swap in the interbank.

i.   Buy USD spot at 64.9050. With this transaction, the exchange position is fully covered. However, there exists a maturity gap in the fund position as USD outflow would be on today, whereas dollar inflow is in spot leg, that is, on T+2 day.

Exchange Position in USD			Fund Position in USD		
	Purchase	Sell		Credit	Debit
Customer		-	Cash	Maturity Gap	-
Interbank	+		Spot	+	Maturity Gap

ii.   To cover this maturity gap bank does a buy/sell swap.

a.   Buy dollar/Sell INR value cash

b.   Sell dollar/Buy INR value spot

iii.   USD is in discount in the spot market compared to cash market. So, the bank pays, and as a market taker, the bank pays high. The swap point is 0.0375.

iv.   The cover rate to buy from the interbank = 64.9050 + 0.0375 = 64.9425.

v.   After adjusting the margin, the forward rate quoted to the exporter = 64.9425 + 0.02 = 64.9625 INR per dollar.

10.10.4 Cash Settlement in Cross Rate

7.   EUR/USD: Spot   1.0606/07
       C/S   31/30
     USD/INR: Spot   68.4500/4700
       C/S   4/5

A customer is having euro receivables.

Exchange Arithmetic
EUR/USD: 1.0606 + 0.0030 = 1.0636
USD/INR: 68.4500 − 0.05 = 68.4000
EUR/INR: 1.0636 × 68.4000 = 72.7502
Customer Rate = 72.7302

Initial Position:

EUR						USD					
Exchange Position			**Fund Position**			**Exchange Position**			**Fund Position**		
	P	S		C	D		P	S		C	D
Customer	+		Cash	+		Interbank			Cash		
Interbank			Spot			Interbank			Spot		
Interbank						Interbank			spot		

The customer has EUR which to be converted into INR. The customer wants value cash. However, the bank cannot cover this position directly.

i.   So bank sells EUR and buys USD value spot at 1.0606.

The exchange position and fund position after the spot transaction are as follows:

EUR						USD					
Exchange Position			**Fund Position**			**Exchange Position**			**Fund Position**		
	P	S		C	D		P	S		C	D
Customer	+		Cash	+		Interbank	+		Cash		
Interbank		−	Spot		−	Interbank			Spot	+	
Interbank						Interbank			spot		

ii. Next, to cover the USD fund and exchange position bank sell USD buy INR value spot is at 68.4500.

EUR						USD					
Exchange Position			**Fund Position**			**Exchange Position**			**Fund Position**		
	P	S		C	D		P	S		C	D
Customer	+		Cash	+	↗	Interbank	+		Cash		
Interbank		-	Spot		-	Interbank		-	Spot	+	-
Interbank						Interbank			Spot		

So, there is no position open in USD. The position that is open is in EUR. So, the bank is required to cover this position through a sell/buy swap.

iii. Sell EUR/Buy USD value cash
Buy EUR/Sell USD value spot

EUR						USD					
Exchange Position			**Fund Position**			**Exchange Position**			**Fund Position**		
	P	S		C	D		P	S		C	D
Customer	+		Cash	+	Sell	Interbank	+	-	Cash	Buy	Maturity Gap
Interbank		-	Spot	Buy	-	Interbank	+	-	Spot	+	-
Interbank	+	-				Interbank			Spot	Maturity Gap	Sell

In spot, euro is in discount; receive is low: 30.

So, the EUR/USD rate is 1.0606+0.0030=1.0636.

EUR						USD					
Exchange Position			**Fund Position**			**Exchange Position**			**Fund Position**		
	P	S		C	D		P	S		C	D
Customer	+		Cash	+	Sell	Interbank	+	-	Cash	+	Sell
Interbank		-	Spot	Buy	-	Interbank	+	-	Spot	+	-
Interbank	+	-				Interbank	+	-	Spot	Buy	-

iv. Sell USD/Buy INR value cash
Buy USD/Sell INR value spot
Sell/buy is in USD; spot is in premium; pay is high: 5
USD/INR: 68.4500−0.05=68.4000.

v. EUR/INR=1.0636×68.4000=72.7502.

vi.   Deduct 2 paise margin as the bank buys euro from the client.

vii. The final rate is 72.7302.

8.   The exporter wants a conversion on value cash for JPY export. The margin for the bank will be 2 paise. Quote for JPY/INR is required to be given to the exporter by the bank. The USD/JPY and USD/INR rates are as follows:

USD / JPY Spot	110.24	110.26
Cash / Spot	20	30

USD / INR Spot	68.5000	68.5200
Cash / Spot	3	4

For this, the exporter will sell the JPY and, hence, the bank will buy JPY from the customer.

Exchange Arithmetic:

USD/JPY 110.26 − 0.20 = 110.20

USD/INR 68.5000 − 0.04 = 68.4600

JPY/INR = (68.46 / 110.20) × 100 = 68.2024

With the margin = 68.1824.

The bank will buy JPY value cash from the customer and will cover its position in the cash and spot market using FX swap. Here, the mechanism of cover operation will be illustrated for both JPY and USD in order to arrive at the final JPY/INR rate. For JPY and USD, the exchange position and the funds position will be as follows:

JPY						USD					
Exchange Position			**Fund Position**			**Exchange Position**			**Fund Position**		
	P	S		C	D		P	S		C	D
Customer	+		Cash	+		Interbank			Cash		
Interbank			Spot			Interbank			Spot		
Interbank						Interbank			spot		

The cover operation in the interbank for JPY will be as follows:

i.   Buy USD and sell JPY value spot at 110.26. With this transaction, the bank covers its exchange position in JPY but there exists a maturity mismatch in the fund position of JPY. Also, the bank opens its position in USD.

JPY						USD					
Exchange Position			**Fund Position**			**Exchange Position**			**Fund Position**		
	P	S		C	D		P	S		C	D
Customer	+		Cash	+		Interbank	+		Cash		
Interbank		-	Spot		-	Interbank			Spot	+	
Interbank						Interbank			spot		

ii. The bank sells USD/buys INR value spot at 68.5000. So, it covers both the exchange and fund position for the bank in USD. However, a maturity gap is still there in JPY.

JPY					USD					
Exchange Position			Fund Position			Exchange Position			Fund Position	
	P	S		C	D		P	S		C	D
Customer	+		Cash	+		Interbank	+	-	Cash		
Interbank		-	Spot		-	Interbank			Spot	+	-
Interbank						Interbank			spot		

iii. To cover JPY fund position, the bank does a swap operation.

   a. Buy USD/Sell JPY value cash

   b. Sell USD/Buy JPY value spot

   Since it is a buy/sell swap in USD, and USD is in premium in the spot segment compared to cash, the bank receives, and receives low; 0.20.

   Hence USD/JPY cash rate will be = 110.26 − 0.20 = 110.06.

JPY						USD					
Exchange Position			Fund Position			Exchange Position			Fund Position		
	P	S		C	D		P	S		C	D
Customer	+		Cash	+	Sell	Interbank	+	-	Cash	Buy	
Interbank		-	Spot	Buy	-	Interbank	+	-	Spot	+	-
Interbank	+	-				Interbank			spot		Sell

iv. This transaction covers all the positions in JPY, however, opens the position in USD. So, the bank has to do a swap operation in USD.

   a. Sell USD/Buy INR value cash

   b. Buy USD/Sell INR spot

   Since it is a sell/buy swap in USD and USD is in premium in spot compared to cash, the bank pays and pays high: 0.04.

v. Hence USD/INR cash rate will be = 68.50 − 0.04 = 68.46.

vi. Hence, the cover rate of JPY/INR to sell JPY in interbank in cash market will be

$$= (68.46 / 110.06) \times 100$$
$$= 62.2024.$$

vii. JPY/INR cash rate quoted to the exporter = 62.2024 − 0.02 = 62.1824.

9. Importer wants a conversion on value cash for JPY import. Margin for the bank will be 2 paise. Quote for JPY/INR is required to be given to the importer by the bank. The USD/JPY and USD/INR rates are as follows:

USD / JPY Spot	110.24	110.26
Cash / Spot	20	30

USD / INR SPOT	68.5000	68.5200
Cash / Spot	3	4

Exchange Position
Customer wants JPY and having INR
USD/JPY: 110.24 – 0.30 = 109.94
USD/INR: 68.52 – 0.03 = 68.49
JPY INR: (68.49 / 109.94) × 100.

For this, the importer will buy the JPY and, hence, the bank will sell JPY against INR to the customer.

Nostro account of the bank in USD would get debited today on account of the payment of the customer. So bank needs to buy JPY against USD to be credited to his nostro account immediately on the same date as the deal date. However, the bank cannot book this directly in cash market segment. The bank, in order to cover its position, will involve the spot leg and the use FX swap in the interbank. Here, the mechanism of cover position will be illustrated for both JPY and USD in order to arrive at the final JPY/INR rate. Initial exchange position and the funds position are as follows:

JPY						USD					
Exchange Position			Fund Position			Exchange Position			Fund Position		
	P	S		C	D		P	S		C	D
Customer		-	Cash		-	Interbank			Cash		
Interbank			Spot			Interbank			Spot		
Interbank						Interbank			spot		

The cover operation in the interbank for JPY will be:

i. Sell USD and buy JPY value spot at 110.24. With this transaction, the bank covers its exchange position in JPY but there exists a maturity mismatch in the fund position of JPY. Also, with this transaction, the bank opens its position in USD.

JPY						USD					
Exchange Position			Fund Position			Exchange Position			Fund Position		
	P	S		C	D		P	S		C	D
Customer		-	Cash		-	Interbank		-	Cash		
Interbank	+		Spot	+		Interbank			Spot		-
Interbank						Interbank			spot		

ii. Bank buys USD/sells INR value spot at 68.5200. So it covers both the exchange and fund position for the bank in USD. However, a maturity gap is still there in JPY.

JPY						USD					
Exchange Position			Fund Position			Exchange Position			Fund Position		
	P	S		C	D		P	S		C	D
Customer		-	Cash		–	Interbank	+	-	Cash		
Interbank	+		Spot	+		Interbank			Spot	+	-
Interbank						Interbank			spot		

iii. To cover JPY fund position, the bank does swap operation.

    a. Sell USD/Buy JPY value cash

    b. Buy USD/Sell JPY value spot

Since it is a sell/buy swap in USD, and USD is in premium in the spot segment compared to cash, the bank pays and as market taker, the bank pays high: 0.30.

iv. Hence USD/JPY cash rate will be $= 110.24 - 0.30 = 109.94$.

JPY						USD					
Exchange Position			Fund Position			Exchange Position			Fund Position		
	P	S		C	D		P	S		C	D
Customer		-	Cash	Buy	-	Interbank	+	-	Cash		Sell
Interbank	+		Spot	+	Sell	Interbank	+	-	Spot	+	-
Interbank	+	-				Interbank			spot	Buy	

v. This transaction covers all the positions in JPY; however, it opens the position in USD. So, the bank has to do a swap operation in USD.

    a. Buy USD/Sell INR value cash

    b. Sell USD/Buy INR spot

Since it is a buy/sell swap in USD, and USD is in premium in spot compared to cash, the bank receives, and as market taker, the bank receives low; 0.03.

vi. Hence USD/INR cash rate will be $= 68.52 - 0.03 = 68.49$.

vii. Hence the cover rate of JPY/INR to sell JPY in interbank in cash market will be

$$= (68.49 / 109.94) \times 100$$
$$= 62.2976$$

viii. JPY/INR cash rate quoted to the importer $= 62.2976 + 0.02 = 62.3176$.

10.11 Some Important Points about Forward Contract

We know that a forward contract is deliverable at a future date, and the duration of the contract is computed from the spot value of the transaction. However, there may be two types of forward contract: (a) fixed forward contract and (b) option forward contract.

a. **Fixed Forward Contract:** If the delivery of foreign exchange takes place on a specified future date, then it is known as the fixed forward contract. As explained earlier, if the customer gets into a fixed forward contract for three months, and the deal date on which the forward contract is booked is June 3, then the customer would be able to present the bill or other instrument on September 5. The customer cannot deliver the forward contract prior to or later than the determined date. We know that the forward contract is an instrument to hedge the fluctuation in foreign exchange. It may be noted that most often it is difficult to know the exact date of foreign exchange delivery. So, the purpose of hedging the risk may be defeated. That is the reason that there is one more instrument, namely, the option forward contract.

b. **Option Forward Contract:** As it is difficult to know the exact date of foreign exchange delivery, the customer is given a choice to deliver the goods during a given period of days. Under this contract, a customer can sell or buy foreign exchange on any day during a given period of time at a predetermined rate of exchange. The rate at which the deal takes place is the option forward rate. For example, if a customer enters into a two month option forward contract on May 15, then he or she can deal with the foreign exchange on any day between July 1 and July 31. This period is known as the option period.

However, it may be noted that for the option period, the delivery date should not exceed one month. For example, the valid option periods can be January 3 to January 10, January 18 to February 17, or April 1 to April 30.

10.12 Swap Points for Broken Dates

It is not that the exporter or importer is always looking for the month end rate. They may be looking for the quote, which can be of any date in a month. We have already discussed that to calculate one month forward rate, we need to first arrive to spot rate. So, if the customer wants to book a deal for one month and if the deal date is July 11, then the spot rate would be of July 13, assuming that July 13 is the second business day for the non-USD center and working day for the USD center.

Suppose an importer of automobile parts for manufacturing of cars orders a few parts from the USA. From the day he or she knows that his or her consignment is on the way to the point of time of actual payment for the same, there is Forex risk exposure on him or her.

The risk is that the spot rate after three months could be higher than what is available today. If the consignment is worth, say, USD 2 million, he or she needs to buy USD 2 million to be paid on October 17. If the aforementioned rates prevail, what rate would the banker quote to the merchant?

In other words, the banker has to quote for a forward contract for delivery on October 17, 2016. Forward rate is calculated by F = Spot + FP.

In India, the FPs are given for only month ends. To calculate the forward rate for the last working day of the month, we need to add the points to the spot rate.

Therefore, one needs to derive the FPs applicable to October 17 through interpolation method using September 30 and October 30 FPs. Let us assume that the month end rates are given in Table 10.8.

As the deal date is August 12, 2016, Friday, the spot would be August 17, 2016. It is because August 13 and August 14, 2016, are Saturday and Sunday, respectively. Also, being Independence Day, August 15, 2016, Monday, is also a holiday. So the T+2 day is August 17, 2016. So, as the customer wants to book a two month forward, the forward value date would be October 17, 2016.

- FP for September 30, 2016 = 11

- FP for October 31, 2016 − 16

- Number of days between September 30 and October 31 = 31

- Number of days between September 30 and October 17 = 17

- FP for 17 days = (16−11)/31 × 17 = 2.74

- FP for October 17, 2016 = 11 + 2.74 = 13.74

- Therefore, the banker's quote for the importer merchant will be current spot of 65.72 + FPs of 0.1374, which together is 65.8574.

As it is an import customer, we need to add the margin with the rate. If the margin is 2 paise then the final rate is 65.8774.

Table 10.8 Interbank Spot (S) and Forward Points (FP) for USD/INR

Current date and time: 12/8/2016 10:32 (Friday)				
Spot: 65.71/72			Forward Points (FP)	
FWD	Settlement Date	No Days	Bid	Offer
C/S	12-Aug-16	2 (before spot)	0.25	0.35
T/S	16-Aug-16	1 (before spot)	0.15	0.2
Spot	17-Aug-16	spot		
S/August	31-Aug-16		3.5	4
1 month	30-Sep-16		10	11
2 months	31-Oct-16		15	16
3 months	30-Nov-16		20	22
4 months	31-Dec-16		28	30
5 months	31-Jan-17		35	36
6 months	28-Feb-17		42	44
7 months	31-Mar-17		51	52
8 months	30-Apr-17		60	61
9 months	31-May-17		76	77
10 months	30-Jun-17		85	87
11 months	31-Jul-17		100	103
12 months	31-Aug-17		120	122

10.13 FEDAI Rules for TT and Bill Buying and Selling Rate

We know that there are two major merchant rates: (s) buying rates, quoted for purchase transaction and (b) selling rates, quoted for sell transaction. Buying rates are divided into (a) TT buying rate and (b) bill buying rate. Likewise, selling rates are categorized into (a) TT selling rate and (b) bill selling rate.

- TT buying rate: This rate is applied for all purchase transactions that do not involve the handling of documents such as draft or bill of exchange where the nostro account of the bank is credited. This rate is calculated by deducting the exchange margin from the interbank buying rate of the currency.

- Bill buying rate: This rate is applied for the foreign bill purchased. Bill transactions generally have a time lag as the bill has to be sent to the overseas center by the banker for payment. This period would increase if it is a usance bill (usance bills are bills which are payable after a certain period of time, say, 30 days from sight, 90 days from acceptance). So this rate is higher than the TT buying rate.

- TT selling rate: This rate is applicable for all sale transactions that do not involve documents such as draft or bill of exchange where the nostro account of the bank is debited. This rate is calculated by adding the exchange margin to the interbank selling rate of the currency. The transaction for which this rate is quoted are as follows:

  o   Issue of demand drafts and telegraphic transfers.

  o   Cancellation of foreign exchange that is already purchased. For example, when an export bill is purchased and is unpaid, then the bank would apply TT selling rate for the transaction.

- Bill selling rate: This rate is applied to foreign bill selling.

Example 1: Bill Buying Rate
Suppose, a bank purchases a usance bill 30 days from the date of sight
  USD/INR: Spot 68.21/23
  S/1M: 10/11
  S/2M: 22/23
  S/3M: 37/38
  Calculate the rate on maturity.
As prescribed by FEDAI, 25 days NTP would be applicable in case of calculating the maturity.

So, if the month end rate is applied, the exporter is supposed to receive 22 points. But FEDAI prescribes that for bill buying rate, if USD is in premium, then the last month premium would not be passed on. The bank has to calculate the rate by rounding it off to the lower month.

So, a premium of 22 would not be passed on. Instead, the premium of lower month, that is, 10, would be passed on.

So, the rate for the exporter for 55 days would be 68.21+0.10=68.31 INR per USD.

With the margin of 2 paise, it would be 68.29.

If suppose the spot date is April 20. In the given example, the 55th day falls in June 15. However, the premium of June would not be passed on; instead, only the premium of May would be passed on.

If in USD/INR pair USD is in discount, then discount should be charged to the exporter.

Example 2: Bill Buying Rate
Suppose, a bank purchase a usance bill 30 days from the date of sight.

USD/INR: Spot 68.21/23 (20th April)

S/May: 11/10

S/June: 23/22

S/July: 38/37

Calculate the rate on maturity.

In this case, 55 days would be taken as the maturity day. However, as USD is in discount, this would be charged to the exporter. So, the bank purchases the bill at 68.21 – 0.23 = 67.98 INR per USD.

Case 3: Bill Selling Rate

Calculate bill selling rate for two months when USD is in premium.

USD/INR: Spot 68.21/23

S/1M: 10/11

S/2M: 22/23

S/3M: 37/38

Calculate the rate on maturity.

FEDAI prescribes that for bill selling rate, if USD is in premium, then last month premium would be charged on the customer. So, a premium of 23 would be charged.

The bill selling rate for two months would be 68.23 + 0.23 = 68.46 INR per USD.

If in USD/INR pair USD is in discount, then discount should not be passed on while selling USD.

Example 4:

USD/INR: Spot 68.21/23 (April 20)

S/May: 11/10

S/June: 23/22

S/July: 38/37

Calculate the rate on maturity of two months.

As USD is in discount, this should not be passed on to the customer while selling the rate. As prescribed by FEDAI, the bank must charge the swap points by rounding it off to the lower point. The bank sells the bill at 68.21 – 0.10 = 68.11 INR per USD.

QUESTIONS

A. Multiple Choice Question

1. Foreign currency against rupee is said to be at a premium it will be
   i. Beneficial to the exporter
   ii. Beneficial to the importer
   iii. Beneficial to the both
   iv. It makes no difference

2. Who prescribes the rules of rounding off for various currencies
   i. FEDAI

ii. RBI

iii. ICC

iv. None of the above

3. Cover operation is
   i. Possible through interbank transaction
   ii. Can be done only by using Forex swap
   iii. Both the above

4. Nostro a/c is
    i. A US dollar account maintained by the Indian bank with Chase Manhattan Bank in New York
    ii. An INR account maintained by Chase Manhattan bank with an Indian bank in India
    iii. A US dollar account maintained by Chase Manhattan Bank with the Indian bank in India
    iv. A yen account maintained by Chase Manhattan with the Bank of Tokyo, Osaka branch
    v. All (i), (ii), (iii) and (iv)
    vi. (i), (ii) and (iii)
    vii. (i), (ii) and (iv)
    viii. (i), (iii) and (iv)

5. If Bob has to ask for a quote of USD/yen he would say
    i. 1 million yen
    ii. 1 million USD
    iii. Either of i or ii

6. NTP means
    i. The average period normally involves from the date of negotiation/ purchase/discount till the proceeds of bill credited in the nostro account of the bank concerned.
    ii. It is used for sight draft or for the usance draft like "90 days at sight."
    iii. It is in general 25 days.
    iv. It is related to the time taken for the arrival of goods at overseas destination.
    v. (i), (ii), (iii)
    vi. Only (ii) and (iii)
    vii. All (i), (ii), (iii) and (iv)

7. After doing a deal with an export customer, INR depreciates; by doing the cover bank earns
    i. More profit
    ii. Less profit
    iii. Only the margin, irrespective of the move in the market

B. Answer the Following Questions

1. AUD/USD 0.7212/14, you can sell AUD at

2. USD/JPY 124.21/23, you can sell JPY at

3. USD/CHF 0.9608/10, you can buy CHF at

8. USD/INR is 57.60/62 and you are long in your position and your limit may hit any time, in an uptrending market the ideal or the best quote would be
    i. 57.61/63
    ii. 57.59/61
    iii. 57.60/62

9. On July 10, 2011, at 10 AM, an exporter requested his or her bank for providing him or her with FCY/LCY rate for conversion of his or her USD deposit to INR. The transaction was concluded at the rate of 45. By default, this would mean that the actual currency exchange between the exporter and bank would happen on
    i. Cash date
    ii. Tom date
    iii. Spot date
    iv. Forward date
    v. None of the above

10. The following quotes are seen on the screen: (1+1)
    USD/SGD spot 1.6225/30
    182-day swap: 35/20
    a. The outright forward USD/SGD 182-day rate is
        i. 1.6190/1.6210
        ii. 1.6195/1.6205
        iii. 1.6245/1.6265
    b. SGD is at
        i. discount
        ii. premium

11. Purchase and sale transaction has to be classified from the point of view of
    a. The customer when it is merchant desk transaction
    b. The bank when it is interbank transaction
    c. Always AD-I category bank

4. If interbank spot rate for USD/INR is 60.60/62 and cash spot rate is 2/3, then calculate value cash for an exporter and an importer.

5. If interbank spot rate is 60.60/62 and cash spot rate is 3/2, then calculate value cash for an exporter and importer

6. USD/INR 64.2100/2300, margin 2 paise, rate for USD exports. Is it required to any swap transaction? Rate for the customer.

7. USD/INR 66.5100/5200, Margin 2 paise, rate for USD import. Cover rate for the customer.

8. If interbank spot rate is USD/INR: 60.60/62 and cash spot rate is 2/3, then calculate
   a) Spot rate for an exporter
   b) Spot rate for an importer
   c) Value cash rate for an exporter
   Value cash rate for an importer

9. USD/INR: 63.9100/9200
   USD/CHF: 0.9399/01
   Margin 3 paise. Calculate the CHF/INR rate for CHF exports.

10. GBP/USD: 1.5564/66
    EUR/USD: 1.1111/13
    EUR/GBP rate for EUR outflows of an Indian Corporate with a margin of 5 pips?

11. ABC Travels wants to cover only the cross leg for its CHF receivables when the spot USD/CHF 0.9174/76 and the margin for bank is 4 pips. Bank X has to quote a rate to the customer.

12. Answer the following questions

	USD/INR	EUR/USD	USD/JPY
Spot	65.71/72	1.2394/96	110.41/42
Forward points for 31st January	35/36	21/22	19/18

   a) An exporter will sell EUR on January 31. What is the rate the bank will offer?
   b) An importer will buy 100 JPY on January 31. What rate will the bank offer?

13. If interbank spot is USD/JPY 110.24/110.26 and cash spot rate is 20/30 and USD/INR 62.50/52

and C/S: 4/3, quote JPY/INR to customer for value today with a margin of 5 pips.

14. TVS motors selling a manufacturing unit in Cheshire London, investing in Hamburg Industrial Estate:
    EUR/USD: 1.0915/17, GBP/USD: 1.5480/82
    Quote a rate to your customer for EUR/GBP with a margin 5 pips.

15. EUR/USD 1.1052/53
    Cash Spot 0.0002/0001
    With a margin of 3 pips, what quote will you provide for a cash EUR import transactions?

16. USD/INR: Cash/Spot 0.0225/0.0200
    You receive.
    Cash/Spot 0.0025/0.0050
    You reverse. Are you in profit or loss?

17. C/S 0.0125/.0100 you receive. Now C/S 0.0000/.0025, you reverse. What is your p/l on a position of USD 10 million?

18. Spot USD/INR 64.8950/9050, C/S 0.0375/0.0300, margin 2 p. What cash rate will you quote ABC Ltd for an inward remittance of USD 10 million?

19. An importer has to pay an advance remittance of CAD 100,000 by TT value spot. Spot USD/INR 64.50/60
    Spot USD/CAD 1.7570/1.8540
    The bank requires a margin of 5 paise on CAD/INR. What rate will be quoted to the customer?

20. Say, it is USD/INR deal. If the deal date is June 27, and June 30 is holiday in India, what would be the one month forward contract maturity date? If on the maturity date if there is a declared holiday in the USA, then what would be one month forward date

21. If the deal date is August 17, and the interbank screen shows
    USD/INR; Spot 67.30/32 (August 19)
    S/August: 3/4
    S/September: 10/11
    S/October: 21/22
    Find the bill buying rate for 30 days usance period.

22. If the deal date is August 17; and the interbank screen shows

USD/INR; Spot 67.30/32 (August 19)
S/August: 3/4
S/September: 10/11
S/October: 21/22

EUR / USD Spot: 1.1112/13
S/August: 2/3
S/September: 5/6
S/October: 9/10

Find the bill buying rate for 30 days usance period.

Appendix

Dealers are governed by the FEDAI code of conduct as well as the RBI's and bank's own rules and guidelines in the matter. Deals should be only with approved counterparties—other banks in India, overseas banks, the bank's overseas branches and the RBI—and within the limits for individual counterparties. Besides adhering to counterparty exposure limits, banks are required to maintain the following limits:

- Daylight Limits
- Net Overnight Open Position Limit
- Dealer-wise Limit
- Individual Gap Limit (IGL)
- Aggregate Gap Limit (AGL)

There are some important guidelines prescribed by FEDAI for dealing in Forex marker. Also, a dealer has to go by the code of conduct prescribed by FEDAI and FIMMDA.

Hours of Business

1. The exchange trading hours for interbank Forex market in India would be from 9.00 AM to 5.00 PM. No customer transaction should be undertaken by the AD branches after 4.30 PM on all working days.

2. Cut-off time limit of 5.00 PM is not applicable for cross currency transactions. In terms of internal control guidelines over foreign exchange, according to the RBI (February 2011), ADs are permitted to undertake cross-currency transactions during extended hours, provided the management lay down the extended dealing hours.

3. For the purpose of foreign exchange business, Saturday will not be treated as a working day.

4. "Known holiday" is one that is known at least four working days before the date. A holiday that is not a "known holiday" is defined as a "suddenly declared holiday."

5. Brokers have to obtain necessary approval from the FEDAI for undertaking broking business in the Indian FX market. The dealers should distribute deals through as many empaneled (by the board of directors) brokers as possible.

Chapter

11

Bank Guarantees in International Trade

In international trade transactions, many a times, the trade establishment happens between a very large party with high international reputation and a small or medium party with low international reputation. In such case, the small- or medium-scale importers may be requested to arrange for a bank guarantee to ensure that payment would be made once the transaction is completed. In such case, the small exporter can request his or her bank to stand as a guarantor for the payment. Also, if the company gets into a cross-border project of a government, it may have to produce a performance guarantee issued by a bank. So, we can say a guarantee is a financial instrument issued by a bank or a financial institution to provide an assurance that the payment would be made or the performance would be accomplished as required per the contract or the agreement.

Under demand guarantee, banks or financial institutions agree to make the payment on request. Consequently, the issuing bank undertakes the risk, although limited.

11.1 Parties to the Guarantees

Applicant: The party who is having its obligation under the underlying relationship supported by the guarantee. It may happen that the applicant is not the instructing party.

Instructing Party: The party, other than the counter-guarantor, who gives instructions to issue a guarantee or counter-guarantee. The instructing party is responsible for reimbursing the guarantor or, in the case of a counter-guarantee, the counter-guarantor. The instructing party may or may not be the applicant.

Beneficiary: It means the party in whose favor the guarantee is issued.

Advising Party: The party or the bank that advises or notifies the party about the issuance of the guarantee.

For example, let us assume that a company, say ABC Private Ltd bags a project from, say the Government of Indonesia, to build 300 power transmission towers. It has applied with many other companies across the world. However, the selection of the company is based on the minimum cost and the past performance of the company. Yet, the government needs an assurance that the project would be finished on time without compromising the quality of the project. To ensure these the government puts a condition that the company ABC-needs to submit a guarantee given by one or more banks. So, according to the above definition of Uniform Rules for Demand Guarantee, publication 758, company ABC is an applicant, its bank is the issuing bank and the Government of Indonesia is the beneficiary.

The bank of ABC would have a detailed analysis on the balance sheet of the company. After having the credit rating and the financial well-being of the company, the bank of ABC decides about the amount sanctioned for issuing a bank guarantee in favor of the Indonesian government. Generally, the amount of bank guarantee is a percentage of the total amount of the contract. It may be noted that bank likes to limit the total risk exposure of its own and if the Government of Indonesia may invoke the bank guarantees against the service of the ABC company, the risk exposure of the bank increases. So, the bank would decide to open a bank guarantee only if the company ABC has not utilized the overall limit for bank guarantees. Once invoked, the bank will have to immediately release the amount to the government.

11.2 Steps to Establish a Bank Guarantee or Demand Guarantee

1. Contract between the two parties, the principal and the beneficiary, must have a mention about the requirement of the bank guarantee.

2. To get a bank guarantee issued, the principal submits a request to a guarantor with all the details of the terms and the conditions. The principal must be able to provide the details of the beneficiary in favor of whom the guarantee must be issued.

3. By using SWIFT format, a bank or a financial institution, which is playing the role of the guarantor, issues the bank guarantee. Through secure online swift platform, the guarantor advises the advising bank about the issuance of the bank guarantee. Generally, the advising bank is located in the beneficiary's country.

4.   The advising bank advices the bank guarantee to the beneficiary by online means.

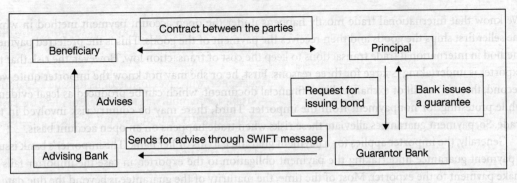

11.3 Types of Bank Guarantees

Initially, banks had two main bank guarantees that were widely used in the international trade finance: (a) Performance Guarantees and (b) Financial Guarantees. However, with the requirement of international trade, the other types of bank guarantees have also become popular. For example, bank guarantees such as (a) performance guarantee or performance bond, (b) advance payment guarantee, (c) payment guarantee, and (d) order or counter guarantee are also used widely in international trade. We would now discuss these different types of guarantees and their usage in different contexts of trade in the international market.

11.3.1 Performance Guarantees

This is a bond or a guarantee to ensure that the seller would be able to perform as per the agreement with the buyer. If any bank or financial institution issues this kind of bond guaranteeing the performance of the seller, and if seller fails to perform, then the buyer can invoke the guarantee as a collateral for any loss suffered due to nonperformance or low-quality performance of the seller.

11.3.2 Advance Payment Guarantees

We know that one out of the four payment methods is known as advance payment method. If one party is sufficiently large or has high international reputation in the market, then he or she may request for advance payment from the importer before the shipment of the goods. Also, advance payment may be asked by the seller if he or she sells to a customer not having good credit worthiness. Besides these two, advance payment may also be called for in a situation where the exporter knows that because of sovereign risk and/or country risk, he or she may not get paid. Advance payment method is practiced in international trade scenarios to protect the interest of the exporter from the nonpayment or partial payment conditions. However, it may happen that the importer agrees to pay in advance only if the exporter can produce a bond or guarantee against his or her performance. So, this guarantee is issued by a bank or a financial institution to safeguard the interest of the importer. In case the seller fails to deliver the goods, then the buyer can get his or her money back. So, in this case, the issuing bank of the guarantee must be able to pay to the buyer who has paid the exporter in advance, maybe for procuring raw materials.

11.3.3 Payment Guarantees

We know that international trade mostly happens under the open account payment method in which the seller first ships the goods and then receives the payment of the goods. This is the preferred payment method in international trade transactions to keep the cost of transaction low. However, the risk that the exporter is undertaking is large for three reasons. First, he or she may not know the importer quite well. Second, there is no bill of exchange, like a financial document, which can be produced as legal evidence while protesting for nonpayment from the importer. Third, there may be country risk involved in the trade. So, payment guarantees alleviate these risks when trade happens on an open account basis.

Generally, the importer applies for a payment guarantee to his or her bank. The importer's bank issues a payment guarantee undertaking the payment obligation to the exporter, in case the importer fails to make payment to the exporter. Most of the time, the maturity of the guarantee is beyond the due date of the payment. This extended time period of the guarantees is to facilitate the exporter to make his or her claim if not paid within the due date. This kind of payment guarantees are also applicable for large spot deals and/or for annual contracts without LCs.

The bank charges the party depending on the risk they take. If the country risk and the credit risk is high, then the fees of the issuance of this guarantee is also high. Fees may be high depending on the documentation requirement.

11.3.4 Retention Money Guarantees

If the export order is related to any capital goods or machinery goods, then sometimes the importer may not like to pay the exporter the full amount of the invoice. This is generally mentioned in the established contract and mutually agreed between the exporter and the importer that the machine must run satisfactorily for some fixed period of time, say 6 months' time, and then only the full payment would be made to the exporter. Also, in case of establishment of a production plant or any such large project, the exporter may not be paid the full amount even after the successful completion of the project. It may be a condition mentioned in the project that 10% of the total invoice amount would be due for payment till the production unit or plantation unit is installed as required by the contract and runs agreeably for next one year from the date of completion of the project. In this process, the exporter's fund gets blocked. To eliminate the problem of part payment or due payment, the exporter may request his or her bank to issue a retention money guarantee in favor of the importer or the buyer. It provides a guarantee that the planation or the production unit or the machinery supplied would run as per the contract. Once the exporter's bank gives the guarantee, the exporter's money would not be held back. So, the exporter gets the full payment of the invoice value. On the other hand, the importer gets an assurance that the loss or damage is covered under the retention money guarantee. So, if anything goes wrong with the installation or with the smooth run of the project, the importer can invoke the guarantee with the bank.

11.3.5 Bid Bond Guarantees

If the project is large enough, and if there are many potential companies to bid for the project, a bid-bond guarantee may be called for. This guarantee is a tool to judge the capability of the company to complete it successfully, on winning the bid. So, a company, say ABC, which requires to bid for a infrastructure project in Ethiopia and would like to win the bid may be submitting a bid-bond guarantee to the Ethiopian government to ensure competence of the ABC company for the project. On the other hand, if the bank is assured about the creditworthiness of the company ABC, then they can issue a bid-bond guarantee, which can be used by the company for bidding for several projects across borders.

11.3.6 Order and Counter Guarantees

This is a surety given by the debtor to the creditor, to protect against the failure to fulfill an obligation as contracted. In case of default, the creditor can demand the payment back.

11.4 Advantages of Bank Guarantees

1. Documentary requirement is comparatively lesser in the bank guarantees compared to LC transactions.

2. Bank guarantees are used for huge amount of a project, especially for infrastructure projects, real estate projects, and power projects.

3. It is an instrument that is invoked only when there is nonpayment or nonperformance. On the contrary, LC is a payment obligation.

4. International forfaiting market largely depends on the bank guarantees.

11.5 LC and Bank Guarantees

Letter of Credit	Bank Guarantees
• LCs are the mechanism to settle the commercial payments towards purchase of goods. • Documentary credits give assurance of payment to the seller against submission of specified documents. • Liability of the LC issuing Bank is independent of the applicant to the LC.	• Guarantees are assurance by a banker for payment against default on the part of principal borrower. • Liability of the guarantor is co existent to the liability of the principal debtor.

Parties to the LCs and Bank Guarantees

Letter of Credits	Bank Guarantees
• Applicant (Importer/buyer), • Issuing Bank, and • beneficiary; • In some case there can be confirming bank.	• Applicant/Instructing party, • Issuing Bank and • Beneficiary; • Applicant may or may not be instructing party.

Governing Rules

Letter of Credit	Bank Guarantees
UCP 600 for documentary LCs.	**URDG 758:** The guarantee/counter guarantee must expressly indicate that it is subject to URDG 758, except so far as modifications and exclusions.

11.6 Important Provisions of URDG 758

Counter-guarantee means any signed undertaking, however named or described, that is given by the counter-guarantor to another party to procure the issue by that other party of a guarantee or another counter-guarantee, and that provides for payment upon the presentation of a complying demand under the counter-guarantee issued in favor of that party;

Counter-guarantor means the party issuing a counter-guarantee, whether in favor of a guarantor or another counter-guarantor, and includes a party acting for its own account;

Demand means a signed document by the beneficiary demanding payment under a guarantee;

Demand guarantee or **guarantee** means any signed undertaking, however named or described, providing for payment on presentation of a complying demand;

Applicability: Applicable only if it is stated in the guarantee that it is subject to URDG 758. A guarantee can exclude/modify certain clauses of URDG.

- The guarantee will be irrevocable whether the guarantee specifically states so or not;

- All parties to the guarantees deal with the documents only and not in the goods/performance mentioned in the guarantee;

- Advising of the Guarantee—Can be advised directly to the beneficiary.
  If advised through another bank, the role of the advising bank is to confirm the apparent authenticity of the document only.

A SBLC can be confirmed by a bank requested to do so by the issuing bank. No such option is available for a guarantee.

Claims payable under the guarantee:

- A demand (Article 2) under a guarantee must be accompanied by the documents specified in the guarantee and a supporting statement (Article 2). in what respect the applicant (Article 2) is in breach of his or her obligations.

- A demand (Article 2) under a counter-guarantee must be supported by a supporting statement (Article 2) having received a complying demand (Article 2) under the guarantee.

Expiry of the guarantee/counter-guarantee:

- Expiry means the expiry date or the expiry event or, if both are specified, the earlier of the two.

- Expiry date means the date specified in the guarantee on or before which a presentation may be made.

- Expiry event means an event that under the terms of the guarantee results in its expiry, whether immediately or within a specified time after the event occurs, for which purpose the event is deemed to occur only:

    o   When a document specified in the guarantee as indicating the occurrence of the event is presented to the guarantor, or

    o   If no such document is specified in the guarantee, when the occurrence of the event becomes determinable from the guarantor's own records.

Partial demand and multiple demand:

- If a demand is made for less than the full amount available, then it is known as partial demand.

- If a demand is made for more than once then it is known as multiple demands.

- The expression "multiple demands prohibited" or a similar expression means that only one demand covering all or part of the amount available may be made.

- Where the guarantee provides that only one demand may be made, and that demand is rejected, another demand can be made on or before expiry of the guarantee.

Advising party means the party that advises the guarantee at the request of the guarantor;

Applicant means the party indicated in the guarantee as having its obligation under the underlying relationship supported by the guarantee. The applicant may or may not be the instructing party;

Application means the request for the issue of the guarantee;

Authenticated, when applied to an electronic document, means that the party to whom that document is presented is able to verify the apparent identity of the sender and whether the data received have remained complete and unaltered; beneficiary means the party in whose favor a guarantee is issued;

Business day means a day on which the place of business where an act of a kind subject to these rules is to be performed is regularly open for the performance of such an act;

Instructing party means the party, other than the counter-guarantor, who gives instructions to issue a guarantee or a counter-guarantee, and is responsible for indemnifying the guarantor or, in the case of a counter-guarantee, the counter-guarantor. The instructing party may or may not be the applicant;

Presentation means the delivery of a document under a guarantee to the guarantor or the document so delivered. It includes a presentation other than for a demand, for example, a presentation for the purpose of triggering the expiry of the guarantee or a variation of its amount.

11.7 Caselets on URDG

Now, in the next section we discuss some of the important provisions of URDG 758 through a few case studies.

Case 1

Bank A issues a performance guarantee in favor of ZBL Ltd, Dubai, for USD 1,450,000, subject to URDG 758. The guarantee states that it will be operative only after the applicant NB Ltd have received payment of USD 145,000 as advance payment. Beneficiary lodges a demand for USD 100,000 with a supporting statement of default by the NB Ltd. Bank A claims that the guarantee is inoperative since advance payment was not received. The beneficiary insists guarantee is valid in terms of URDG 758.

The condition in the guarantee does not specify any document to verify the compliance. Hence the condition will be ignored.

The guarantee therefore will be operative from the date of its issuance.

Therefore the claim is binding on the issuing bank, if otherwise in order.

Case 2

A guarantee was issued for USD 1,000,000 for payment of 500 tons of goods. 100 tons were to be shipped each month from July to November and the claims for USD 200,000 were to be drawn for each month's shipment. The demands for the first two months were duly paid. There was no shipment in the month of September. In the month of October, the bill for USD 200,000 was received by the opening bank, covering 100 tons of goods. The issuing bank refused to pay.

Had this case been under the LC, the rejection by the LC-opening bank would be in order as noncompliance of shipment schedule will cancel the LC itself. However, since this is under demand guarantee, as per URDG 758, each presentation is treated separate and, hence, despite noncompliance of schedule of shipment, payment will have to be made by the guarantee-issuing bank.

Case 3

A demand guarantee stipulated a condition that "goods should be inspected before shipment." A demand is received accompanied other stipulated declaration but without the inspection certificate. Is the bank issuing the guarantee is bound to make payment?

As per Article 7, a condition without stipulating a document to indicate compliance will be disregarded.

In this case, a condition has been stated but no document specified to verify the compliance, and hence the condition will be disregarded and the guarantee-issuing bank must make the payment, if the claim is otherwise in order.

Case 4

At the request of your customer, M/s BL builders, you have requested Rafidain Bank, Baghdad, Iraq, to issue a performance guarantee in favor of ABC Ltd. The guarantee has been issued by that bank against the counter guarantee of your bank. The guarantee is valid up to August 31 2014, and your counter guarantee is valid up to September 30, 2014. On September 8 the beneficiary lodges a claim with Rafidain Bank and in turn Rafidain Bank invokes your counter guarantee. The Rafidain Bank claims that the delay in lodgment of claim was due to force majeure.

Confirm whether the guarantee is issued subject to URDG 758.

Article 26 provides that when presentation is not possible due to "force majeure," the guarantee and the counter guarantee will be extended *once* by 30 calendar days.

The presentation, therefore, is within the extended validity of the guarantee in terms of this article and therefore binding on the banks.

Case 5

Your bank has issued a guarantee favoring the Trade Fair Authority of India against the counter guarantee of your foreign correspondents for clearing the goods without payment of customs duty (for participation in the International Trade Fair). The guarantee is valid up to August 31, 2014. The counter guarantee is valid up to September 30. On August 28 you receive a letter from the beneficiary of the guarantee to extend the guarantee by another six months or alternatively make payment of the guarantee amount. On contacting the foreign bank, you are informed to withhold the payment to enable parties to sort out the matter. How will you react?

Article 23 of URDG provides that in case of such a demand (extend or pay), the guarantor bank at its discretion suspend the payment for 30 days. The bank at its discretion may pay the guarantee amount despite applicant's instructions to extend. The applicant is bound to reimburse the guarantor the amount so paid to the beneficiary.

Case 6

Your bank has received a demand guarantee in favor of your importer customer to cover the advance payment remitted by the importer for supply of machinery. The guarantee requires an inspection certificate from the Indian Inspection Agency as a supporting document if claim is to be made on account of quality of the material.

The importer has lodged a claim stating that the instructing party has failed to supply the goods of ordered quality and in support he or she has submitted the certificate from the named inspection agency.

The foreign bank refuses the claim on the ground that the certificate by the inspecting agency is in Hindi instead of English, the language of the guarantee.

Article 14 provides that any document issued by the beneficiary or the applicant has to be in the language of the guarantee.

If such document is issued by any other party, then it can be issued in any language.

Therefore, the claim cannot be rejected on account of the supporting document being in a language other than the language of the guarantee.

Case 7

ABC Bank has issued a guarantee on behalf of D for an amount of USD 25,000 in favor of X and valid up to December 31, 2013, with an additional claim period up to January 15, 2014.

X lodges a claim on ABC Bank on 16th January 2014.

Is the claim tenable?

Claim is lodged after the expiry of guarantee and is therefore not tenable as per Articles 2 and 3 of URDG 758.

Case 8

Bank ABC issued a guarantee in India favoring a customs authority against the counter-guarantee of their overseas correspondent XYZ Bank on behalf of the client of XYZ Bank. The guarantee was valid up to October 31, 2013 while the counter-guarantee was valid up to November 15, 2013.

The customs authority lodged a claim under the guarantee with ABC Bank on October 30, 2013.

ABC Bank lodged claim under the counter-guarantee of XYZ Bank after November 15, 2013, which was refuted as it was made after the expiry of the counter-guarantee.

Bank refuted the claim of the beneficiary on the grounds that its claim under the counter-guarantee was not honored.

Was the stand taken by Bank ABC correct?

The beneficiary has made a valid claim under the guarantee and is entitled to receive the claim.

The guarantee and counter-guarantee are two separate transactions independent of each other, though they may contain a reference to each other, for the purpose of identification as per Article 5 of URDG 758

Case 9

At the request of X, a guarantee was issued by ABC Bank on January 1, 2013 in favor of beneficiary Y. Subsequently, an amendment was issued containing three changes in terms of the guarantee. The beneficiary Y was agreeable to two changes but not the third one. Can the amendment be treated as a valid one?

The amendment cannot be treated as valid, as partial acceptance is tantamount to rejection of the amendment as per Article 11 (e).

Case 10

At the request of X, guarantee was issued by ABC Bank on November 1, 2013, in favor of beneficiary Y. Subsequently, an amendment was issued on December 1, 2013, stating that it shall take effect unless rejected within 15 days from date of amendment.

Can the amendment be treated as a valid one?

The amendment cannot be treated as valid, as provision in an amendment to the effect that the amendment shall take effect unless rejected within a certain time, shall be disregarded as per Article 11 (f) of URDG 758.

Case 11

At the request of X, a guarantee was issued by ABC Bank in favor of Y, valid up to December 31, 2013. The guarantee had specified that any claim thereunder should be made in writing, duly signed by the beneficiary and sent by DHL courier to the guarantor in Mumbai. The beneficiary submitted the claim by ordinary post, which reached ABC Bank well within the validity of the guarantee.

ABC Bank refused to honor the claim citing that the claim was not sent by DHL courier, though delivery by any other mode was not specifically excluded in the guarantee.

Was the bank's stand correct?

The Bank's stand was not correct, since as per Article 14 (d) if such other mode of delivery is not specifically excluded, it shall be effective, provided that claim is made within the validity of the guarantee.

Case 12

At the request of X, a guarantee was issued by ABC Bank in favor of Y, valid up to December 31, 2013. The guarantee stipulated that the demand was to be accompanied by a written statement duly signed by the beneficiary. Y submitted a demand on December 1, 2013, without the written statement, as required in the guarantee, which was refused by the bank. Subsequently, a demand, duly accompanied by a written statement, as required in the guarantee, was submitted by Y on December 21, 2013. ABC Bank refused to honor the claim, stating that the guarantee prohibited "multiple demands."

Was the stand correct?

The stand of the bank was wrong, as in terms of Article 18 of URDG— making a demand that is not a complying demand or withdrawing a demand does not waive or otherwise prejudice the right to make another timely demand, whether or not the guarantee prohibits partial or multiple demands.

Case 13

At the request of X, ABC Bank issued a guarantee favoring Y, valid up to December 31, 2013.

Y lodged a claim under the same on the December 10, 2013.

ABC Bank conveyed its rejection on the December 21, 2013.

Y refused to accept rejection as it was in in contravention of Article 20.

Was the stand taken by Y correct?

The stand taken by Y is correct as in terms of Article 20 (a) of URDG 758, the guarantor, has to, within five business days, following the date of presentation, examine the demand and determine if it is a complying demand.

Case 14

Banks in Guwahati were closed for three consecutive days from August 8,2012 to August 10, 2012, due to riots. On August 12, 2012, the beneficiary of a guarantee made a demand to the guaranteeing bank, seeking payment under the guarantee that was valid up to August 10, 2012.

The guaranteeing bank refused to honor the demand stating that the guarantee had already expired.

The beneficiary claimed that he or she could not submit the claim before August 10, 2012, since the banks were closed on such dates.

Was the stand of the bank correct?

The bank's stand is incorrect, as in terms of Article 25 (b), should the guarantee expire at a time when presentation or payment under the guarantee is prevented by "force majeure," the guarantee shall be extended for a period of 30 calendar days from the date on which it would otherwise have expired and shall be bound by any such extension.

Case 15

At the request of X, ABC Bank issued a guarantee in favor of Y, wherein the charges were to the beneficiary's account and the guarantee was conditional upon payment of such charges.

The beneficiary refused to pay the charges and the bank therefore claimed the amount of charges from X.

In the meantime, the beneficiary lodged a claim under the guarantee, well within its validity and as per terms of the guarantee.

X refused to pay the guarantee amount as well as the charges, stating that the guarantee was conditional upon the payment of charges by the beneficiary.

Was the stand of X correct?

The stand of X is inconsistent with Article 32 (b) and (d) in terms of which the instructing party is liable for charges if not paid by beneficiary and that the guarantor cannot stipulate that the guarantee is conditional upon receipt of charges.

Case 16

At the request of X, ABC Bank issued a guarantee favoring Y, valid up to December 31, 2013.

In terms of the guarantee, any demand by the beneficiary was required to be accompanied by a "certificate of noncompliance."

A demand was made by Y duly accompanied by the "certificate of noncompliance" in accordance with the terms of the guarantee.

ABC Bank paid the claim under the guarantee and claimed the amount from the instructing party, under their counter-guarantee

X refused to pay stating that the "certificate of noncompliance" was not signed by the beneficiary.

Was the stand of X correct?

The stand of X is incorrect as in terms of Article 19 (c), if the Guarantee requires the presentation of a document without stipulating whether it needs to be signed and by whom it is to be issued/signed or its data content, the Guarantor shall accept the document as presented if its content appears to fulfill the condition of the document required by the Guarantee.

Case 17

At the request of counter guarantor, a bank issues a demand guarantee under URDG. However, the issuer of demand guarantor required the counter guarantee to be subject to URDG 758. The bank that issues counter guarantee does not mention that it is opened under URDG 758. When the bank is notified and requested for an amendment, it is argued that URDG 758 is by default applied to counter guarantee once the guarantee is opened under URDG 758? Is the claim of the bank correct? If a counter guarantee is subject to URDG 758, then does it mean that the demand guarantee is also subject to URDG 758?

According to URDG 758, Article 1 (a), where, at the request of a counter-guarantor, a demand guarantee is issued subject to the URDG, the counter-guarantee shall also be subject to the URDG, given that the counter-guarantee excludes the URDG. However, a demand guarantee does not become subject to the URDG merely because the counter-guarantee is subject to the URDG.

Case 18

One bank guarantee is opened subject to URDG 1992 version. The other parties has objected, stating that it is not allowed. Any bank guarantee when opened has to be with reference to the latest publication version of URDG. Is the bank correct in opening a bank guarantee subject to older version of URDG?

Yes the bank is right in opening the bank guarantee with reference to the URDG 1992 publication. Only if demand guarantee and/or counter guarantee does not have any reference to the year of publication or publication number in particular then that bank guarantee or the counter guarantee is subject to the latest version of URDG 758. According to Article 1 (d), where a demand guarantee or counter guarantee issued on or after July 1, 2010 states that it is subject to the URDG without stating whether the 1992 version or the 2010 revision is to apply or indicating the publication number, the demand guarantee or counter-guarantee shall be subject to the URDG 2010 revision.

Case 19

If a guarantee is opened with the following phrase, then which dates are to be considered as the relevant date for the fulfillment of the relevant event?

Scenario 1: Guarantee is valid till January 31, 2017.

Scenario 2: The shipment should happen between January 1 and January 31, 2017.

Scenario 3: The guarantee can be invoked from January 2 to January 10, 2017.

Scenario 4: The shipment should happen before January 23, 2017.

Scenario 1: The maturity day of the guarantee is January 31, 2017.

Scenario 2: The shipment should happen between January 1, and January, 31 2017, means that including January 1 and January 31, the shipment can happen on any day in between.

Scenario 3: The guarantee can be invoked from January 2 to January 10, 2017, means that the two dates, January 2 and January 10, are included.

Scenario 4: The shipment should happen before January 23, 2017. It means shipment should be made latest by January 22.

Case 20

A guarantee is issued without stating if it is irrevocable. The issuer of the demand guarantee states that even if it does not mention if it is irrevocable, the demand guarantee has to be treated as irrevocable. Is the bank right?

Yes, the bank is right as per the clause of URDG 758, Article 4 (ii). A guarantee is irrevocable on it issue even if it does not state so.

Case 21

On January 10, 2017. Punjab National Bank (PNB) has received a request to open a demand guarantee on the basis of counter guarantee from a South Indian bank. However, due to inexperience in opening a guarantee, the officer at the desk has kept it pending and on January 25, 2017, the officer has communicated to the other bank about the inability to open the guarantee. The party has incurred financial loss. Which bank should be held responsible for this?

URDG 758, Article 9 clearly states that if a guarantee is requested and for any reason the guarantor bank fails or not in a position to open it, then it has to communicate immediately without any delay. In the above case, PNB to be held responsible.

Case 22

A demand guarantee was issued by PNB and was advised by State Bank of India, Dubai. The guarantee required a complying certificate that the packing list should be issued not before January 21, 2017. When documents were submitted, PNB has rejected the payment stating that the packing list was not issued by an internationally reputed agent although it is issued on January 20, 2017. So the guarantee was rejected on noncompliance. The party requested the payment from the State Bank of India, Dubai, which was the second advising bank. Is the rejection correct? Why? What is the role of the second advising bank?

The bank is incorrect in rejecting the document as it never mentioned who should be the issuing agency to issue the packing list. As per Article 19(c) we know that if the guarantee requires the presentation of a document without stipulating whether it needs to be signed and by whom it is to be issued/signed or its data content, the guarantor shall accept the document as presented if its content appears to fulfill the condition of the document required by the guarantee.

As the second advising party, the role of the bank is to signify that that it has satisfied itself as to the apparent authenticity of the advice it has received, and that the advice accurately reflects the terms and conditions of the guarantee as received by the second advising party. The second advising party or the advising bank do not have any further responsibility to the beneficiary. This is as per Article 10 (b).

Case 23

A demand guarantee was issued by an Ethiopian bank and was requested to be advised by State Bank of India, Dubai. However, State Bank of Dubai was not sure about the apparent authenticity of the credit. So it has communicated immediately to the bank in Ethiopia about its inability to advise the credit. However, the party in whose favor the guarantee is issued insists the bank to advise the guarantee. On the request, the advising bank agrees to advise the guarantee. Can the bank deny advising a guarantee? If a bank is not satisfied with the apparent authenticity of the guarantee, what should be the role of the bank?

According to URDG 758, Article 10 (e), if a bank is requested to advise a guarantee, and agrees to do so, but cannot satisfy itself as to the apparent authenticity of that guarantee or advice, it shall without delay so inform the party from whom the instructions appear to have been received.

If the advising party or second advising party elects nonetheless to advise that guarantee, it shall inform the beneficiary or second advising party that it has not been able to satisfy itself as to the apparent authenticity of the guarantee or the advice.

Case 24

A bank guarantee has called for an amendment. However, the beneficiary does not give his or her consent to the amendment. Does this amendment apply to the beneficiary?

As per URDG 758 Article 11 (b), an amendment made without the beneficiary's agreement is not binding on the beneficiary. Nevertheless the guarantor is irrevocably bound by an amendment from the time he or she issues the amendment, unless and until the beneficiary rejects that amendment.

Case 25

A demand guarantee is issued with two clauses that (a) the guarantee is valid till January 31, 2017 and (b) the guarantee is valid till two days of the complying presentation. The presentation happens on January 21, 2017. Which date is to be considered as the expiry date in this case?

The expiry date should be January 23, 2017. As per URDG 758 Article (2), expiry means the expiry date or the expiry event or, if both are specified, the earlier of the two.

11.8 Difference Between SBLC and Guarantees

SBLC is a commercial LC, although it is invoked only when at the time of nonpayment. However, payment against the SBLC depends on the documentary compliance under the LC. Guarantee is not a commercial LC and documentary compliance is not a mandatory criteria for invocation of guarantee.

SBLCs are governed either by ISP 98 or by UCP 600. However, it is beneficial to open the SBLC under ISP 98. Bank guarantees are governed by URDG 758.

References and Resources

https://www.cleverism.com/lexicon/bank-guarantee/
http://www.letterofcredit.biz/Bank-Guarantee-Sample-in-MT-760-Swift-Format.html
http://www.letterofcredit.biz/Advance-Payment-Bank-Guarantee-Sample.html
http://www.letterofcredit.biz/Retention-Money-Guarantee-Sample.html
http://www.letterofcredit.biz/Performance-Guarantee-Sample.html
https://www.tradefinanceglobal.com/letters-of-credit/difference-between-lcs-and-bank-guarantees/

QUESTIONS

Answer the Following Questions

1. What are bank guarantees? Why are they used in the international trade?

2. Who are the different parties in bank guarantees? Explain their role in the transaction flow of guarantee.

3. Write down the steps in establishing a bank guarantee.

4. How many types of bank guarantees are there in international trade? Define the role of each of them.

5. Explain performance guarantee with an example.

6. Explain the role of payment guarantee with an example. In which situation does this kind of guarantee become useful?

7. What is advance payment guarantee? Explain the scenarios in which advance payment guarantee is called for. Give an example with the flow chart of an export transaction in international trade

8. What is payment guarantee? Describe a scenario when it is used in international trade.

9. Explain retention money guarantee? Why and how is it used in international trade? Explain with a scenario.

10. Write a short note on bid bond guarantee?

11. What is order and counter guarantee? Describe the role of it.

12. What are the advantage of using bank guarantee in international trade?

13. Write a few differences between LC and bank guarantees

14. What are the major difference between SBLCs and bank guarantees?

15. What are the differences between payment and advance payment guarantee?

16. What is "presentation" as per the definition of bank guarantees and URDG 758?

17. Can bank guarantee be opened under ISP 98? Can URDG 758 govern the functioning of SBLC?

18. Which all countries were restricted from issuing bank guarantee? Which documentary credit works in the similar way like bank guarantees?

19. At the request of A, a guarantee was issued by State Bank of Hyderabad (SBH) in favor of B, valid up to December 31, 2016. The guarantee had specified that any claim should be sent by DTDC courier to the guarantor at Mumbai. The beneficiary submitted the claim by ordinary post, which reached SBH well within the validity of the guarantee. SBH Bank refused to honor the claim citing that the claim was not sent by DTDC courier, though delivery by any other mode was not specifically excluded in the guarantee. Was the bank's stand correct?

20. At the request of A, SBH Bank issued a guarantee favoring B, valid up to December 31, 2016. Guarantee required that any demand by the beneficiary should be accompanied by a "certificate of noncompliance." The guarantee was invoked by B with a demand duly accompanied by the "certificate of noncompliance" in accordance with the terms of the guarantee. SBH Bank paid the claim under the guarantee and claimed the amount from the instructing party, under their counter-guarantee. A refused to pay stating that the "certificate of noncompliance" was not signed by the beneficiary. Was the stand of A correct?

21. Banks in Kolkata were closed for two consecutive days on January 13 and January 14, 2017, due to a strike called by all political parties. On January 16, 2017, the beneficiary of a guarantee made a demand to the guaranteeing bank, seeking payment under the guarantee, which was valid up to January 14, 2017. The guaranteeing bank refused to honor the demand stating that the guarantee had already expired. The beneficiary claimed that he or she could not submit the claim on or before January 14 as the banks were closed on such dates. Was the stand of the bank correct? What would have happened if the same situation comes under an LC product? Would the bank be given a chance to submit the documents after the expiry if the product is SBLC and is opened under ISP 98?

22. At the request of A, guarantee was issued by SBH Bank on December 10, 2016, in favor of beneficiary B. Subsequently, an amendment was issued on the December 15, 2016, stating that it shall take effect unless rejected within 15 days from date of amendment. Can the amendment be treated as a valid one?

23. At the request of A, State Bank of Patiala (SBP) issued a guarantee favoring B, valid up to January 31, 2017. B lodged a claim under the same on the January 5, 2017. SBP Bank conveyed its rejection on the January 21, 2017. B refused to accept rejection as it was in in contravention of Article 20 of URDG 758. Was the stand taken by B correct?

24. At the request of A, a guarantee was issued by SBP Bank in favor of B, valid up to January 31, 2017. The guarantee stipulated that the demand was to be accompanied by a written statement duly signed by the beneficiary. Y submitted a demand on the January 3, 2017 without the written statement, as required in the guarantee, which was refused by the bank. Subsequently, a demand, duly accompanied by a written statement, as required in the guarantee was submitted by Y on the January 17,

2017. ABC Bank refused to honor the claim, stating that the guarantee prohibited "multiple demands." Was the stand correct?

25. A demand guarantee is issued with two clauses that (a) the guarantee is valid till January 21, 2017 and (b) the guarantee is valid till two days of the complying presentation. The presentation happens on January 20, 2017. Which date to be considered as the expiry date in this case.

26. A demand guarantee was issued by an Ethiopian bank and was requested to be advised by State Bank of India, Dubai. However, State Bank of Dubai was not sure about the apparent authenticity of the credit. So it has communicated immediately to the bank in Ethiopia about its inability to advise the credit. However, the party in whose favor the guarantee is issued insists the bank to advise the guarantee. On the request, the advising bank agrees to advise the guarantee. Can the bank deny advising a guarantee? If a bank is not satisfied with the apparent authenticity of the guarantee, what should be the role of the bank?

27. At the request of counter guarantor a bank issues a demand guarantee under URDG. However, the issuer of demand guarantor required the counter guarantee to be subject to URDG 758. The bank that issues counter guarantee does not mention that it is opened under URDG 758. When the bank is notified and requested for an amendment, it is argued that URDG 758 is by default applied to counter guarantee once the guarantee is opened under URDG 758? Is the claim of the bank correct? If a counter guarantee is subject to URDG 758, then does it mean demand guarantee is also subject to URDG 758?

28. What is the meaning of partial drawing and multiple drawing as per URDG 758?

29. What is the difference between guarantee and counter guarantee?

30. If the guarantee says that date on BL shows that shipment should happen after February 2, 2017, and if shipment happen on February 2, is it treated as noncompliance?

Appendix

Form of Demand Guarantee under URDG 758

[Guarantor Letterhead or SWIFT identifier code]

To: [Insert name and contract information of the Beneficiary]

Date: [Insert date of issue]

- **Type of guarantee:** [Specify tender guarantee, advance payment guarantee, performance guarantee, payment guarantee, retention money guarantee, warranty guarantee and so on]
- **Guarantee No.:** [Insert guarantee reference number]
- **The guarantor:** [insert name and address of place of issue, unless indicated in the letterhead]
- **The applicant:** [Insert name and address]
- **The beneficiary:** [Insert name and address]
- **The underlying relationship:** The applicant's obligation in respect of [Insert reference number or other information identifying the contract, tender conditions or other relationship between the applicant and the beneficiary on which the guarantee is based]
- **Guarantee amount and currency:** [Insert in figures and words the maximum amount and the currency in which it is payable]
- **Any document required in support of the demand for payment, apparent from the**

(Continued)

(Continued)

- **supporting statement that is explicitly required from the following text:** [Insert any additional documents required in support of the demand for payment. If the guarantee requires no documents and the supporting statement, keep this space empty or indicate "none"]

- **Language of any required documents:** [Insert the language of any required document. Documents to be issued by the applicant or the beneficiary shell be in the language of the guarantee unless otherwise indicate herein]

- **Form of presentation:** [Insert paper or electronic form. If paper, indicate mode of delivery. If electronic, indicate the format, the system of data delivery and the electronic address for presentation]

- **Place of presentation:** [Guarantor to insert address of branch where a paper presentation is to be made or, in case of an electronic presentation, an electronic address such as the guarantor's SWIFT address. If no place of presentation is indicated in this field, the guarantor's place of issue indicated above shall be the place of presentation].

- **Expiry:** [Insert expiry date or describe expiry event]

- **The party liable for the payment of any charges:** [Insert the name of the party]

As a guarantor, we hereby irrevocable undertake to pay the beneficiary any amount up to the guarantee amount upon presentation of beneficiary's complying demand, in the form of presentation indicated above, supported by such other documents as may be listed above and in any event by the beneficiary's statement, whether in the demand itself or in a separate signed document accompanying or identifying the demand, including in what respect the applicant is in breach of its obligations under the underlying relationship.

For identification purposes, the beneficiary's demand and statement have to be presented through the intermediary bank, which shall confirm the authenticity and validity of your signatures or the same shall be accurately registered by a public notary who shall confirm the authenticity and validity of your signatures.

Any demand under this guarantee must be received by us on or before expiry at the place of presentation.

This guarantee is subject to the Uniform Rules for Demand Guarantees (URDG) 2010 revision, ICC Publication No. 758.

Signature(s)

Optional clauses:

- Time as from which a demand can be presented if different from the date of issue:

A demand under this guarantee may be presented as from [indicate date or event], e.g.:

- The crediting of [insert currency and exact amount to be received as advance payment] to the applicant's account [indicate account number] maintained with the guarantor, provided such remittance identifies the guarantee to which relates;

- **The receipt by the guarantor of** [insert currency and exact amount to be received as advance payment] for further credit to the applicant's account [indicate account number] maintained with the guarantor, provided such remittance identifies the guarantee to which it relates;[1] or

---

[1] This suggested operativeness/entry into effect clause, like the one in the bullet immediately preceding it, is frequently used in advance payment and retention money guarantees. In both cases, the clause ensures that the guarantee is not available for drawdown before the amount due by the beneficiary

- **The presentation to the guarantor of a statement stating** [the release of the tender guarantee] [the issue of a documentary credit fulfilling the following terms: indicate amount, issuing or confirming party, and goods/services description] or [the entry into effect of the underlying contract].
- **Variation of amount clause:**

The guarantee amount will be *reduced* by [insert percentage of guarantee amount or exact amount and currency] upon [chose one or more of the options below:

- **Presentation to the guarantor of the following document(s):** [insert list of documents]
- **In the case of an index specified in the guarantee as triggering reduction** [insert index figure triggering the reduction in the guarantee amount]; or
- (in the case of a payment guarantee): the remittance of [insert exact amount and currency] to the beneficiary's account [indicate account number] held with the guarantor, provided the record of such remittance enables the guarantor to identify the guarantee to which it relates [for example, by referring to the guarantee's reference number.]

   The guarantee amount will be increased by [insert percentage or exact amount and currency] upon [chose one or more of the opinions below:

- Presentation to the guarantor of the following document(s): [insert list of documents];
- Presentation to the guarantor of the applicant's statement stating that the underlying contract was amended to increase the scope or value of the works and specifying the amount and currency of the new value; or
- In the case of an index specified in the guarantee as triggering increase [insert index figure triggering increase in the guarantee amount]
- Sample terms for Article 15(a)'s supporting statement to be provided by the beneficiary:

1. In the case of a *tender guarantee*, the supporting statement could state:

The applicant:

- has withdrawn its offer during the tender period, or
- while it was declared the successful bidder, the applicant did not sign the contract corresponding to its offer and/or failed to provide the guarantee(s) requested in the call for tenders.

2. In the case of a *performance guarantee*, the supporting statement could state: The applicant is in breach of its obligations with respect to the underlying relationship because [of late delivery] [the contract's performance was not completed by the due date] [there was a shortfall in the quantity of the goods supplied under the contract] [the delivered works are defective] etc.

3. In the case of a *payment guarantee*, the supporting statement could state:

---

under the underlying contract is paid to the applicant. There are two ways to draft this clause. The first one, reflected in the first bullet, is to consider the guarantee operative only when the amount is effectively credited to the applicant's account. This leaves the beneficiary/payer with the risk of errors in credit transfers or third party attachments. Another way to draft this type of clauses, reflected in the second bullet, considers the beneficiary's obligations as satisfied when the payment is received by the guarantor holding the applicant's account. Any delay in crediting that payment to the applicant's account is left to sort out between the applicant and the guarantor according to the bank–customer relationship agreement or rules law.

(Continued)

(*Continued*)

The applicant has not fulfilled its contractual payment obligations. 4. Supporting statements required under other types of guarantees (advance payment, retention money, delivery, warrantee maintenance and so on) are likewise expected to be general in their drafting without the need for the beneficiary to substantiate its claim or to provide meticulous technical detail of the breach absent an express requirement in the guarantee itself. Available at http://www.procreditbank.com.mk/WBStorage/Files/Form%20of%20Demand%20Guara.ntee%20under%20URDG%20758%20EN.pdf on January 7, 2017.

Bank Guarantees in SWIFT Format

----------------------INCOMING MESSAGE----------------------

Message Receive Time: 11.07.2016 - 10:30

Message Type: 760 - GUARANTEE / STANDBY LETTER OF CREDIT

Delivery: N

Record Number: 0005000451200

Sender: Industrial Development Bank of India, Mumbai, India

Receiver: Commerzbank, Frankfurt.

Value Date: Spot

Currency: EUR

Amount:10,000000

Branch: Frankfurt

Department: International Banking

Session Number: 3200

Sequence Number (ISN): 750000

==

7: Sequence of Total	1/1
20: Transaction Reference Number	120BGS500000
23: Further Identification	ISSUE

30: Date	10.07.2016
40C: Applicable Rules	URDG

77C: Details of Guarantee

We hereby request you to advise the following guarantee to beneficiary without any obligation on your part:

PAYMENT GUARANTEE NO.   120BGS500000

DATED 10 July 2016

THE GUARANTOR: Industrial Development Bank of India, Mumbai, India.

THE APPLICANT: Ashok Kumar Yadav, Kubera Kalani, 2nd floor, V.N. Road, Churchgate, Mumbai, 400 020.

THE BENEFICIARY: Gareth James Wall, Roßmarkt 14, 60311 Frankfurt am Main, Germany.

As guarantor, we have been informed that the beneficiary and the applicant, have established a contract No.1 DD March 16, 2016, CALLED 'THE CONTRACT', FOR SUPPLY OF 30,000 T-SHIRTS, CALLED 'THE GOODS' FOR THE TOTAL AMOUNT OF EUR15 MIO.

According to the contract terms, the applicant's obligations to pay for the supplied goods must be secured by a bank guarantee issued in the beneficiary's favor in the amount of EUR 10 MIO.

We, as guarantor, hereby irrevocably undertake to pay to the beneficiary any amount(s) in Euro claimed by the beneficiary up to the maximum of EUR 10 MIO. (in words: one hundred million euro) upon presentation of the original of the beneficiary's complying demand in paper form with reference to this guarantee number stating that the beneficiary supplied the goods to the applicant in conformity with the contract terms and the applicant has failed to meet a part of or all his payment obligations thereunder in due time in the amount claimed by the beneficiary under this guarantee, but not exceeding EUR 10 MIO in the aggregate.

Any demand under this guarantee will be *honored by the guarantor only when*:

1. Presentation has to be done within 30 calendar days from the date of shipment indicated in any relevant international Air transport bill (including the date of shipment in calculation).
2. Supported by copies of the following documents presented in paper form:
   a. Beneficiary's invoice indicating the contract number and date, and
   b. International air transport document containing date of shipment.
3. Presented through the intermediary of State Bank of India, Mainzer Landstraße 61, 60329 Frankfurt am Main, Germany, which will
   a. Forward it to the guarantor under their cover letter together with the documents as per point 2. of present paragraph, and
   b. Confirm to the guarantor by authenticated swift message format MT799 to the guarantor's swift address IDBIIN–XXX the authenticity of signature(s) appearing on the beneficiary's demand.

Language of all required documents under this guarantee is English.

(Continued)

(Continued)

This guarantee is valid until September 29, 2016. After the expiry date the guarantor's liabilities hereunder will expire in full and automatically. The original of the beneficiary's demand together with required documents must be received by the guarantor

1. On or before the expiry date,
2. At the place of presentation, State Bank of India, Mainzer Landstraße 61, 60329 Frankfurt am Main, Germany, except for document 3b of present guarantee, which must be presented in electronic form to guarantor's swift address.

All charges under the guarantee are for the principal's account.

This guarantee is subject to *the uniform rules for demand guarantees (URDG) 2010 revision, ICC publication no.758.*

Please Confirm Execution

Retention Money Guarantee

Beneficiary: ABC International Plant

Date : 31.July.2016
1st Floor, 2A Rainbow Building,
Singapore

Retention Money Guarantee No. : 2016/0351

We have been informed that Advanced Manufacturing Systems Corporation, G Wall, Singapore (hereinafter called "the principal"), has entered into contract No. 32140931 dated July 8, 2016 with you, for the supply of semiconductor machinery manufacturing.

Furthermore we understand that, according to the conditions of the contract, retention money in the sum of 7,500,000 covering the principal's warranty obligations will be released against a retention money guarantee.

At the request of the principal, we, XYZ Bank, hereby irrevocably undertake to pay you any sum or sums not exceeding in total an amount of 7,500,000USD (say seventy-five thousand USD) upon receipt by us of your first demand in writing and your written statement stating that the principal is in breach of his obligations under the underlying contract, and the respect in which the principal is in breach.

Your demand for payment must also be accompanies by the following documents: (a) Copy of commercial invoice and (b) Proof of identity certificate issued and signed by our branch in beneficiary's country or else one of our corresponding bank's located in beneficiary's country stating that the bank has verified beneficiary's signature(s) appearing on the first demand of payment. It is a condition for any claim and payment under this guarantee to be made that the advance payment referred to above must have been received the principal on his account number 12345678 at ABC Bank (Head Office), Singapore. This guarantee shall expire on November 30, 2016 at the latest. Consequently any demand for payment under it must be received by us at this office on or before that date. This guarantee is subject to the Uniform Rules for Demand Guarantees, ICC publication No. 758.

Advance Payment Bank Guarantee

Advance Payment Bank Guarantee

Beneficiary: Kohinoor Ltd. Mumbai   Date : 30.July.2016
23A Nariman Point
69000 Mumbai
India

Advance Payment Bank Guarantee No. : 2016/0034

We have been informed that ABC Multinational Ltd, Singapore (hereinafter called "the principal"), has entered into contract No. 111222999 dated 19.July 2016 with you, for the supply of 200 Metric Ton/ Metric Tons Basmati Rice.

Furthermore we understand that, according to the conditions of the contract, an advance payment in the sum of 200,000 USD is to be made against an advance payment guarantee.

At the request of the principal, we State Commercial Bank Mumbai. hereby irrevocably undertake to pay you any sum or sums not exceeding in total an amount of 150,000 USD (say One Hundred Fifty Thousand USD) upon receipt by us of your first demand in writing and your written statement stating: that the principal is in breach of his obligations under the underlying contract, and the respect in which the principal is in breach.

Your demand for payment must also be accompanies by the following documents:

Copy of commercial invoice

It is a condition for any claim and payment under this guarantee to be made that the advance payment referred to above must have been received the principal on his account number 99999944455 at the State Commercial Bank Mumbai, India.

This guarantee shall expire on 30th August 2016 at the latest.

Consequently any demand for payment under it must be received by us at this office on or before that date.

This guarantee is subject to the Uniform Rules for Demand Guarantees, ICC publication No. 758.

Performance Guarantee Sample

Beneficiary: ABC Infrastructure ltd.   Date : 30.July.2016

23A Nariman Point
69000 Mumbai
India

Performance Guarantee No. : 2016/032-PFRM

We have been informed that XYZ Development Corporation Tokyo, Japan, (hereinafter called "the principal"), has entered into contract No. 2016/0531/Cnt dated 15 June 2016 with you, for the supply of 3000 Metric Ton/Metric Tons of Steel.

(Continued)

(Continued)

Furthermore we understand that, according to the conditions of contract, a performance guarantee is required.

At the request of the principal, we The International Commerce Bank of Tokyo. hereby irrevocably undertake to pay you any sum or sums not exceeding in total an amount of 300.000,00USD (say Three Hundred Thousand USD) upon receipt by us of your first demand in writing and your written statement stating:

that the principal is in breach of his obligations under the tender conditions, and the respect in which the principal is in breach.

Your demand for payment must also be accompanies by the following documents:

Proof of identity certificate issued and signed by our branch in beneficiary's country or else one of our corresponding bank's located in beneficiary's country stating that the bank has verified beneficiary's signature(s) appearing on the first demand of payment.

This guarantee shall expire on 15 November 2016 at the latest.

Consequently any demand for payment under it must be received by us at this office on or before that date.

This guarantee is subject to the Uniform Rules for Demand Guarantees, ICC publication No. 758.

Index